Helen Gould Was My Mother-in-Law

By

Celeste Andrews Seton

AS TOLD TO

Clark Andrews

Helen Gould Was My Mother-in-Law
By Celeste Andrews Seton
As told to Clark Andrews

Copyright 1953 by Celeste Andrews Seton and Clark Andrews

First published, 1953
Third Printing, 2020
Grateful thanks to Neils Bodeker and Tumbledown Editions for the digital redo of N.M. Bodeker's wonderful map of Lyndhurst.

Library of Congress Catalog Card No. 53-8438

FOR OUR MOTHER

Foreword

Jay Gould died in his home at 579 Fifth Avenue, New York, in 1892. During his lifetime he amassed one of the largest fortunes in the United States. It is estimated that at one time his ownership of stocks and bonds in railroads covering 18,000 miles of track, transatlantic cables, mining, land and industrial corporations, totaled over a billion dollars.

This story is based on the life of Jay Gould's eldest daughter, Helen Gould Shepard. Her four adopted children agree that this book is the emotional and spiritual image of their foster mother. They disagree, however, about some of the facts. Helen Anna says the sweet peas did not win a prize in the flower show — the lilies did. Finley Jay says he doesn't remember the flower show at all. Louis will not commit himself. Olivia says she is, frankly, a little fuzzy about it, but doesn't see what difference it makes.

A few liberties have been taken with geography and time. And one other thing: Some of the minor characters have been given fictitious names. For example, Osato, the Japanese gardener, in chapter 10, was really named Hiro-hito.

And many thanks to Mr. B. H. Leather of *The New York Times*, Mr. Henry Nicholas Snow, and Mrs. Helen Rose for their courtesies.

A New Foreword Many Years Later!

Helen Gould Was My Mother-in-Law was a best-seller in the 1950s. The authors, my aunt and father, wrote this hilarious true story which revolves around the Gould family's life at their beloved Lyndhurst. Celeste wanted it to be called Far Above Rubies and Clark wanted it to be titled The Guest Book. The publisher, however, insisted on the Helen Gould title and won the debate. Clark was a successful radio and movie writer, who after leaving Hollywood for service in World War 11 and a bad marriage to the actress Clair Trevor, returned to his roots in New York. He and his sister then set to work putting to page the tales of her courtship and marriage to Louis Seton, a grandson of the (in)famous railroad tycoon, Jay Gould. Together, Celeste and Clark produced one of the best books of the era.

Some time has passed, and *Helen Gould is My Mother-in-Law* remains a wonderful portrait of a fascinating influential family during a poignant chapter in American history. In bringing this book back to light, Gael Seton Habernickel, Celeste's daughter, and I hope to share this wonderful story with new generations. All 21 of Clark and Celeste's descendants (as of this writing, that's 3 on Clark's side and an impressive 18 on Celeste's) would love to see the wonderful characters in this story brought to life!

Some time has passed, and *Helen Gould is My*

Mother-in-Law remains a wonderful portrait of a fascinating influential family during a poignant chapter of American history. In bringing this book back to light, Gael Seton Habernickel, Celeste's daughter, and I hope to share this wonderful story with new generations.

Two fun facts about the incredible artwork from the original book. The witty map of Lyndhurst was drawn by the renowned children's book illustrator and author, N.M. Bodecker, who charmingly claims to have never been there. The book's cover was also created by the iconic artist Helen Borten, who was only 23 at the time and who also went on to become a beloved children's book writer and illustrator.

The location of much of the book, Lyndhurst on the Hudson in Tarrytown, New York is now a signature property of the National Trust for Historic Preservation and has many interesting tours and events. Additionally, their gift shop is very well curated and a treasure chest of related items and, of course, books.

Lyndhurst itself is a magnificent film location, and has hosted, among others, the show Dark Shadows and the recent films "Seven Deadly Sins," and "A Winter's Tale."

The Lyndhurst experience is well worth one or many visits! www.lyndhurst.org

I'm sure you will enjoy the book. Celeste and Clark would have wanted you to read it in the company of a cocktail – or as our grandmother, Mrs. Andrews in the book, might suggest, with a nice seventh cup of coffee. Happy Reading!

Candace Andrews Dollahite

PS We welcome all questions and comments at <u>helengouldwasmymotherinlaw@gmail.com</u>

Contents

1	THE ADIRONDACKS	1
2	TEA	11
3	FAY AND DARIO'S	25
4	THE SABBATH	39
5	ROAST BEEF AND YORKSHIRE PUDDING	51
6	FAITH, HOPE, AND CHARITY	65
7	NIGHT TRAIN	77
8	LYNDHURST	89
9	THE RITES OF SPRING	105
10	PLAN OF BATTLE	115
11	LE GRAND PRIX	129
12	SEVEN DAYS SHALT THOU LABOR	137
13	THE WEDDING	153
14	THE CATSKILLS	167
15	FANCYWORK	179
16	FORE!	195
17	PICNIC WITHOUT ANTS	211
18	SWORDFISH	225
19	SOUTHWARD BOUND	239
20	BATTER UP	257
21	GATHERING OF THE CLAN	275
22	SNOWSTORM	291

1

The Adirondacks

I FIRST MET LOUIS Seton on the Lake Placid Club golf course in the summer of 1933. He shot a seventy-one, and I, not counting the water hole where I lost three balls and my temper, shot a hundred and sixteen. We were forty-five strokes apart—a world of difference on a golf course. By the end of the week we were a little closer together, and then in the lengthening shadows of an August afternoon, two events of great and lasting proportions happened; I broke a hundred, and he kissed me.

After that Louis and I saw a great deal of each other. One Saturday, we motored up to Quebec. We followed the guide book page by page, including a climb up the goat path to the Plains of Abraham. I learned a lot about Quebec that day. I also learned a lot about Louis. When we drove into a gas station, he asked for ten gallons of Ethyl— in perfect French. At dinner that evening in the Chateau Frontenac, he was positively amazing; he ordered *medaillons de saumon a l'aspic and bouchees de ris de veau aux truffes*, with the savoir-faire of a pretender to the French throne.

"Louis," I asked, "where did you learn to speak French so well?"

"Long ago when I was a little boy. It was a punishment."

After dinner we started home. It was a beautiful starry night, and I leaned my head back on the seat and tried to find the Big Dipper. Suddenly, Louis began to hum the overture to *Pagliacci*.

"Louis," I said, "you're marvelous. How did you happen to learn that?"

"A punishment," he said.

"Do you know *Aida*?" I said.

Sure.

"Cavalleria Rusticana?"

"Sure.

"Samson and Delilah?"

"Every note."

"Louis," I said, "in your youth you must have been a scoundrel."

But this was nothing. I found out Louis could recite almost entire chapters of the Bible by heart. Such talent, I thought, should not be wasted. One rainy Sunday, sitting around the club house, I casually dropped the information that Louis could recite the first twenty-five verses of Genesis without an error. This incredible boast led to a few bets, but Louis performed without a single error and threw in for good measure ten verses of The First Epistle of Paul to the Corinthians. We made fifty-three dollars.

"It pays to know the Scriptures," Louis said.

During the summer I lived with my mother in a cottage called "Moosewood." We always had breakfast together. Mother was usually very gay and chatty, but when she had anything serious to discuss, she always began with a long prelude of silence—then suddenly it would burst forth: "Celeste, what do you *really* know about Louis Seton?"

"Not much, really," I answered, somewhat surprised.

"Surely you must know something about him? You've been with him constantly for two weeks."

"He goes to Princeton. He'll be a senior this fall. He might make Phi Beta Kappa."

"That's nice. Anything else?"

"Well," I answered brightly, "he got a birdie on that long fourteenth yesterday over at Saranac."

"All right, Celeste; you don't have to be flippant about this. It's only natural for me to be interested in your friends."

"Yes, Mother."

"I know most of the people here, but I can't seem to place a Mr. and Mrs. Seton. I've never met them at Saturday tea, or any of the bridge parties."

"As a matter of fact, Mother, his family's not up here."

"Oh! Where does he live?"

"New York."

"And you've never asked about his family?"

"No, I haven't—and he's never asked me about you." That stopped Mother's questions temporarily and she changed the pace.

"Do you want another cup of hot coffee, dear?"

"No, thank you, seven is enough."

Mother poured herself a fresh cup, and after a few sips continued the conversation. "Seton . . . Louis Seton? I'm positive I've heard that name somewhere—I just can't place it. Well, I'm sure he's a perfectly nice boy, but I'd just like to know who he is. After all, I *am* your mother."

"And I'm twenty-one, Mother dear," I answered. "But if it will make you happier, I'll try and find out."

"Of course, you will. You're sure you don't want another cup of coffee?"

"No thanks. I'm late now. I should have been at the golf

club fifteen minutes ago."

I got up from the breakfast table, kissed Mother goodbye, and whispered in her ear: "Ye are all the children of light, and the children of the day; we are not of the night, nor of darkness."

"What's that, dear?" Mother said in a very surprised tone of voice.

"It's from the Bible. Louis taught it to me."

"How interesting! Is he a minister's son?"

"I don't know. Goodbye."

Louis left for New York at the end of the week, and Mother no longer questioned me directly, though there was a significant inflection in her voice whenever she said: "Here's another letter for you this morning, dear!" During the month of September, Father came up and joined us. He liked to have his vacation then because he could see the leaves change, and as the first faint patches of autumn color appeared on the mountainsides, I wondered if Father could see me changing too. I was falling in love, and I felt that the blush on my cheeks was sometimes as vivid as the maple leaves that came trembling down.

It seemed only a brief moment after Father arrived until we were all getting into our car one morning to go home. And when Mother said, "Now, are you perfectly sure we have all fifteen suitcases," I knew it was the end of summer.

Princeton played a schedule of nine football games that fall, and Louis asked me to *all* of them, including the last one when three inches of snow fell in the fourth quarter. The final whistle blew just in time; it saved me from frostbite. It was good to get on the train back to New York. I did my best to keep up the old college spirit, but I was exhausted and fell asleep. I didn't wake up until my eardrums began to crack in the tunnel under the Hudson River.

We got out at Penn Station and jumped into a Black and White cab. The snow had turned to a steady drizzle as we skidded around Thirty-Fourth Street for the long drive up Park Avenue. We were huddled close together to keep warm, and it was comforting to know that the football season was over. At Seventy-Second Street we had to stop for a red light. Louis suddenly turned his head a little and said as casually as he might have asked for a cigarette: "Will you marry me?"

My answer was immediate, but not conclusive: "What?" He repeated: "Will you marry me?"

This time I answered more decisively: "Yes."

"That's good," he said. "That's swell."

That was all there was to it, except that I began to feel the need of a little ceremony.

"Aren't you going to kiss me to make it official?"

"Not in front of the taxi driver."

The traffic light suddenly snapped green, and we were on our way again. At Seventy-First Street I was just coming home from a football game. At Seventy-Second Street I was engaged. A city block can mean a lot in a girl's development. The taxi pulled up in front of my house, and we went upstairs.

We were both much closer to marriage and lobar pneumonia, and it wasn't a bad feeling at all.

Father and Mother were out when we came into the apartment. We mixed a highball, clicked our glasses, and Louis kissed me as I stood by the shelf of the entire *Encyclopedia Britannica*. Then we sat down.

"Louis, I don't know exactly how to say this, but there is something I must ask you. Father and Mother will want to know."

"Certainly, dear," he replied, "what is it?"

I hesitated a moment, then I said: "I hope you won't be offended, what I want to know is—who are you?"

Louis jiggled the ice in his glass and didn't say anything.

"Please understand, Louis," I went on, "I know your name, and that's about all. I've never met your family, and these questions are bound to come up—tomorrow, the next day, even tonight," and I glanced apprehensively at the clock.

Louis stood up and said deliberately: "You've never met my family for a very good reason. I haven't any. I was an orphan. Now I have foster parents. They took me out of the State Charities Aid when I was five years old. Their names are Mr. and Mrs. Finley Shepard. My mother's name was Helen Gould."

I answered as calmly as I could: "You mean that your mother is Jay Gould's daughter?"

"My *foster* mother, yes."

I didn't say anything for a moment. I couldn't. I didn't feel anything either except a kind of buzzing in my ears. Then I burst out laughing.

Louis looked at me rather surprised and said: "What's so funny?"

"What's so funny, Louis darling?" I answered. "Wait till I tell Mother."

"What will she say?"

"She will ask a few questions. Mother will want to know how they found you, where you came from—everything!"

"It's all a little complicated," Louis answered, "and it happened a long time ago. Mother was forty-five years old when she married. She had always loved children. She was brought up in a home with five other children herself, but as she put it—it was God's will that she would never be blessed by any of her own.

"One day she was entertaining some orphan children when one little five-year-old boy suddenly became ill. The doctor came and solemnly pronounced: 'Measles!' It was a heaven-sent diagnosis. She put him to bed, nursed him, and fell in love with him."

"Were you that little boy, Louis?"

"No, he was my brother—or rather, he was going to be. Mother and Father adopted him, and his name was changed from a number to 'Finley Jay Shepard.' In those days it wasn't so complicated to adopt babies, least of all for Mother."

"Where do you come in, Louis?" I asked.

"Next. One afternoon Mother went into the nursery, and Finley Jay said eagerly: 'Mother, would you like to meet my best friend?' He dove under the bed, took out a shoe box, and opened it carefully: 'Here he is, Mother, my best friend.' She peered into the box, but instead of saying 'How do you do,' she screamed. It was a daddy longlegs.

"That evening, at dinner. Mother said to Father, 'Our son must have someone to play with besides insects.

"I quite understand your apprehensions, my dear," he answered, 'but we must deal intelligently with the problem. I should like to suggest that we consider another little boy.

"Mother did not consider this a suggestion; she thought it was an inspiration. So down she went to the State Charities Aid to find a five-year-old brother for Finley Jay. That was me. I was presented to Finley with a great deal of ceremony, but I was received a bit coldly at first.

"He has only two legs, take him away!' Finley Jay said. It was some time before I made up for that deficiency. I could play jackstraws, but I couldn't walk up the wall."

"Louis," I broke in, "there's one thing I don't understand.

Why is your name Seton? Why isn't it Shepard?"

He answered slowly and methodically: "When my parents adopted me I didn't have a number; I had a name—the same one I have now—Seton. When I grew up I naturally wanted to know why."

"Didn't they tell you?" I asked.

"In a way—yes. I was told that when I was left with the State Charities Aid my name was Seton and legally it couldn't be changed. Whenever I mentioned the subject it was always dropped like a hot potato. But that's all ancient history. Why do you look so startled?"

"You must admit that finding out the man you're going to marry is an orphan adopted by Helen Gould is a little unexpected. It's even more unexpected than finding out you can sing *Aida*"

Louis smiled and answered, "I understand that, but there's one thing I must tell you. Finley Jay and I prefer to be called waifs—not orphans. Finley, you see, was discovered on the steps of St. Patrick's Cathedral."

"Stop, Louis, you're joking," I interrupted.

"No," Louis contradicted, "that's the honest truth. A policeman found him one rainy morning and he was immediately sent to the State Charities Aid. When Mother adopted him, the papers played it up for everything it was worth. I've seen the clippings: 'Waif adopted by the richest family in America'; 'Waif abandoned at St. Patrick's finds home on Fifth Avenue.' We still kid each other about it.

Good morning, waif'—'pass the butter, waif'—'loan me a million, waif.' "

"Where did your sisters come from?" I asked.

"Same place. The State Charities Aid. One day Mother gave a party for two little girls next door. When they left, Finley screamed, 'I want a little sister like that! I want those little girls to live here all the time.' If Finley Jay had asked for the moon, Mother would have tried to get it for him, so a week later she trotted back and found Helen Anna and Olivia. The State Charities Aid did a land-office business."

"It's an incredible story, Louis," I said. "The four of you from rags to riches because Finley Jay came down with measles."

"But it's not going to be that way forever."

"What do you mean?"

Louis explained: "When Jay Gould died, he left a fortune to his six children, but his will had a curious paragraph in it. It stated that when his children died, the money they had inherited from him could be left only to their blood issue. Finley, Olivia, Helen Anna and I are not blood issue so none of us will legally inherit a dollar of Jay Gould's money."

"What a curious thing to have put into a will."

"It almost seemed that Jay Gould divined the future, and didn't like it."

"I'm sorry about that, Louis."

"I am too."

Just then I heard the elevator door open in the foyer outside the apartment. It was Mother and Father.

2

Tea

LOUIS SAID HE would come by for me at four o'clock sharp. We would call on his mother at four-thirty sharp, and it was Louis' estimate that the first drop of *Lapsang Souchong* tea would fall into a Sevres cup shortly after five.

That morning Father was a little surprised to see me at the breakfast table for my first appearance in nine years. But I needed time. A day is none too long to choose the correct dress for your first encounter with your future mother-in-law. At eleven o'clock I thought I should wear my good black crepe. At twelve my choice was a tailored navy blue wool with pique collars and cuffs. At one o'clock Mother suggested my brown duvetyn. I tried it on, but decided it was too low in the neckline by a good inch. An inch on a map isn't much, but on a lady's neck it cuts across natural boundaries.

It was after three-thirty when Mother and I came to a decision. We agreed that I shouldn't wear a dress at all! A suit would be more appropriate for the occasion; a simple gray suit. A hand-made white blouse with drawn work, and a small gray hat with a red cockade of ribbon completed the ensemble. I looked right. I felt right. I almost felt like having a cup of tea.

Louis arrived promptly. He was a little ill at ease as he shook hands with Father, and when he kissed Mother his ruddy complexion changed abruptly to scarlet. My kiss was delayed until we stood in the hall waiting for the elevator. Then we went out and jumped into Louis' car. After we got settled, he looked at me and said approvingly.

"That's a very attractive outfit you have on."

"I hope it's all right. I just picked the first thing off the rack."

"Well, it's very nice," he said as he started the car. As we were crossing the trolley tracks at Fifty-Ninth Street, I said a little nervously, "It's a very warm day for November. We could almost put the top down."

Louis nodded.

"Much too nice a day to spend indoors," I amplified. Louis smiled and answered sympathetically, "We won't stay more than an hour."

"I didn't mean it that way," I added hastily. "I just hope your mother likes me. It would be awful if she didn't. Mother and Father like you. They're very happy about everything."

"Mother will like you, all right," Louis reassured me. "She won't be able to help it, but there's a good chance you may not like her."

"Why not?" I asked.

"Some people consider her eccentric."

"In what way, Louis?"

"For example, she reads the Bible a great deal."

"Is that eccentric?"

"No, but she lives by it, and what's more, she may discuss it."

"This afternoon?" I asked quickly.

"Anytime."

"You're the Bible expert," I said. "All I know is the Twenty-Third Psalm, and the Lord's Prayer. I know half of that in Latin. What else, Louis? We're almost there."

"No one is allowed to drink in the house."

"That's not so bad."

"And don't cross your legs."

"Why not?"

"Mother considers it unladylike. Another thing, smoking is verboten for ladies."

"How about breathing?" I asked.

Louis laughed and said, "It's all right in moderation."

"Has your mother always been like this?"

"Always. Nothing will ever change her. She's very nice and very generous, and she spends her whole life trying to do good. She's easy to make fun of, and we all do it sometimes because you can't help it. But we all love her, and we're all a little afraid of her."

"Me, too—I'm scared stiff," I said.

"Just agree with her about everything and don't say too much, and she'll like you very much. Besides Miss Stebbins and Miss Davis will be there."

"Who are they?"

"Mother's social secretaries. They're with her all the time—morning, noon and night. She hardly winds a clock without them. They'll help the conversation along."

"That's good; but really, Louis, I don't know how I'm going to get through this. I just can't change my basic personality in five minutes."

"Your basic personality is highly acceptable," he answered.

We pulled up in front of 579 Fifth Avenue, a handsome

four-story Victorian brownstone, and stopped between two white police signs that read "No Parking." Louis switched off the motor and said, as grimly as if we were going into battle: "All set?"

"Yes," I replied, "to the last drop of tea."

We got out of the car, walked across the sidewalk and up the highly polished marble stairs of the vestibule to the heavy glass door. Louis rang the bell. A few couples strolling along Fifth Avenue glanced curiously at us. On the corner a man was selling apples. The depression was everywhere around us. While we were waiting Louis said:

"There's one thing I forgot to tell you."

"What's that, Louis?"

"Mother wears a wig."

"Oh, I'm sorry," I said.

"It's called a transformation," Louis explained.

The door was opened by a butler. He was dressed in a cutaway and a wing collar one size too small. A bald spot on his head acquired by years of devoted service was bordered by faint wisps of gray hair. His greeting was friendly but brief: "Good afternoon."

Louis said: "Here we are, Sitwell. On time, I hope?"

"On time, Master Louis." Then he moved back a step to let us enter. I did not falter. I crossed the threshold, and I was in the Victorian Era.

Louis motioned toward a small reception room, and I went in and took off my coat. There were two small gilded opera chairs with their backs primly turned toward Fifth Avenue and a couch covered in plum-colored velvet. A marble-topped table, overhung by a tall oval mirror, stood against the wall. There was a silver tray on it holding a few calling cards. I casually picked one up. It read, "Bishop Manning." I put it back quickly.

Then standing in front of the mirror I looked at myself appraisingly. Suddenly my suit seemed all wrong. It was too severe. It was out of place in this house. I should have worn a dress. But it was too late now. The hands on the elaborate Ormolu clock said four-thirty sharp, and I heard Louis discreetly cough in the hall. So I straightened my blouse, gave one final flip to the brim of my hat, and went out.

Louis took my arm, and we started down the long hall together. Above me crystal chandeliers hung with heavy dignity, and the gilded pipes of an organ rose like stalagmites towards the towering stairwell. We passed the grand staircase, an elevator, and then, far away, in half shadow, I saw Sitwell. He was waiting for us patiently. As we approached, he turned a half step, faced the living room like a sergeant-at-arms, and in a deep sonorous basso prof undo announced:

"Miss Andrews and Master Louis."

My name sounded awkward and insipid.

We turned at a right angle and entered. Louis' mother ran smiling and toddling over to greet us, a little, plump lady of sixty-odd years, with full rosy cheeks and tiny feet. She bent forward, kissed Louis lightly on the cheek, and said:

"It was sweet of you to come."

Then she turned to me, kissed me lightly on the cheek, and said:

"It was sweet of you to come."

It was a gracious welcome.

Mrs. Shepard was wearing a simple draped black dress with a modest neckline. Around her throat was an East Indian silver necklace, and on her wrist was a small, square gold watch on a grosgrain ribbon band. On her wedding finger was a heavy gold ring. Her attire was unpretentious and unadorned, but it was obvious that Mrs. Shepard was not the simple person she appeared to be. Her thin, tight lips, her sharp penetrating blue eyes, and her firm chin were the outward features of great strength and stubborn determination. Instinctively I felt there was little chance of ever being yourself in her presence. I must put on a mask of rigid formality and play a part. My duty would be to please her—never myself. She might have many naive beliefs and customs, but she would project them with a will of iron. She reminded me somewhat of pictures I had seen of Queen Victoria. If Mrs. Shepard said, "Gentlemen, the earth is a parallelogram," no one would dispute it in her presence.

"And now I want you to meet everyone," Mrs. Shepard said expansively. "This is Miss Stebbins," and she nodded toward a tall imposing gray-haired lady who came forward boldly and said in a big, hearty voice:

"Good afternoon," and then she sneezed a little half sneeze that was ludicrously out of proportion to her strong frame.

"Excuse me, dear," she said. "Excuse me. I do so wish I could sneeze like a human being." There was a twinkle in her eye as she spoke, and I felt immediately that I was going to like her.

Mrs. Shepard interrupted the twinkle and continued: "And this is Miss Davis."

Miss Davis was short, and a little chubby and mild as May. She smiled broadly and said almost inaudibly:

"It was sweet of you to come." It was like a faint echo of Mrs. Shepard.

Then after I thought I had met everyone, Mrs. Shepard said:

"And now I want you to meet Chinky."

I was not aware that anyone else was in the room, but as I followed her gaze, I realized I was mistaken, for there on a small velvet cushion on a petit point footstool a Pekingese dog was reclining in regal splendor. I hesitated, not knowing what the exact protocol was in cases of this kind, and there was a momentary silence as if Mrs. Shepard were waiting for me to make some gesture. So I said:

"Hello, Chinky."

I was a little surprised when I was answered immediately by a shrill soprano bark. I am not sure, of course, but I think Chinky tried to say:

"It was sweet of you to come."

The introductions were over.

Mrs. Shepard took me gently by the arm and said: "Now, Celeste, dear, you must sign the guest book," and she led me over to a Chinese Chippendale desk on which a huge hand-tooled leather volume lay open. Miss Stebbins picked up a peacock quill pen, dipped it into a jade inkwell, and handed it to me ceremoniously. The feather made a long, graceful arc, and I couldn't help thinking. This would be something to be tickled with!

Miss Stebbins whispered, "Go ahead. Take your time and write distinctly."

I bent down and wrote for the ages: "Celeste Andrews, November 25th, 1933."

As I finished, I noticed a familiar name directly on the line above mine. "Evangeline Booth." Well, *she* certainly didn't have my penmanship! I gave the pen back to Miss Stebbins, and she said quietly, "You spilled a little ink on your thumb, dear, but it's nothing to worry about." Then in her shrill, high voice, Mrs. Shepard chirped brightly:

"Now shall we all have tea?"

We sat down around a large refectory table in the middle of the room, and immediately Sitwell entered with a huge silver tea service. It looked to me as though he were carrying part of the Comstock lode.

Mrs. Shepard officiated like a high priestess, assisted by Agnes, the parlor maid, whose expression was as grim as if she were passing out quinine. At length we were all served, including Chinky, to whose very teeth Mrs. Shepard personally delivered a small alligator pear sandwich.

We sipped in a silence broken only now and then by silver spoons striking against Sevres china like grace notes and the little off-key squeak my chair made every time I shifted position.

Looking casually about the room I found it gloomy and unfriendly. The upholstery was a heavy gray-taupe plush which blended in solemn harmony with the carpets and woodwork. The room had three immense windows and heavy curtains and blinds were drawn against any chance ray of sunlight. Nearby, a marble statue of a Fifth Century Greek meditated in classic serenity. He was decorated by two kinds of foliage — laurel and fig. Huge glass bookcases stood formidably in front of each wall. I could not make out the titles of the books, although I was sure that among them lurked such childhood enemies as Thackeray, Sir Walter Scott and Anthony Trollope.

The only light touches were innumerable pictures of Mrs. Shepard's four adopted children and a card table on which was a gigantic jigsaw puzzle in process of solution. I squinted, and it looked like a half-completed profile of Herbert Hoover. On a side table there was a huge bowl of fruit. I thought of the man outside selling apples.

Mrs. Shepard gently interrupted my speculations:

"My dear Celeste, I have heard a lot about you. I understand you attended Smith College?"

"Yes, I did, Mrs. Shepard, for two years."

"I have heard some rather unpleasant things about it."

I hadn't the faintest idea what she was talking about, and I raised my head a little in surprise.

"Unpleasant things?"

"Yes," she continued, "Communism, you know."

"I was never aware of it," I said.

Mrs. Shepard continued as though she had not heard me.

"They have parades there. At night. By torchlight. And they don't believe in God. It's too bad." Then abruptly she changed the subject.

"What do you do with your time now, my dear?"

"Oh," I stammered, "I read a little, go to the theater."

"Oh, how nice. How very nice. What have you seen?"

"*Tobacco Road*"

"That's too bad," she answered, and her forehead knitted a little frown.

"Too bad?"

"Yes, I've heard it's about very benighted people—and there's a lot of smoking in it. Very wicked, indeed. I really don't understand why they allow such things." These conclusions were accompanied by little affirmative nods from Miss Davis. Then Mrs. Shepard said, "What are your other activities, Celeste?"

"I play golf a little. As a matter of fact, Louis and I are going to play tomorrow—at Sleepy Hollow."

"I can hardly believe it, Celeste!"

"Yes, I know it seems strange playing in November, but a lot of our friends do it. Of course, there are no caddies."

She commented simply, "Tomorrow is the Lord's Day."
Why hadn't I thought of that? Tomorrow was Sunday. What could I say? I glanced over at Louis for a little support, but he looked like The Great Stone Face. Even Miss Stebbins whom I had counted on, was staring high above the ceiling. I was alone in a great plush Victorian desert.

The questions continued—sweetly, yet proddingly, "What do you read, my dear?"

This time I could not afford to make a mistake. I thought carefully for a moment, and made my decision, and with a smile of self-confidence, said, *"Little Women."*

Mrs. Shepard nodded approvingly and reminisced, "Dear Jo—and lovely Amy."

But victory was brief, for Mrs. Shepard next inquired: "Do you ever read the Bible, my dear?" This question I was prepared for.

"Oh yes," I answered rapidly, "often—almost every day. Sometimes at night before I go to bed."

"Do you have any favorite verses?" she asked.

"Of course," I said brightly, "the Twenty-Third Psalm." "How nice. How very nice, indeed. It is my favorite passage. Do recite it for me. Do please, Celeste. We would all love to hear it."

I had to go through with it. There was no retreat. I said meekly, "Shall I stand up, Mrs. Shepard?"

"That would be nice."

I stood up, and after a self-conscious cough, slowly began:

The Lord is my shepherd; I shall not want.
He maketh me to lie down in green pastures.
He leadeth me beside the still waters.
He restoreth my soul.

Then I stopped, because for the life of me, I couldn't think of the next line. Struggle as I might, I just couldn't think of it. It wouldn't come. I repeated the last line, hoping to coax the next one from my memory, but it was useless. Then I heard the loud prompting voice of Miss Stebbins:

"He leadeth me in the paths of righteousness for his name's sake."

I could have kissed her. I could have thrown my arms around her.

"Of course. Of course. Of course." And I continued in a burst of confidence:

> *Yea, though I walk through the valley of the shadow*
> *of death*
> *I will fear no evil: for thou art with me.*

In another moment I was safely at the end, and I finished the last verse proudly and reverently.

> *And I will dwell in the house of the Lord forever.*

Then I sat down.

My heart was pounding, and if I had not covered myself with glory, I certainly was a little nearer grace. Mrs. Shepard's face was wreathed in a beatific smile.

The evensong was interrupted by a nurse, in a spotless starched uniform, who rustled efficiently into the room. She stopped behind Mrs. Shepard's chair.

"I think it's time for our nap. Don't you?"

"I don't think five minutes more could hurt me, could it?"

"Remember our doctor's orders, Mrs. Shepard," and she looked pathetically at Miss Stebbins and Miss Davis, as if asking for cooperation. They immediately stood up and hovered over Mrs. Shepard like drones around the Queen Bee. Mrs. Shepard took the hint gracefully and said to me apologetically:

"You will excuse me, my dear. I know you will understand," and then she stood up, and we all rose with her. It was time to go. The tea party was over.

Louis said, "It has been a most enjoyable afternoon."

"Indeed, it has," I added.

Mrs. Shepard smiled, and Miss Davis added, "Yes." Miss Stebbins enlarged the sentiment to, "Yes, it has," and suddenly sneezed again.

"Oh my, there it goes again," she apologized. "I *wish* I knew what could be done."

Mrs. Shepard took me by the arm. "Celeste, we have many things to talk about. Will you and Louis come with me to church tomorrow morning? Afterwards we can all have dinner together. Finley Jay and Helen Anna will be here and so will my husband. I want everyone to meet you."

Louis said quickly, "We'd love to come, Mother."

Then Mrs. Shepard came forward and kissed me lightly on the cheek, but suddenly in a surprised, frightened little spasm she drew back and cried:

"Oh! Oh! We have forgotten. We have forgotten." Miss Stebbins inquired hastily: "What is it, Mrs. Shepard?"

"We have forgotten, we have forgotten the remembrance. Oh dear! Oh dear!"

Miss Davis seemed to understand and quickly left the room.

"I am so sorry, Celeste," Mrs. Shepard remonstrated. "We have been so negligent. So thoughtless. You must forgive me."

Miss Davis came running back. She was carrying a huge corsage of white orchids. She handed them carefully to Mrs. Shepard, who muttered: "Yes, the remembrance, the remembrance. How could we have forgotten. Miss Davis?" And then before I knew it, she was pinning them on my shoulder, fussing over them, arranging them with loving care. At last she was satisfied.

"There, there," she cried. And she stepped back to look at her creation.

"They are wonderful," I said.

Miss Stebbins said, "They are from Mrs. Shepard's green house. They are called *Cattleya trianae*"

"And how beautiful they are on you!" Mrs. Shepard said.

"How very beautiful," said Miss Stebbins.

"How beautiful," echoed Miss Davis.

Then with one final gesture, Mrs. Shepard kissed me again on the cheek and whispered a parting sentiment, "It was sweet of you to come."

A moment later the heavy grilled door of 579 Fifth Avenue closed behind us. Louis and I stood for a moment, lingering on the marble steps while our eyes accustomed themselves to the bright crimson glare of the sunset and the world outside.

3

Fay and Dario's

LOUIS STARTED TO drive up Fifth Avenue but before we had gone two blocks, he said: "Would you like a quiet drink?"

"Would you?" I asked hopefully.

"Yes, how about Fay and Dario's?"

"Any place, any place at all."

Louis turned west on the next corner toward Sixth Avenue, and halfway down the long block, he stopped in front of an old brownstone. We stepped down to the service entrance and rang the bell. A little peephole opened and one eye peered out suspiciously to see if we were friend or foe. Recognition was immediate and amiable:

"Oh, it's you, Mr. Seton! Just a moment, please. It's nice to see you."

A buzzer hummed from somewhere far back in the building and the black iron-grilled door clicked open. It was an unconventional welcome, but reassuring and friendly. We walked up the dark stairway of the speakeasy, through a long, narrow dining room to the bar which was empty, except for one couple holding hands. Louis had taken me here a few times during the fall and every time we came back it was always with a little suspense: Would it still be open? Speakeasies had a habit of closing at a moment's notice, but so far, Fay and Dario's had escaped the indignity of a police padlock.

On this late Saturday afternoon, it was business as usual, and everything was the same: A life-sized pastel of a reclining nude hung behind the bar. An old lithograph of the Roman Coliseum was tacked on one side of it, and on the other, a faded Princeton banner completed the triptych.

The rest of the room was decorated with empty magnums and jeraboams. On the tables were plates of Saratoga chips, and hand-woven peasant baskets full of pretzels. The decor was hardly elegant but there was no plush and clutter, and not an antimacassar in sight! Fay and Dario's was dimly lit, romantic, highly illegal, and at this moment, very comfortable. Of course we might be raided by the prohibition agents, but even then, the most I would have to recite would be my name and address.

If by some fantastic mischance Mrs. Shepard ever entered this place, she would have recoiled in horror at the fifteen kinds of scotch, four kinds of gin, the endless array of wines and liquors, including Benedictine, distilled by the holy Monks in the ancient Abbey of Fecamp. But though she would disapprove of the merchandise, she could not fail to approve of the clientele. The sons and daughters of some of her closest friends, including a minister's son, often dropped in for refreshments.

We sat down at one of the little calico-covered tables in the corner and Louis asked me what I'd like to have. He suggested, with a little embarrassed smile: "A nice cup of Lapsang Souchong tea, and some thin buttered bread?"

"No thanks, Louis," I said. "Tea is over now. I'd like a cocktail and if it isn't too wicked to smoke, a cigarette."

Suddenly, Dario, the proprietor, saw us and rushed over with a big polished smile and a hearty welcome:

"*Celesta, Celesta, buona sera, car a signorina*" and he bent low and kissed my hand. "And what exquisite orchids," he said.

"They are called *Cattleya trianae*," I answered.

"They look beautiful on you, and you are looking so well! Now, what is your pleasure? Nice dry martini? Old fashioned? Sidecar, maybe?"

"No, thank you, Dario; it's got to be something special today," Louis said. "We're going to be married as soon as I graduate this spring."

"How wonderful! *Che bella motizia! Questo mi fa piacere!* You will be very happy. And you must have something extra special—as my guests—champagne, yes? A fine Charles Heidsieck? Just came off the boat!"

"That would be fine," Louis said.

I murmured absent-mindedly: "How sweet!"

"How dry!" Louis corrected.

Dario snapped an order to the bartender and in a moment the champagne popped; we clicked our glasses and drank, and Dario added a final sentiment:

"*Salute e felicita!*"

There was no doubt of it—Dario approved of our marriage.

"Now, you want to be alone," he said. "Later, maybe, I will come back and play you a love song on my guitar," and his hands gracefully pretended to caress the strings. Dario backed away from our table and went over to see if the couple who were still holding hands wanted anything beside each other, and Louis and I started to sip the champagne.

The tall cold goblet felt better in my hand than the tiny

Sevres cup at 579, and it was a relief not to be afraid that any moment you might do something wrong, or say something that would be misunderstood.

I had never met anyone like Mrs. Shepard before and now, as I thought of her as my mother-in-law, I was a little apprehensive about the future. Really! Reciting Bible verses like a child at Sunday School! Many of my friends had told me about their mothers-in-law; they had spoken of them with affection, with humor, and sometimes with embarrassment. But for pure originality, Mrs. Shepard was unique!

Louis seemed to be reading my thoughts—and my doubts.

"Celeste, you see what I mean about Mother?"

"Indeed, I do."

"Tell me what you think."

"I don't know exactly, Louis; your mother is sweet and charming, but she's like something out of a book. She lives in a world that doesn't exist. I feel uncomfortable and ill at ease in it."

"We all do at times. But gradually, you'll get used to her and come to understand her. Anyway, Celeste, she'll be very good to you."

"I'm sure of that, but what can we *talk* about? I could never be myself with her. Besides, how do you know she has accepted me? She didn't *say* anything. She just decorated me."

"Everything is okay," Louis said. "The orchids and the invitation to church are her way of showing approval. They're symbolic."

"So tomorrow we go to church and receive her blessing?"

"Yes, at the Collegiate Dutch Reformed Church."

"I'm Episcopalian, myself."

"That's all right," Louis said. "It won't show."

Then suddenly, I don't know why, a little suspicion crossed my mind; rather playfully, I gave way to it: "Louis," I asked, "you said your mother approves of me because she gave me orchids, invited me to church, and to Sunday dinner?"

"That's right."

"Are you positive?"

"Yes," he said, and then he stopped short.

"Yes, what?" I asked.

"Well, you see," he replied with a little blush, "I'm positive Mother approves because—well, because, this has happened before."

"What has happened before? You've been married?"

"No—no—no," he laughed, "not married—just engaged."

"What was she like, Louis? Intelligent?"

"Yes."

"Beautiful?"

"Very."

"Nice figure?"

"Superb."

"Her name wasn't Venus by any chance?"

"No, it was Peggy."

"That's a nice name. How did Peggy do on the Twenty-Third Psalm?"

Louis didn't answer. He just smiled and reached for the champagne bottle to fill our glasses.

I said, "A little more wine for 'her stomach's sake.'" "That's very good," Louis said proudly, and completed the verse. " 'And for thine often infirmities.' " Actually, I drank very little, one or two cocktails, a glass of wine or champagne, but even this amount could be subject to widely contrasting interpretations. My own mother would have claimed most emphatically that I seldom drank, but I am sure Mrs. Shepard would say, "It's a pity Celeste drinks!" Both would be right and both would be wrong. And now when I asked Louis if he didn't agree that his mother would condemn me he replied that whenever the subject of liquor came up, she always quoted a little poem:

The drop leads to the glass,
The glass to the bottle,
The bottle to the drunkard's death,
Remember Uncle Harry!

The meaning of the first three lines was crystal clear, but the last was clouded in obscurity. It seems that no one knew the identity of Uncle Harry, and the numerous genealogical charts of Mrs. Shepard's family provided no clue. So Uncle Harry was remembered by posterity only as a horrible example.

Suddenly Louis cried:

"Look, Celeste, there! Over on the bar!"

I looked over and saw Dario's beautiful black Persian cat. It moved gracefully along the bar and sniffed in succession a Bacardi cocktail, a strega, a double scotch and soda, and a Pimm's cup belonging to a man who had just come in alone. Then the cat jumped down, came over to us, and leaped up onto our table and investigated our champagne. It took a tiny lick and shivered disdainfully. Obviously, it preferred mice. Dario rushed over and shooed the cat away and apologized. I didn't mind. - A black cat and Charles Heidsieck made a good omen. Better I thought, than Lapsang Souchong and a petit point Pekingese.

"I owned a cat once," Louis said when the excitement had died down.

"What kind of a cat?"
"A Swiss cat."
"What kind of a cat is that?"
"It's a cat that lives in Switzerland!"
"Were you in Switzerland?"
"Long ago. I went to school there for a while when I was thirteen," and then Louis began to talk about his brother and sisters, and of the early days of his childhood, after he was taken from the Charities Aid Society to live in the big house at 579.

When Mrs. Shepard adopted the four children, she tried to raise them practically single-handed. She awakened them in the morning, arranged their meals, taught them, supervised their play and their prayers, and tucked them in bed at night. She was assisted in her labors of love by a governess and a staff of fifteen servants, though most of the time they functioned more as spectators than as assistants.

They were, however, invaluable for search parties because the children were constantly vanishing. A house of four floors and over thirty rooms afforded innumerable secret hiding places and the children knew every one of them. It was impossible for Mrs. Shepard to patrol the entire territory by herself. She even experimented with a two-tone whistle as a sort of assembly call, but no matter how hard she blew it, the whistle would not carry above the third floor, let alone to the attic.

One day was especially frustrating. Two of the children disappeared. When they were finally found, the *governess* disappeared. Unable to tell Mrs. Shepard face to face that she was leaving, she left a note with the lady's maid saying that "she could not work in the same house with a Hindu butler."

"Louis, Sitwell isn't a *Hindu!*" I interrupted emphatically.

"No, Sitwell is American, but at that time, a missionary friend of Mother's recommended Hiralal and she couldn't refuse. She tried to make a Christian out of him and suggested that he join the Dutch Reformed Church, but he didn't want to be converted. He left soon afterwards for Hyderabad."

After this particular governess quit, weeks were spent finding a new one. Every morning, between the hours of ten and eleven, there were more governesses in the house than children. Mrs. Shepard talked to hundreds of applicants. Finally, the choice was narrowed down to two charming ladies, but Mrs. Shepard could not make up her mind which to favor. It was almost more than she could bear to have to choose between them.

Suddenly, it occurred to her that there was a very simple solution. She would have two governesses; one for the boys and one for the girls. So she engaged them both and immediately a certain amount of order was restored to the household. Of course, there was an occasional incident. Once the living room was temporarily converted into a soccer field and two hand-carved Balinese heads were used as goal posts, but all in all, there was peace and quiet.

As soon as the two governesses became accustomed to the general routine of the household, Mrs. Shepard devoted more and more of her time to her children's education. Others might take care of their physical needs, but she would take care of their brains and their souls. She was most ambitious that they mature into highly intellectual and God-fearing and neither time, nor money, nor discipline would be spared. Louis, Finley Jay, Helen Anna, and Olivia would grow up to be philologists, philatelists, botanists, ornithologists, musicologists, Biblicists, bibliologists, and ladies and gentlemen. They would avoid the tedium of the social world.

Mrs. Shepard did not enjoy the society of Newport, Southampton, Bar Harbor, or any place that was associated with famous people like the Astors, Vanderbilts or the Belmonts. She preferred her philanthropies and charities. She cared more for her four children than she did for the four hundred.

Unfortunately, this obsession for culture and doctrinaire Christianity made her an austere mother. She loved her children, but she did not accept the ways of childhood. She had no patience with the human and natural problems of growing up. Mrs. Shepard set a rigid and almost unattainable standard of righteousness. But whatever her training program lacked in psychological soundness, it never lacked in rigor. From earliest morn to latest night the sins of her children were itemized, corrected, prayed for, and expiated.

Listening to Louis tell me this I didn't see how any of the children ever lived through it.

"Louis," I said, "is your father as exacting as Mrs. Shepard?"

"No," Louis said, "he is strict, but he was easier with us in many ways. He always liked sports and games, and even today, he plays a pretty good game of golf. You'll meet him tomorrow."

Now as we sipped our champagne, the couple at the bar kissed each other and it reminded Louis of his mother's obsession for that particular form of affection. He said that as far back as he could remember, none of the children had been permitted to enter or leave a room without kissing Mrs. Shepard. Louis calculated that, on the average day, the four of them together kissed Mrs. Shepard thirty-six times. Mr. Shepard did not think such a continual display of affection was necessary, but he did not say anything about it.

Over a period of some ten years there were many governesses who came from abroad. One was Dutch, one was Scottish, one was English, and one was German. So, Louis picked up a smattering of many languages.

The learning of French, however, was not left to chance. Every Wednesday a French teacher came and torture was methodically inflicted on the children from four-thirty until dinner time. What happened to the French language during these hours shouldn't have happened to a French poodle! A new maid who passed by the room where the lessons were held wanted to know if the children were sick. The chef who knew the habits of the household said there was nothing to worry about; they were just conjugating the verb *connaitre*. The teacher usually escaped just before dinner and then a new teacher took over: Mrs. Shepard.

It was an inflexible rule that during the evening meal not a word of English was to be spoken. Mrs. Shepard guided the conversation—what there was of it. Louis recalled that before he became fluent in the language, his vocabulary limited him somewhat in his choice of food, but left him completely powerless to quench his thirst. He could not remember the word for "water," and for three consecutive Wednesdays he left the table with his tongue hanging out. Mrs. Shepard referred to Wednesday evening as "French Night," and she took great pride in watching her children's progress.

"Don't you think they're doing splendidly?" she would say to her husband.

"I don't really know, my dear," Mr. Shepard always answered. "I don't speak a blooming word of French myself."

Spanish night came on Thursdays and the identical procedure was followed. The tutor came in the afternoon, and Mrs. Shepard took over at dinner. On this evening there was a slight variation. Mrs. Shepard did not understand a word of Spanish, so she used the honor system. If her children did not know the Spanish word for "butter," they would simply go without, and she trusted them not to deceive her. Although she couldn't follow a single bit of the conversation, she enjoyed listening to it. She thought Spanish "so musical" and never seemed to tire of hearing the children say "Please pass the bread," and "Please pass the butter." *Sirvase darme el pan,* and *Pasame la mantequilla por favor* were to Mrs. Shepard as enjoyable as listening to the lilting phrase of a *fandango*. Once when Louis dropped his knife, he said sharply: "La *gran puta*."

"What does that mean, dear?" his mother asked. "It sounds lovely!"

Louis said the phrase was a little difficult to translate literally, but that it meant the knife was no good. If Louis had really translated the words, he would have been forced to say that the knife had no father. Louis' vocabulary was advanced for a boy of twelve—but so was his tact.

Mr. Shepard was always happy when Friday came around; for English was once again the official language of the household.

Apparently as I had already gathered from Louis Mrs. Shepard never made any allowances for differences in the children's personalities. No individuality was ever encouraged. They all did exactly the same things exactly at the same times. It was a wonder that they didn't all end up looking like identical quadruplets.

Their music lessons were a painful example of their mother's passion for conformity. Each child played the same exercises and practiced the same pieces, to the dismay of the entire household. Louis claimed that the parlor maid's nervous twitch was the direct result of Felix Mendelssohn's "March of the Priests."

On top of the music lessons, the children were carted each Saturday morning to Dr. Walter Damrosch's concerts at Carnegie Hall, and once a month to Box 25 in the Golden Horseshoe of the Metropolitan Opera House. When Helen Anna caught a cold during "The Valkyrie," all the children were given liberal doses of a special cough mixture. A cure for Helen Anna—a preventative for the others.

The children had an elaborate course in accounting. A monthly allowance of fifty cents had to be itemized down to the last penny. A glance at the bookkeeping showed five cents went each week to the Sunday School collection, and five cents to the church collection. During a month, with forty cents irrevocably pledged, ten cents was left for "miscellaneous."

"I still have my account book," Louis said. "I can show it to you."

By this time, it was getting late. A lot of people had come into the bar, but we hadn't noticed them. Friends were greeting each other noisily, and someone had discovered the cat and was trying to wean it away from cream with a piece of pineapple out of an old-fashioned. Everyone felt a personal obligation to change this animal's diet. After all it was almost Saturday night, and no school tomorrow, and no church except for us. Louis picked up the Charles Heidsieck bottle, and there was one glass left for each of us. Suddenly, I heard some chords on a guitar, and Dario walked over to our table.

"Are you happy?" he asked.

"Yes," I said.

"How's the champagne?"
"Wonderful!"
"Is there anything else you wish?"
"Yes, please sing us a song. You promised."
"All right. Let me think. Oh yes! I remember a song I think you'll like. It's an Italian folk song about a boy and girl. They're going to get married."

Dario strummed a few chords and then began to sing in a rich, full tenor voice. The song was haunting and melodious and the noise in the little speakeasy quieted down. Dario's audience listened intently. Even the cat had a moment of peace. I was happy and contented, and 579 Fifth Avenue seemed remote and far away.

4

The Sabbath

LOUIS AND I were to meet his mother and father on the church steps at eleven. Louis rang our apartment bell at ten. He was invariably prompt; this morning I thought he was premature. He looked extremely dignified in a dark-blue serge suit and a stiff collar, but something seemed to be the matter with his neck.

"Louis," I asked, "isn't your collar a bit tight?"

"Yes," he said, "I borrowed it from Sitwell."

We arrived at the Collegiate Reformed Church in good time—in fact we had twenty minutes to spare. The church was a block and a half north, and across Fifth Avenue from 579. And Mrs. Shepard, who attended services regularly, found it most convenient. Walking briskly, she could cover the distance in something under five minutes.

Convenient though it was, I didn't think the church was very beautiful. It was a formidable building, cold and drab like so many of the early brownstone churches in New York. How different, I thought, from the magnificent cathedrals I had seen one summer vacation in Europe. However, one shouldn't judge a church by its architecture, but by its good works, and I saw by the announcement box near the front archway that the Collegiate Church was doing its best.

Sunday

9:30	Church School
11:00	Morning Worship The Rev. Malcolm James MacLeod will preach: "The Parable of the Wise and Foolish Virgins"
4:30	Organ Recital—Palestrina and Bach
5:00	Vespers
7:00	Women's Bible Class—Church Library

For Monday, the schedule was less spiritual. There was only one item on the agenda:

5:00	Basketball

By the time I had read all this it was almost eleven o'clock, and the steps were crowded with last-minute arrivals. Limousines were driving up to let out cargoes of the faithful. Most of the women wore mink coats and the men were dressed in the conventional costume for Sunday worship—cutaway and high silk hat.

Suddenly Louis turned to me and said:

"Here they are—Mother and Father—right on time; and Celeste," he added, "Father's eyes are very bad. He can hardly see at all. We have to watch him carefully so he doesn't stumble over anything."

I turned, and saw the Shepards coming up Fifth Avenue. Mrs. Shepard was toddling along with nervous little steps and clinging tightly to her husband's arm. She had on a broad-brimmed Sunday bonnet with a high, round crown, and on her black coat was a huge corsage of her favorite flowers – *Cattleya trianae*.

As she approached, a white pigeon suddenly swooped down from nowhere and flew directly at her. It looked as though there might be a little accident, but at the very last moment, Mrs. Shepard fortunately bowed to a passing friend and the pigeon fluttered harmlessly over her hat. The bird made a graceful U-turn at the end of the block and headed back towards St. Patrick's to join its friends.

"Good morning, my children," Mrs. Shepard said, and kissed us each lightly on the cheek.

Then she added, a little out of breath:

"My daughter Helen Anna is so sorry to miss church. She does get these headaches quite often. You must excuse her."

Then Mrs. Shepard said to me:

"Celeste dear, this is my husband," and there on the steps of the Collegiate Church I met one of the handsomest men I had ever seen. He was tall and dignified, straight as an arrow, and as he doffed his high silk hat I saw he had silken white hair which exaggerated his kindly blue eyes and firm-set mouth. Although he was in his late sixties, there was hardly a wrinkle on his face, and I thought how distinguished he would look presiding at a directors' meeting or leading a grand march.

"I think we should go in," Mrs. Shepard suggested after a moment "We don't want to be late, do we?"

She took Louis' arm, and I took Mr. Shepard's. As we started slowly toward the big oak doors, he leaned down, squinted over his rimless glasses, and said apologetically: "Celeste, I hope we didn't keep you waiting, but my wife mislaid her gloves – you know how women are."

I smiled understanding, and we went inside together. The organ was playing a mournful prelude. We walked down the right aisle and bustled into a pew reserved for us by a little bronze plate inscribed "Mr. and Mrs. Finley Shepard." We all sat down and bowed our heads for the customary silent prayer. I said:

"Dear Lord, please make me a good girl and a good wife, and don't let me say anything which my future mother-in-law will not approve of. Amen."

I sat back in the pew, and for a moment I was a little dismayed because I saw that I had finished first. My brevity might have seemed irreverent and I was about to lean down and say another prayer, but just then Mr. Shepard completed his devotion, so I was not alone. Mrs. Shepard and Louis were still praying. After a few moments Mrs. Shepard finished her communion, but Louis was still at it.

The minutes were going by. I couldn't imagine what he could be saying all this time. I had a most horrifying suspicion. What if Louis wasn't praying at all? What if he had fallen asleep—suppose he snored?

But just as I was about to warn him by dropping a prayer book, he finished and sat back in the pew. I breathed more easily. The organ prelude ended, everyone rose to chant the doxology, and formal worship began.

Except for a few variations, the ritual was much the same as in my own church, and by keeping one eye on Mr. Shepard I was able to make the minor adjustments. During the responses he answered clearly and distinctly. It seemed almost as if he were carrying on a private conversation with the Reverend Mr. MacLeod. When it came to the singing part of the services, my future father-in-law was magnificent. He knew all the hymns by heart, and sang them in a fine bass voice. Mrs. Shepard, on the other hand, sang not a single note. She followed every word in the hymnal with her finger, pronounced each one silently—but that was all. Later I learned that she couldn't carry a tune.

The climax of all services in Protestant churches, is of course, the sermon. When Doctor McLeod ascended the pulpit, there was a general squirming and settling down. Everyone wanted to get as comfortable as possible to receive his message. He began in a portentous voice with just a touch of laryngitis:

"The text for today is from the Twenty-Fifth Chapter of St. Matthew—Verses: One to Thirteen. The parable of the Wise and Foolish Virgins."

At once I began to feel a trifle uncomfortable.

"Then shall the kingdom of heaven be likened unto ten virgins which took their lamps and went forth to meet the bridegroom. And five of them were wise, and five were foolish..."

From my sketchy biblical reading I remembered what came next. Five of the virgins ran out of oil for their lamps, but the wise ones wouldn't come across with a drop.

The Reverend Doctor MacLeod finished the Thirteenth Verse:

"Watch, therefore, for ye know neither the day nor the hour wherein the Son of man Cometh..." Then he skillfully and flamboyantly showed how this parable applied to life today.

Mrs. Shepard listened intently to every word because she was afraid of God, and Louis and I listened to every word because we were afraid of Mrs. Shepard.

I heard the church bell strike twelve-thirty and felt that it should be about time for Doctor MacLeod to conclude. He must have heard the bell, too, because he began his closing paragraphs. Gravely he implored everybody present never to forget what happened to the five foolish virgins who ran out of oil. And he said he hoped this parable would assist us all to live our daily lives in more Christian harmony. The sermon was over! Then after a short prayer, the minister walked down the steps of the pulpit to the chancel and intoned:

"Remember the words of the Lord Jesus Christ: 'It is more blessed to give than to receive." and immediately everybody started to put his hands in his pockets. Eight ushers wearing white carnations and carrying huge silver plates began to carry out their duties. There was nothing for me to do now for a few minutes, so I sat back and enjoyed the music. The soprano and alto were singing the Offertory, "Arise, O Lord God." It was a pleasant obligato to the crisp folding of new bills. I was contented and relaxed. I half-closed my eyes in peaceful reverie and was only dimly aware that the ushers were getting closer.

Suddenly a thought raced through my mind; my eyes opened and I became panicky. I remembered I had only ten cents in my purse! I had neglected to take more money with me. What a dreadful predicament! I couldn't cash a check, I couldn't faint, and I couldn't leave—and the usher was now only two pews in front of us. In a moment he would pass the plate to us and, sitting in the pew that belonged to one of the richest families in the world, I would make my contribution—one dime. I edged as close to Louis as I could, cupped my hand over my mouth, and whispered:

"Louis, will you loan me a dollar until Tuesday?"

Louis seemed not to hear me, and the usher was now only a single pew away. I had to try once more, a little louder:

"Louis, Louis, please help me! If you give me a dollar, I'll pay it back double. I promise."

This time he heard me. He turned his head slightly and answered:

"Sorry, you're in a spot. I only have a five-dollar bill."

There went my last hope.

The usher descended quickly upon us and gave the plate to Mr. Shepard who passed it to me. I handed it to Louis who passed it to Mrs. Shepard, and she put in a twenty-dollar bill. Then the plate began its return journey. Louis put in his new five-dollar bill. It was my turn. I had no choice. I put in my old dime, and it made a little clink as it hit bottom. As Mr. Shepard put in another twenty-dollar bill, I winced, but at last the ordeal was over. Total receipts from the Shepard pew: Forty-five dollars and ten cents.

The benediction was said, the organ played the postlude, and church was out.

There remained one final duty to perform: To pay our respects to the minister. He was standing in the alcove resplendent in a white surplice and silk stole, surrounded by his flock. As we walked up, he took Mr. and Mrs. Shepard each by one hand, exclaiming:

"How *do* you do? So refreshing to see you both here every Sunday."

Mrs. Shepard smiled and answered: "We enjoyed your sermon *so* much. It was a wonderful message."

"Thank you, thank you," the reverend gentleman replied, "but I think I ran a little overtime," and he winked at Louis. Then he turned to me:

"And who is this lovely young lady?"

Mrs. Shepard spoke for me: "This is Celeste Andrews," and then she said something that took me completely by surprise: "She is going to be my daughter-in-law."

"Well! Well! Well!" Doctor MacLeod reacted expansively. "Well! Well! Good news indeed!" and he placed both of his hands over one of mine:

"Dear, dear, Celeste! You must be very happy to be on the threshold of such a glorious adventure. Please come and see us often and allow an old man to give you his heartfelt blessing."

We said goodbye and walked back to 579 in silence. Sitwell opened the door, and as we went in, a girl about my age in a smart green dress and beautiful pumps ran down the red-carpeted stairs two at a time. It was Helen Anna.

"Hello, everybody," she said, as she kissed her mother. "How was the sermon?"

"It was a wonderful message," Mrs. Shepard answered. "I'm so sorry I missed it. I've been thinking about you all morning."

"How sweet. Is your headache any better?"

"It's gone. I took ten grains of aspirin."

"Five grains would have been sufficient," Mr. Shepard said.

"Yes, Father," Helen said contritely and then turned her attention to me.

"And you're Celeste! I'm so glad to meet you. Wouldn't you like to come up to my room for a few minutes before dinner?"

"I'd love to," I said and we started upstairs as Mr. Shepard issued a warning: "Just twenty-five minutes before dinner."

Helen Anna was a slender, pretty brunette. She had vitality, and verve, and a cute little upturned nose and a friendly laugh. Her hands were thin and artistic and matched her dainty waist and graceful feet. She was half ballerina and half tomboy, and there was mischief in her big blue eyes. No Victorian chains would ever be strong enough to hold her.

We climbed two flights of stairs, turned down a hallway, and stopped in front of a door. Helen Anna opened it and said ceremoniously: "Enter, this is where I live."

It was a large, bright room with chintz curtains. The tall windows looking down on Fifth Avenue let in shafts of sunlight, and it was gay and inviting. This was an oasis in a Victorian desert. On the wide canopy bed was a huge quilt of lively colors, and on the little mahogany reading table was a copy of *Anthony Adverse* and a movie magazine with a picture of Ronald Colman on the cover. Next to a frilly dressing table in the corner was a bird cage big enough to hold an eagle, though its only tenant was a little Hartz mountain canary. Then remembering my first meeting with Chinky, I said: "Hello, Dickie."

"His name is Concerto, but don't waste your time. We've had him eleven years, and he's never peeped once."

"Doesn't he like it here?"

"He should. He eats more than I do. Sit down, Celeste, and make yourself comfortable. Would you like a drink?"

"I am rather thirsty," I said, "but I'll get it myself," and I started to get up...

"No, no," Helen Anna interrupted. "I mean a real drink. You know — a martini."

This was one word I never expected to hear in this house. For a moment I thought she was joking.

"Helen Anna," I asked, "are you quite sure this is all right?"

Then Helen Anna opened a drawer of her chiffonier, fumbled under some white satin slips, and brought forth a quart of gin and a bottle of vermouth. Holding them aloft, one in each hand, she said mockingly:

"The Helen Anna collection; in this house, as rare as laughter."

She went into the bathroom for a thermos of cracked ice, and made the drinks.

"To you, Celeste," she said, "my future sister-in-law," and two rather nervous young ladies drank two rather strong martinis. After we recovered from the sting of the first swallow, Helen Anna started talking. She spoke in quick little staccato sentences with the most fervent curiosity about the most commonplace things: Did I go dancing often? Did I ever go shopping at Saks Fifth Avenue? Was I always allowed to see Louis without a chaperone? She hardly waited for my answer to the last question before she was on to the next. She acted like someone who had been away a long time and wanted to catch up with the world in five minutes.

"How was church today?" she continued and leaned forward on the edge of her chair.

"It was about virgins and oil—." I changed the subject and inquired about her headache.

With a little laugh, she said, "Better now, but it's a strange coincidence. I seem to get them almost every Sunday—just before church." Then, like quicksilver, she was off on another topic: "Tell me, Celeste, how do you like our happy home?"

"I've never been anywhere quite like it. I think it's very interesting."

"I suppose it is unless you live in it. Oh, I'm so jealous of you I could spit."

"Why, Helen Anna, what in the world have you got to be jealous of me for?"

"Everything. You're getting married. You'll have a

home and life of your own. If you want a drink, you won't have to be a sneak to get it. If you want a cigarette, you won't have to lock yourself up in the johnnie."

"Helen Anna," I said, "you're not going to spend your *life* here. You'll get married, too."

"And just who am I going to marry? I know exactly two men. Sitwell and our minister. In a pinch, I suppose I could marry Finley Jay, except I think there's a law against marrying your own brother."

"He's only your adopted brother," I said. "That would be all right."

"Well, he wouldn't have me. He treats me like a baby. You'll see when you meet him at dinner."

"Will there be anyone else at dinner besides the family?" I asked.

"I don't think so."

At that moment the little house phone started ringing on the wall, and Helen Anna answered it. It was Sitwell. And from the conversation I gathered that he was telling her it was almost time for dinner. She thanked the butler for the warning, and just before she hung up, she said: "Sitwell, thanks a lot for the liquor. I'll do the same for you sometime."

Mrs. Shepard's house was full of little surprises. It might be a little foreboding, but it certainly wasn't dull.

"Dinner's in ten minutes," Helen Anna said. "Do you want to wash up or anything?"

I went into the adjoining bathroom and closed the door. It was only a little smaller than a squash court and there was ample room for two adults in the old-fashioned bathtub. Hand-stitched monogrammed towels lined the racks, and all the soap was molded in the form of little cherubic angels. Godliness and cleanliness obviously went hand in hand. When I shut the door, I had to look twice to believe my eyes, for hanging down from a brass hook was a huge scroll. And on it, printed in large, bold Gothic type, was this message:

Wine is a mocker, strong drink is raging;
And whosoever is deceived is not wise.
Proverbs 20:1

Now I knew we shouldn't have had those martinis. "Hurry up," Helen Anna shouted, "we'll be late."

I ran out of the bathroom, and she shoved a peppermint Lifesaver into my mouth "to take away the gin smell." "Tell me, Helen Anna, where did the scroll come from?" "Mother. She puts a new one in the bathrooms every week."

I thought to myself if you don't achieve divine grace in this house one way, you surely will in another.

Then as the house phone started to buzz we ran quickly out of the door. It was Sitwell again — always at his post — sounding the dinner alarm like a good sentinel.

5

Roast Beef and Yorkshire Pudding

WHEN HELEN ANNA and I came into the living room, we found there an unexpected guest, a plain, middle-aged lady who was whispering with Mrs. Shepard in the corner. She was introduced to us as Miss Quincy from Chatham. Her cheeks were drawn and gaunt, and her simple gray dress was the soul of New England primness. Mrs. Shepard said it was a great privilege to have Miss Quincy for dinner, and Miss Quincy replied it was a great privilege to be there.

As soon as Mr. Shepard saw us, he rose politely, but then he sat down again quickly at the card table. He was working on the enormous, unfinished jigsaw puzzle of Herbert Hoover. Somehow it had never occurred to me that Mr. Shepard was connected with this gigantic project. There were hundreds of little pieces still to be assembled. I watched him carefully and methodically searching for the precise ones; he was a study in patience and concentration. Every now and then, when he discovered a certain segment of an arm or a nose, he exclaimed, "There, there, I found you, you little devil!"

Once as he labored I heard him mumble:

"Mr. President, I don't know if you are really worth all this trouble!"

The large oak door to the dining room opened and Sitwell announced dinner. I wondered where Louis' brother was, but Mr. Shepard explained his absence: "Finley Jay is late again. I think we must proceed without him." At 579 time, tide and Sunday dinner waited for no man.

The dining room was a large room handsomely appointed. Four tall candles in silver holders burned like torches on the table, and in the center there was an exquisite array of flowers. From the frescoed ceiling a choir of cherubs looked down upon us. Although there were only seven places set now, 1 saw that the seating arrangements would not be decided extemporaneously; there were place cards leaning against each long-stemmed water goblet.

I was to sit on Mr. Shepard's right, and next to Miss Quincy and across from Louis and Helen Anna. But my place card was artistic as well as functional. Below my name was a miniature photograph with a caption: "Swans on the Delaware River." Helen Anna picked hers up and said in an unmistakable tone of disappointment: "Another view of Mount Ida from our place in the Catskills. Same as last week."

As we sat down, Mr. Shepard explained that their married daughter, Olivia, and her husband, John Burr, would not be with us.

"But you'll meet all of us in time," he said, "sooner or later."

Then Mrs. Shepard, seated at one end of the long table, said in a voice that barely carried to her husband seated at the other:

"Finley, dear, *will* you?"

He closed his eyes, bowed his head, and said, "For what we are about to receive, may the Lord make us truly thankful. Amen." And dinner began.

For a few moments the only sound in the great room was the gentle lapping of turtle soup. There was a tremendous bowl before me and my immediate concern was not so much to enjoy it as to avoid spilling it.

During the first course there was no attempt whatsoever at conversation; no one ventured so much as a casual reference about the weather. Even Helen Anna seemed completely subdued by the formality of the atmosphere. We were home, but not *at home*. After what seemed like an eternity of silence, Louis came through with an icebreaking statement.

"Good soup, isn't it?"

This certainly wasn't a particularly brilliant remark, but, under the circumstances, it was audacious. Immediately, everyone chimed in enthusiastically to agree. Helen Anna and I, and even Mrs. Shepard proclaimed wholeheartedly that it was indeed a good soup. It was pleasant to hear the human voice again. Louis had thrown us a lifesaver . . . But alas, nothing much came of it; this little flicker of life started with "good soup" and died with "good soup."

The walls of the dining room were completely done in fine brown Moroccan leather. This dull, monochromatic effect was broken only by two pictures hung in heavy, hand-carved gilt frames. One of them was of a cow, just under life-size. I think it was painted by that famous French cow-painter, Rosa Bonheur. She had idealized the creature with all the holy fervor of a Hindu. The cow was a Guernsey, and it appeared contented. I did not know to whom this particular piece of livestock belonged, but the owner must have considered it an exceptional likeness. It was big and realistic down to the last detail; you felt as if you could milk it right there in the dining room.

On the opposite wall, directly facing the cow, hung the picture of "Grandpa" — that fabulous American financier. Jay Gould, forever perpetuated in oil and varnish.

From what I remembered of his life, there were many who would have preferred to burn him in oil rather than paint him in oil. I had read chapters in American history telling how "Grandpa," John Jacob Astor and Cornelius Vanderbilt had started out as barefoot boys and ended up as freebooters, rich as Croesus.

They had swindled the Indians, hacked down the forests, built the railroads, mined the gold, coerced their fellowmen, built pompous Victorian houses, and rode into respectable society in coaches and four. Their exploits sounded like the stories of Captain Kidd and the Spanish buccaneers. All these things had actually happened, yet somehow you didn't quite believe it, and in the dining room candlelight Jay Gould, himself, seemed unreal, romantic and preposterous. His forehead was high, his complexion was swarthy, and his face was partly hidden by a flourishing beard draping him from chin to chest. His eyes were deep and penetrating and very frightening.

I glanced down the long table at his eldest daughter — my future mother-in-law. She not only looked kind, she was kindness itself. I am sure that in her entire life she had never once intentionally hurt a single living creature. Perhaps, unconsciously, she was atoning for the sins of her father. Yes, it was possible that I was sitting between an angel and a pirate. Still it was comforting to realize that while Jay Gould once built an empire with ruthless ambition, the strength of an ox and the cunning of a fox, all he could do now was gaze forever at a cow.

Immediately after the turtle soup, the plates were whisked away, and we were ready for the next course—oysters. Gourmandically speaking, we were still on the high seas. Placed before me were six of the largest oysters I had ever seen. I was terrified, not so much on account of their size, but because I had to *eat* them. Strange as it may seem, I had never in my life eaten an oyster. Some childhood conditioning, some deep aversion had always denied me this experience. How I wished that it had been May or June; any month without an "R" in it. While I was wracking my brain for a polite excuse which would allow me to skip this course, Mr. Shepard said expansively:

"Celeste, these are the finest oysters in the world, even though ordinarily they are served before the soup."

"Sitwell just became a grandfather," Mrs. Shepard explained, "he's a little excited. We'll pretend not to notice." "Of course, my dear," Mr. Shepard said, "it will not hurt their flavor at all. Celeste, you will never in all your life taste anything more delectable."

Even Mrs. Shepard could not control her enthusiasm. "I do so love oysters. Don't *you*, Celeste, dear?"

I was trapped. By sheer will power I managed to answer: "Yes, Mrs. Shepard," and then she nodded her little head; it was the signal for the massacre to begin. Helen Anna gave me a moment's reprieve by an interesting question:

"Is it true that oysters are alive when you eat them?" "Absolutely," Louis said, "alive and fighting."

It was reassuring to have an expert's opinion. I waited till the last possible moment. Finally, I said to myself, "Courage," picked up my fork, aimed it at an oyster, closed my eyes, and, half expecting to hear it utter a little cry—I stabbed it mercilessly. Then I opened my mouth, steeled myself for the great, slippery swallow, and an oyster slid down my esophagus to the great beyond.

After the last one disappeared, I thought, "My God, to think I've got six of those things swimming around inside me!" The course was over, and I had survived it, but I felt I had aged a great deal in the last few minutes.

Now I wondered what was next on the menu. I prayed that it would be something simple and familiar. It was—solid roast beef and Yorkshire pudding. This was nothing to be afraid of, and I hoped that the funny little jostling in my stomach was just my imagination.

The roast beef actually generated a flicker of conversation. An observation or two was made about the weather, and Mr. Shepard said that the sermon that morning had "quite a lot of teeth in it." The remark was trite but comfortable. Anything was preferable to silence—a silence so pure that you could hear yourself think—and worse—eat. Every time Louis took a bite of celery it sounded as if he were crunching bone.

This brief flare of dialogue held its own pretty well during most of the roast beef. Mr. Shepard would occasionally say something like, "How is everything at college, Louis?", or "How is your golf coming along?"—and Louis would answer that college was fine, although he was having a little trouble with his chip shots. Mrs. Shepard sometimes came in at the end of these forays with a "That's nice," or "How sweet," or "That's too bad." This was the extent of our dinner conversation.

There was never any discussion or elaboration. The syntax of communication had been pruned down to the irreducible minimum: Subject, object, verb, period—and a long pause.

I felt that I should contribute a word or two to the forum;

a comment on the flowers in the center of the table might be appropriate. So, I jumped headfirst into the middle of the next pause: "Mrs. Shepard, those are beautiful flowers. I think the roses are exquisite."

"Yes, my dear," Mrs. Shepard said, "the *Rosa spinosissima* is indeed lovely."

"Yes, yes, Mrs. Shepard; they certainly are," I answered, a little taken aback. A jingle went through my mind: 'Mother, Mother, pin a *Rosa spinosissima* on me. Mr. Shepard joined the conversation: "My dear, the *Spinosissima* is, indeed a fine specimen, and I think the *Gypsophila paniculata* they sent down from the greenhouse this weekend is also remarkable. Celeste, I do want to take you up there sometime."

At that moment Louis laughingly interrupted: "I feel that the *Pelargonium terebinthinaceum* is the most beautiful of all." Personally, I didn't feel this remark was necessary.

During these moments of scintillating repartee, I was aware that the little lady to whom Mrs. Shepard had introduced me before dinner had said nothing all this time. But her silence could not be a sign of shyness—because she was now on her third helping of roast beef. Still she was sitting next to me, and common politeness required that I should talk to her. I tried to recollect her name, but I could not quite remember if it was Miss Quincy from Chatham or Miss Chatham from Quincy. So I decided to take a chance.

I began: "Miss Chatham."

She turned her head, smiled, and replied: "My name is Miss Quincy."

"Miss Quincy," I went on, "you must come from Massachusetts."

"Yes," she replied, "I do."

"How interesting," I said.

"I live in Chatham," she added. "That's on the Cape, but I'm not there very much."

Then she went back to her roast beef.

Mrs. Shepard leaned across the table and said:

"Miss Quincy is a reader, you know."

I'm glad she's something, I thought, she certainly isn't a conversationalist. Perhaps, though, we could strike up a little chat about books. I asked her if she had read *The Bridge of San Luis Rey* by Thornton Wilder.

"No," she answered. "I've never heard of it."

Then I asked her if she had read *Elmer Gantry* by Sinclair Lewis.

"No," she answered.

I decided to try again; perhaps something along classical lines would ring a bell. So I asked her if she had read *Wuthering Heights.*

"No," she said, "but I've heard of it."

At least I was getting warm. Maybe I should try her out on detective fiction. "Have you read *The Case of the One-Eyed Corpse?*"

"I *never* read horror stories."

"Miss Quincy is a *Bible* reader," Mrs. Shepard explained. "She travels all over the country reading the Bible." "Mostly to church groups and schools,"

Miss Quincy clarified. "I've just been all through New England — except Connecticut."

"It is very important work," Mrs. Shepard commented. "It must give you great satisfaction," I said, beaming at her admiringly.

"It does," Miss Quincy said flatly.

Mrs. Shepard looked thoughtful for a moment and then asked, "Is there anything else you wish, Miss Quincy? Perhaps some more roast beef?"

"No more, thank you, Mrs. Shepard." Just then we heard a loud, hearty voice from the foyer. "Sorry, everybody!" And in a moment a tall, dark-haired, attractive young man strode into the room, full of confidence, and more than an hour late. It was Finley Jay, Louis' brother.

He descended first on Mrs. Shepard, kissed her with enthusiasm, and shouted: "Mother, how are you? You look wonderful!" When he shook hands with his father, he simmered down a little but burst into flame again as he smacked Helen Anna on the lips and shook hands with Louis. "How's my beautiful sister and handsome brother?" Finley Jay had invaded the room rather than entered it. There were life and sunshine in this boy, and a great deal of courage too. Being an hour late for dinner in this house was, I thought, practically a federal offense, but Finley Jay took it right in stride.

"You'll all have to forgive me for being late. I was over in Brooklyn with a friend of mine, and we went to church. We couldn't leave before it was over."

This was apparently a flagrant lie but no one questioned it. Mrs. Shepard simply said:

"It's quite all right, dear."

She never doubted for a moment the most outlandish things that were said to her. Invariably she endowed her family and her friends with the virtues that exist only in heaven.

Now Finley Jay's laughing eyes darted around the table, and I saw them stop at Miss Quincy.

"And you," he said expansively, "you must be the girl my brother is going to marry. You are Celeste."

She blushed crimson and replied, "No, I am Miss Quincy—from Chatham."

Finley Jay looked at me. "Then *you* are Celeste, and

you're going to be my sister-in-law!" He ran over, threw his arms around me and kissed me. "Congratulations," he said. "Congratulations." At arm's length, he surveyed me, and asked, "I want to know just one thing. How did Louis ever find anyone so beautiful?"

"Have some dinner," Louis suggested rather annoyed. "It'll get cold."

"Let it," his brother answered. "But where's the ring? Doesn't Celeste get a ring?"

Mr. Shepard interrupted with a little cough. "All in due time, Finley Jay. Sit down and have some dinner."

"I guess I *am* a little hungry, Father."

Finley Jay did not speak again until the pistachio ice cream. Then, to my surprise, I heard him say:

"The *Rosa spinosissima* is beautiful."

Et tu, Finley, I thought.

Helen Anna said a little sarcastically, "We decided the flowers were beautiful almost an hour ago—while you were in church, Finley, dear—in Brooklyn."

After dessert there were only three more items on the agenda: Fruit, nuts and caramel candy. Allowing conservatively forty-five minutes for this combination, the entire Sunday dinner would consume almost three hours —a nice, leisurely meal. Gracious living was not dead on Forty-Seventh Street.

But all things come to an end: Life, Sermons and Sunday Dinners. Life ends with a sigh, the Sermon ends with a prayer, and the Shepard's Sunday dinner, too, had its own special kind of closing signature. It was: "Has Father finished his caramels?" Later I was to learn that Mrs. Shepard always asked this question. And that Helen Anna always answered: "Yes, Father has finished eating his caramels."

After caramels came coffee. We followed Mrs. Shepard into the living room just as the evening sun was going down.

Miss Quincy said, "Excuse me, please. I must leave. I have to go to Connecticut." We said goodbye in turn and she left on a wave of cordiality.

Immediately after Miss Quincy had departed, Mrs. Shepard took my arm: "Celeste, dear, now you must sign the guest book."

"I would love to, Mrs. Shepard, but I signed it yesterday. Don't you remember? At tea."

"Of course, I remember, dear," she answered, "but you must sign it again."

So, I obediently went over to the guest book. This time I showed a distinct improvement; I spilled no ink. Signing the book, in this house, was a continual chore. If you went there seven days a week, you signed seven days a week. I do not know where this mighty book rests today with its thousands of signatures, but whoever turns its pages will look too often upon mine. Please remember it was custom, not vanity, that caused my name to be inscribed so many times.

Right after the guest-book ceremony Sitwell and Agnes, the parlor maid, working beautifully together, brought in the coffee; and Mrs. Shepard at once assumed her duties. We were each asked if we wanted "Cream? Sugar? One lump or two?" Sometime later Louis told me that, after exhaustive domestic research, he had determined that since they were married, Mrs. Shepard must have asked Mr. Shepard eleven thousand seven hundred and forty-three times what he liked in his demitasse, and eleven thousand seven hundred and forty-three times Mr. Shepard had replied: "Nothing." To her dying day, Mrs. Shepard remained unconvinced that her husband might not change his mind. Life at 579 was made up of a series of little habits, little formulae—never varied—never compromised.

After we had been served, Mr. Shepard asked me if I would like to finish my demitasse with him in the salon. I had never been in this room before, and as we entered, I saw a huge couch upholstered in brilliant vermilion Chinese silk. A ferocious, fire-breathing dragon was painted on it in vivid gold. It was as unexpected as coming upon a sea serpent in a mountain lake or a dinosaur in Central Park. Had some grateful Chinese missionary sent this Oriental nightmare to me, I would have hidden it. Not Mrs. Shepard—she made a shrine of it! She considered the couch so priceless an object that she had stretched a red velvet rope across it to prohibit anyone from sitting there. I felt this was an unnecessary precaution. Even St. George would have shunned this monstrosity.

On the other side of the room was a huge Wurlitzer organ. Mr. Shepard went over and motioned me to sit beside him on the bench.

"Celeste, could you stand a little concert?"

"I'd love it," I answered.

He started to play. I didn't know the name of the piece, it was a song—a song without words. It was somber, but melodious and beautiful; and the deep, sonorous tones of the organ reverberated through the house. Mr. Shepard's hands moved gracefully and lightly across the keyboards. He loved music, and his touch was tender and reverent. The song developed dramatically and majestically, and finally, after a series of resolving arpeggios, it ended on a long, sustained chord.

"Mr. Shepard, it was beautiful!" I exclaimed. "I didn't know you played."

"I don't very well," he answered modestly, "just enough to give me pleasure—and perhaps a few others."

"Won't you play something else for me?"

"Of course. Is there anything particular you'd like to hear?"

"No. You choose something."

He looked up thoughtfully at the ceiling, trying to think of a composition I might enjoy. Finally, he said, "Do you like Wagner, Celeste?"

"Yes," I said, "I like Wagner, but I don't know his work very well. How about 'The Evening Star?' "

"It's beautiful. But there's another piece of his I think you know, too," and Mr. Shepard began to play.

I blushed a little as I recognized the opening measures of the Wedding March from *Lohengrin*. But somehow it seemed as if I were hearing it for the first time. It meant something now. It was mine for a fleeting moment, and as he played, I felt saddened and put my head gently against his shoulder.

Presently, the children started to come in from the other room and group themselves quietly around the organ, Louis, Finley Jay and Helen Anna. Mrs. Shepard followed her children and sat down alone by the window. No one spoke. When Mr. Shepard finished playing the Wedding March, he put his arm around me and kissed me.

6

Faith, Hope, and Charity

AT PRECISELY TWO o'clock on February second, two important luncheons took place. Downtown, Mr. Shepard was lunching with my father at the Bankers Club, and at 579 Fifth Avenue my mother had lunch with Mrs. Shepard. Though the luncheons were held a considerable distance apart, and though the menus were entirely different, the main topic of conversation was identical: My marriage to Louis.

Both meetings were pleasant, and all four parents were in unanimous agreement that marriage for their children was practical and desirable. The two luncheons ended at approximately the same time on a happy note, but with widely contrasting amenities. Mother and Mrs. Shepard concluded their "sweet little talk" with a kiss; Father and Mr. Shepard ended theirs with two ponies of brandy.

Mother agreed I was right when I told her that Mrs. Shepard was a little conservative but very well informed. She said that as she was leaving, Mrs. Shepard asked her if she knew what day it was. Mother replied that she thought it was the second of February.

"Yes, Mrs. Andrews," Mrs. Shepard replied, "but it's

also Groundhog Day—just six more weeks of winter." Father, on the other hand, said I was wrong about Mr. Shepard; he was obviously not a teetotaler. When I told Louis about the brandy, he confessed that on more than one occasion, his father had come sailing into the house with a breath that would fell an ichthyosaurus, but Mrs. Shepard's faith was considerably stronger than her sense of smell. She would no more imagine that her husband would touch the wine of the grape than she would suspect Helen Anna of serving cocktails in her bedroom.

In late March my parents gave a small reception to announce my engagement, and the next morning most of the newspapers carried the news, simply and without embellishments. A typical headline read:

"Celeste Andrews to marry Louis Seton, ward of the philanthropically inclined Mr. and Mrs. Finley J. Shepard. Nuptials planned for November."

There were, however, a few headlines that were not so restrained. One of the papers screamed in a bold type: "Celeste Andrews to wed scion of Gould family."

The New York *Herald* said I was going to marry "Louise" Seton, and another paper in giving a short biographical sketch of the families, said my father was a great naturalist. He was very flattered by this confusion with Ernest Thompson Seton until someone phoned to ask him if it was true that the praying mantis eats its mate.

But my own name took the worst beating, particularly in the Midwest. One gazette spelled my first name correctly—backwards: "Etselec Andrews to Wed." Mother said, "Whatever will people think? Your father has business connections out there!"

Mother was right. A few days later Louis received a letter from an old friend expressing surprise that he was marrying the descendant of an Aztec Indian. Louis, bless his heart, thought this the very essence of humor. For days he would repeat: "Do you, Louis, take Etselec to be your wedded wife?" and, occasionally, to this day, he will come home from the office, open the door, and shout, "Is Etselec back from Chapultepec!"

After my engagement was announced I went to 579 Fifth Avenue more and more often. Church services, the long Sunday dinners, and innumerable tea parties became part of a natural routine, and gradually I made the transition from guest to a member of the family. The fear I used to have every time I walked up the marble steps became partially conquered by habit and because I now "belonged."

Belonging had its obligations as well as its pleasures, and Mrs. Shepard called on me occasionally to assist her with her charity work, her entertaining, or just "to take a little walk with her around the block."

One Saturday she was not feeling well, and Miss Wilson, the nurse, insisted that she go to bed at once. Every now and then her heart would flutter, and the prescription was complete rest and quiet. But Mrs. Shepard was opposed to such sedentary therapy and resisted with two powerful weapons: Politeness and momentary deafness.

"I'm sorry, dear lady," she would say, "I can't understand a word you're saying. Now, don't you think you should go down to the kitchen and make yourself a nice cup of tea: You've been working much too hard."

Young nurses, just out of training, were powerless to combat these tactics and had to be replaced by older, more experienced veterans. Such a nurse was Miss Wilson who, when necessary, could quote from the Bible an appropriate verse on the wisdom of cooperation: "If ye be willing and obedient, ye shall eat the good of the land." This was more effective than a sleeping pill; Mrs. Shepard was not prepared to compromise the Scriptures.

Perversity, however, was not the sole reason for her occasional insubordination. She hated to break an appointment, important or trivial, for in her social code a broken date was a broken promise, and a broken promise was a sin.

One morning Mrs. Shepard fought against staying in bed because she had planned to visit her father's grave in Woodlawn Cemetery. When Jay Gould died in 1892, most of the mourners at his interment made this their last visit to his grave. But not his eldest daughter.

Several times a year she journeyed to Woodlawn to take fresh flower wreaths and to say a prayer. Only a nurse with a will of iron and a knowledge of Holy Writ could keep her from this sacred duty.

Since she was unable to go this time, Mrs. Shepard did the next best thing: She asked Louis and me to go in her stead. Her instructions were minute. The chrysanthemum wreaths were ready for us in the conservatory. We must place them on the marble steps of the mausoleum, and she wanted Louis to take a few pictures with the Leica camera she had given him for Christmas. She kissed us goodbye with a parting suggestion that Louis should have the sun over his left shoulder when he took the pictures.

An hour later, Louis and I drove up before Jay Gould's mausoleum, which stood alone in the exact center of a large circular plot of ground. We got out of the car, stood reverently in front of it, and Louis removed his hat. The mausoleum had Ionic columns and looked like a Hellenic temple. Two huge weeping willow trees stood on either side, and nearby, with less natural piety, was a stunted pine. A little faded American flag was stuck in the earth just in front of the marble steps. There was no name on the mausoleum. Apparently, this anonymity discouraged curiosity seekers.

We took the wreaths out of the car, and I arranged them carefully on the front marble steps. Then I pulled the little American flag out of the ground.

"Jay Gould needs a new flag," I said.

Louis nodded and said we'd better get busy and take the pictures. So he got out the camera and set up the tripod, carefully noting the position of the sun. After he had used up two rolls of film, it was time to leave. The sun was going down, and shadows were making crisscross patterns on the tombstones.

As we drove out of the cemetery, Louis said: "Jay Gould's mausoleum cost one hundred and ten thousand dollars."

When we returned home, we told Mrs. Shepard that everything was all right except that the grass needed cutting around the sides of the mausoleum. This information seemed to annoy her almost as much as if we had said that someone had stolen her father's tomb. Frantically she called for Miss Stebbins, and a letter of complaint was mailed as soon as her nervous little hands could write it.

Although Mrs. Shepard had been deeply saddened by her father's death, it was Louis' opinion that only then had she begun to live. Jay Gould left her a huge fortune and she was free now to do almost anything she wished. She could help the sick, educate the ignorant, convert the infidel, and build a highway to Heaven.

One of the things Mrs. Shepard inherited from Jay Gould was an interest in New York University. She remembered that her father had occasionally made donations to that institution, and she felt that by continuing to assist the university she was dutifully carrying out her father's wishes. Certainly if Jay Gould could have known the extent of her interest, he would have been more than satisfied. Altogether she gave almost two million dollars to the university, in addition to the Jay Gould Memorial Library and The Hall of Fame. Mrs. Shepard had never gone to college, but for all practical purposes, she built one.

The week following the trek to Woodlawn Louis came up from Princeton again, and Mrs. Shepard suggested that we visit The Hall of Fame. She had not seen it for many years and was anxious to know how things were getting along. We obediently went up to University Heights, and there in the imposing Roman colonnade overlooking the Harlem River and a gas company, we paid our respects to many famous Americans eternally preserved in bronze and cold winds. I learned that there were three basic requirements for such frigid immortality. You must be famous, you must be elected by a majority vote of a hundred electors, and you must be twenty-five years dead. This last condition was not always so difficult to satisfy. Prior to 1922, a candidate had to be dead for only ten years.

In 1934, there were sixty-nine Americans who had satisfied all requirements for a place in The Hall of Fame. Some of them were known to every schoolboy: George Washington, Thomas Jefferson, Abraham Lincoln, Henry Wadsworth Longfellow, and Edgar Allan Poe. One of them was known by every schoolboy who went to Horace Mann School: Mr. Horace Mann, the Headmaster. Some of them were hardly known by any schoolboys: James Kent, Matthew Maury, and John Lothrop Motley. One of them I am sure was known by *no* schoolboy: Maria Mitchell, who taught at Vassar College from 1865 to 1888.

When we completed our inspection of these celebrities, we reported back to Mrs. Shepard that, with the exception of a few orange peels lying around, and a chip off the left ear of Patrick Henry, (1736-1799), everything was in good order. We did *not* tell Louis' mother that on balmy spring evenings students of New York University were said to consider The Hall of Fame not so much a testament to fame as a convenient setting for romance.

From then on, every now and again Mrs. Shepard would have little bursts of efficiency and ask us to look at this or that monument or drop into some college or institution which she had helped build or endow. Many weekends Louis and I became sort of roving, unofficial inspectors for the Gould philanthropies in the metropolitan area.

Louis knew a lot about the early life of his mother and told me a great deal about it. During her twenties, Helen Gould had been called the "Richest Girl in America" and Louis showed me an old newspaper clipping from *The New York Times* listing some of her contributions for just a single year:

New York University	$435,000
Navy Y.M.C.A.	500,000
Aid to U.S. Government for Spanish War	100,000
Scholarships	40,000
Y.M.C.A. Norfolk, Va.	25,000
National Women's Relief	25,000
Crusade Against Mormonism	6,000
Manhattan Eye and Ear Hospital	5,000
Endowment Fund, Berea College	5,000
Relief for Texas Flood	5,000

This added up, and I checked it twice, to a total of

one million, one hundred and forty-six thousand dollars. I thought of the ten dollars I had just sent to the Smith College Alumnae Fund.

When I told my father about Mrs. Shepard's donations, he made only one comment: "Good diversification."

I said to Louis that some of the items on the list seemed a little peculiar and, I thought, needed a little explanation. He replied that some of them needed a *lot* of explanation.

He told me Mrs. Shepard became interested in the Y.M.C.A. as early as 1897. She had heard disquieting rumors that men in our Navy were not welcome in the better New York hotels and restaurants and consequently drifted into saloons, and gambling dens. Conditions were exceedingly bad in the vicinity of the Brooklyn Navy Yard. One estimate held that there were more dens of iniquity in Brooklyn than sailors. So the Y.M.C.A. went up as fast as a construction company could build it, and it was such a success that Mrs. Shepard's lifelong friend, Mrs. Russell Sage, added an extension.

But my mother-in-law never thought that money was all-sufficient. She went often to the "Y," took flowers from her own greenhouse, and saw to it that the men were kindly treated and cared for. This "Y" became so well known that Theodore Roosevelt made a special trip to see it. And later she returned the visit by lunching with the president in the White House. During the next administration President Taft also visited her building. He too heartily voiced his approval, but did not invite Mrs. Shepard to lunch.

Her association with the Brooklyn Navy Yard was long and enduring, but she did not forget the Army. One afternoon she had an appointment to try on a new dress that she was planning to wear to the opera. She told her secretary to cancel it, saying that she would "make an old dress do." A few days later she gave a complete Y.M.C.A building to Fort Monroe in Virginia.

Louis said that although his mother's interest in the Y.M.C.A. extended from coast to coast, she became particularly interested, during one year, in the state of Kansas and gave large donations to the Y.M.C.A.s at Fort Leavenworth, Kansas; Fort Riley, Kansas; Coffeyville, Kansas; Argent, Kansas; Housington, Kansas; and last but not least, Moberly, Kansas.

I looked again at the clipping of *The New York Times* and stared at one item in particular:

"Crusade against Mormonism . . . . $6,000."

"Louis," I said, "why did your mother give $6,000 for a crusade against Mormonism?"

"To stop it."

"To stop it! What in Heaven's name for?"

"It's easy to explain," Louis said. "Mother doesn't believe any man should have more than one wife. She thinks bigamists with two wives are bad enough. But when she learned that Mormons used to have as many as ten wives, she wrote out a check for six thousand dollars. It was a protest rather than a donation."

"That's incredible!"

"Mother has never been afraid of the impossible. She's done lots of things which seemed to her natural and logical, but which to most everyone else seemed perfectly ridiculous. Why one year she even tried to stop Mohammedanism single-handed!"

"Louis, I can't believe it!"

"It's the honest truth."

"How much did she contribute to that crusade?"

Louis explained patiently that Mrs. Shepard didn't try to stop Mohammedanism with money, but by the word of

God. She had thousands of Bibles printed and distributed all over the Middle East. Apparently, she hoped that every copy of the Koran would be destroyed and a copy of the Bible put in its place. In every peaceful way she knew how she tried to revive the spirit of the Crusades and to convert all Islam to Christianity—and if she made a few inroads on Buddhism and Hinduism, she thought that would be all to the good.

Now I understand better why Mrs. Shepard was so interested in missionaries and contributed to their work all over the world: Money was sent to Peking, Foochow, the Nanking Theological Seminary, the Philippines, Japan, Korea, Africa, and over ten thousand dollars to the Istanbul College for Women. It followed logically that she also contributed generously to the Travelers Aid Society.

"Your mother should have lived in the Middle Ages," I said. Louis agreed.

"Mother," he said, "would have loved to have carried the cross with Richard the Lion Hearted or Prince Frederick Barbarossa."

In some ways Mrs. Shepard did seem out of place in the Twentieth Century, though in others, she was far ahead of her times. But her good deeds far outweighed her foolish ones. Louis was sure that his mother had given away so much money that she hadn't nearly as much left as most people thought. Her contributions to charity and philanthropy amounted, he thought, to over ten million dollars!

He said that Mrs. Shepard received, even now, over three hundred letters a week asking for contributions. Most of them were legitimate, but a few came from cranks and fanatics, who asked for dishes, croquet sets, her picture, her autograph, or a lock of her hair. Some of the demands were not so modest: A few women desired mink coats and dresses. One day she received a letter written, it said, with homemade ink, asking for a silver tea service. Another letter politely inquired:

"Dear Mrs. Shepard: I understand you have nine cars. Would it be convenient for you to loan me one of them for the weekend? I am expecting guests."

At one time Mrs. Shepard had in her employ a very enterprising secretary who went to Tiffany's and had beautiful cards printed which said in elite type that, worthy as the request was, Mrs. Shepard could not comply with it. Unfortunately, Mrs. Shepard would seldom use these cards.

Yes, it was true that the good lady spent her money on everything from supporting a university to contributing to a group in upstate New York who wished to wipe out cigarette smoking.

"Hasn't anyone ever tried to curb this generosity?" I asked.

"Everyone including mother's lawyers, her best friends, her secretaries, but it's no use. It's like trying to stop the tides. Why, during the Spanish-American War, in addition to money, she wanted to give the Navy a destroyer. She was so patriotic that she practically tried to finance the whole war single-handed."

"That's delicious," I said, "a destroyer! Oh, I'm so sorry she didn't give it. Can't you imagine Admiral Dewey writing a letter: 'Dear Miss Gould: Thanks so much for the destroyer. It was just what we needed.' "

"As a matter of fact," Louis said, "something almost as interesting really happened. Shortly after the Spanish-American War was over, Admiral Dewey marched up Fifth Avenue in a great parade. The bands were playing and people crowded on each side of the avenue to see the famous hero.

As his carriage passed in front of 579, he stood up, faced the house, and raised his hand in a gracious salute—a symbol of his appreciation for Helen Gould's magnificent work in the cause of her country. The crowd applauded, and the parade passed by."

Louis said that he had heard his mother remark many times that this was almost the happiest day of her life.

"What do you think her happiest day really was?" I asked Louis.

"Probably the day when Congress voted her a medal for her generosity and her patriotism—far above the call of duty for a private citizen."

7

Night Train

THE MORE LOUIS told me about his mother, the more I wanted to know. Some of her early life and activities had been written up in the newspapers but generally in a cheap or sensational manner—or as "scoops." As a result, Mrs. Shepard had continued her charities and philanthropies as anonymously as possible, assisted by only a few relatives and close friends. But Louis felt that her good works should not go unremembered, even if some of the facts would have to be handed down by word of mouth from one generation to the next.

Mrs. Shepard was especially interested in the broad field of education. Besides New York University, she gave grants and scholarships to a great many other institutions, including Hunter College, Vassar, Rutgers, Delaware County Scholarships, Northfield Seminary for Girls, Mount Hermon School for Boys, Mount Holyoke, Wellesley (three scholarships in honor of her mother), Irvington High School, the Washington Irving High School, and Berea College in Kentucky.

Among so many and diverse schools of learning, it was not surprising that there were occasionally unexpected consequences. At one university Mrs. Shepard endowed the department of science, but unfortunately it did not teach that the world was created in six days. Students heard not the word of God but the word of Darwin. The gospel was not the *Old Testament*, but *The Origin of Species* and *The Descent of Man*.

In time Mrs. Shepard heard about this profanation. Now she knew little about pure science, but she had been to the zoo often enough to remain unconvinced that she herself in any way resembled an organgutan. Miss Stebbins tried to placate her by saying that there was nothing personal in the Darwinian theory, but Mrs. Shepard thought she had been betrayed. She felt that the Creation should be taught as it was in Genesis or not at all — at least with her money.

After this experience Mrs. Shepard thought she should investigate the classrooms of other universities to which she had contributed; very likely she would find other deviations. She did. At one theological seminary there was dancing on Sunday night. At her request it was discontinued. She canceled four scholarships at Vassar, because she did not entirely approve of the teaching methods. At Mount Holyoke, $40,000, which she had given to the Bible Department, was transferred to the Department of Romance Languages. It is said that at the beginning of his lecture the following day a young Bible instructor announced: "Mrs. Shepard giveth, and Mrs. Shepard taketh away."

There was a similar occurrence at Wellesley: One evening the Bible Department was poorer by $50,000 while the Department of Mathematics was richer by an identical amount. Undoubtedly Mrs. Shepard felt that in a changing world, the Bible was open to interpretation, but the square of the hypotenuse still equaled exactly the square of the other two sides.

"Of course," Louis explained, "Mother is more than just a human checkbook."

She went to as many meetings of her organizations as she could. One evening she arrived a little late at a meeting of the Kashmir-Ludhiana Fellowship Committee. She was greeted with more than the usual enthusiasm and could not understand the exaggerated cordiality. Later she learned that her presence permitted the committee to function — she made a quorum.

Louis' mother particularly enjoyed attending sessions of her Bible Clubs and frequently was asked to speak. Her speeches were customarily models of brevity:

"My dear friends, I think the world is drifting dangerously toward atheism, and I believe everybody here tonight should do everything he can to stop it. Don't you think so?"

Mrs. Shepard was often seen in less conservative gatherings. She often went to the Bowery Mission and talked to the deadbeats and derelicts. The Bowery was a tough district, and her friends pleaded with her not to go there, but in vain. She wanted to take the bottle personally from the drunkard — the morphine from the addict.

"You've certainly got to admire her for that," I said.

"I do," Louis replied. "However, it wasn't a very safe idea. So after a brick came through that window, Father put a stop to it," and Louis pointed to the large window overlooking Fifth Avenue. "Mother helped all sorts of people, and sooner or later there was bound to be trouble."

"Who threw the brick?"

"They never found out. The only comment Mother made was that whoever threw it was unfamiliar with the

Ten Commandments. But after she was married Father gradually cut down on a lot of her activities. There were no more jaunts down to the Bowery—no more evangelist meetings at night under tents in vacant lots, and he made her resign from many of her committees. She had been a member of so many societies that she couldn't possibly keep track of them."

Louis showed me one list which he said was rather comprehensive:

Societies — Membership Dependent on Ancestry

Daughters of Colonial Wars of the State of New York

The Dutch Settlers' Society of Albany

The Huguenot Society Daughters of the American Revolution Daughters of American Colonists

Daughters of Founders and Patriots of America

National Society of Magna Charter Dames

National Society of New England Women

New York City Colony

Colonial Daughters of the Seventeenth Century

United Daughters of 1812

Andrew Jackson Chapter Colonial Dames of America

The Fairfield Society

National Society Women Descendants of the Ancient and Honorable Artillery Company

The Daughters of Holland Dames

Historical, Genealogical, and Patriotic Groups

The Milford (Connecticut) Historical Society

New York State Historical Society

The New York Genealogical and Biographical Society

The New England Historic Genealogical Society

Allied Patriotic Societies

American Coalition of Patriotic Societies

Religious Organizations

American Bible Society

New York Auxiliary Bible Society

Union of Churches of Christ in Poland

American Christian Literature Society for Moslems Prothumian Society

Delaware County Council of Religious Education Association for the Re-emphasis of New Testament Missions Women's Board of Domestic Missions, Reformed Church in America

Women's Board of Foreign Missions, Reformed Church in America

Friendly League for Christian Service, Inc.

Women's National Sabbath Alliance American Tract Society

International Order King's Daughters and Sons Margaret Bottome Memorial

Seamen's Christian Association

American Hussite Society

World Dominion Movement Committee

Family Groups

The Society of the Hawley Family John More Association

Miscellaneous
Alumni Association of the Women's Law Class
New York University
Tarrytown Horticultural Society
Gardner School Alumni Association
Russell Sage Foundation Soldiers and Sailors
Club Parent's League of New York American
Geographical Society
American Red Cross
The American Museum of Natural History
Metropolitan Museum of Art
Women's Roosevelt (Theodore) Memorial
Association

When I reached the end of this impressive list I was flabbergasted. There were fifty organizations. Louis said there were a lot more, and he distinctly remembered that Mrs. Shepard was a member of the World Narcotic Association and The Lantern League of the Old North Church.

"No wonder she has a heart murmur," I said.

"That's exactly why Father interfered," Louis replied, "and it would have been better," he continued, "if someone had been able to stop her sooner."

Before her marriage, Mrs. Shepard had never had the advice or companionship of any men except the family lawyer and doctor, and they had very little influence on her. The lawyer was appalled at the way she was giving away her inheritance, and the doctor was appalled at the amount of work that was required to do it. But when I learned this it struck me as extraordinary that her acquaintanceship should have been so limited.

"Didn't she ever go out on dates," I asked, "when she was a young girl?"

"Hardly ever."

"But, Louis, those pictures of her—she was stunning. I should think that every man in New York would have wanted to marry her."

"I guess a lot of them did."

"Didn't she get a lot of proposals?"

"Quite a few."

"Who from?" I asked. "Artists? Bankers? Famous men?"

"No," Louis said, "mostly from crackpots."

Then he explained that actually his mother received quantities of mail from men suggesting marriage. One gentleman said that "any woman who served on so many committees would make a fine wife." These proposals were often pathetic and sometimes very disturbing. One "lover" wrote that he thought of her as the American Florence Nightingale, and if she would be his betrothed, no harm would ever befall her.

But some of the letters were not quite so noble in spirit, and there were investigations and a few arrests. Still in every case Mrs. Shepard went out of her way to obtain clemency for these people wherever she could.

I asked Louis where his mother had met Mr. Shepard.

"In a train wreck," he said.

"In a what?"

"That's right, in a train wreck—just outside of Syracuse. The newspaper clippings are upstairs in a scrap book. If you knew the background the whole thing was perfectly natural."

And then Louis told me how love came to Helen Gould one night just outside of Syracuse.

It seems that she was the majority stockholder in many railroads, including the Missouri Pacific, the Iron Mountain, and the Denver and Rio Grande. It was a large empire, and when she became its queen, she made an occasional inspection trip throughout her kingdom. Once a year a private car carried her and her entourage, including Chinky, the Pekingese, across her domain.

To the railroads it was a serious responsibility, but to her it was an exciting event, and she looked forward to it with bubbling child-like enthusiasm. She made the most elaborate preparations weeks in advance and carefully supervised the packing of some ten trunks, thirty odd suitcases, and countless handbags. Each item, down to the tiniest silk handkerchief, was checked against a huge master list: There was enough equipment to go twice around the world—enough to go to Mars and back.

But Helen Gould was no neophyte traveler. When her father was alive, she used to accompany him on periodic trips. Jay Gould, realizing that someday his daughter would inherit great interests in his railroads as well as responsibility, felt that she should know something about them. He was insistent that she become familiar with the territory, the personnel, and the vocabulary of railroading.

So as they sat comfortably in the red plush seats of their luxurious private car, Helen Gould learned about roadbeds, roundhouses, signal towers, terminals, and rolling stock. And one year, protected in a linen duster with hat and veil, white silk gloves, and a pair of goggles, she was escorted to the locomotive to take a peep at "how things worked from that end."

She was intensely interested, and after listening to the engineer explain what made it tick, she wondered if she might try. Then she sat down beside the engineer and guided the train. It really wasn't as hard as driving a horse and carriage. And while they were rolling along she inquired if it would be all right if she blew the whistle as they approached a station. The engineer pointed to a lanyard and said: "Pull it gently."

"Toot, toot!" and a herd of grazing beef cattle looked up in mild surprise as the train sped past.

Just before they arrived at the station, the engineer reached across her, took the throttle, and the train puffed slowly to a stop. Passengers began to get on and off. One gentleman, hurrying past the locomotive, stopped dead in his tracks when he saw Helen Gould still seated in the little window: "What's this country comin' to?" he said in exasperation. "Now they've got wimmin runnin' the railroads!"

Helen Gould had other practical instruction. Jay Gould knew that communication was inevitably linked up with railroads and felt that his children should learn something about that, too. Once a week a Western Union telegraph operator came to the house, and Helen Gould learned the Morse code and how to apply it on the telegraph key. On one occasion a friend who came for tea was politely told by the butler that her hostess would be a little tardy because she was busy "sending."

Helen Gould was an apt pupil and pretty soon she was quite facile with this new language, except that she did have a little trouble remembering that "dash-dash-dot" was the letter "G" and "dot-dash-dot-dot" was the letter "L." A small telegraph set was installed, and the operator sitting in the living room sent messages to his student sitting in the dining room. Two words a minute is not exactly rapid-fire communication, but soon they could send four, and before long, the operator and Helen Gould were talking to each other at the rate of eight words a minute:

"ARE YOU THERE, MISS GOULD?"
"YES, I AM HERE."

"HOW DO YOU FEEL?"
"MY FINGER HURTS."
"PRESS THE KEY MORE GEOPXY."
"I DIDN'T GET THE LAST WORD."
"GENTLY."
"THANK YOU."
"YOU ARE DOING VERY WELL."
"HOW SWEET."

Helen Gould found riding over the tracks of her railroads very educational and a great deal of fun. While everybody was reading or napping, her face would be glued to the car window like a child peering into a toy store. The Hudson River, the Great Lakes, the farming country of Ohio, the great plains, the corn in Kansas, and the Rocky Mountains were an endless wonderland. She loved her country, and she loved to travel from one exciting end of it to the other.

She also liked to travel quite a bit on foot. Whenever the train stopped, she would pace rapidly up and down the station platform. She was always entranced by the romantic Indian names of the different cars—*Chippewawa, Flying Cloud, Hiawatha,* and she remembered them, too. One day while the train was stopped at a water tower, she paused before a car called *Okefenokee.*

"What's that," she asked, a little puzzled.

"It's just an Indian name," someone said.

"Yes, I know," she replied with a little frown, "but *what* tribe?" No one could supply the information. "Well," she said in a disappointed tone, "I'll look it up as soon as we get to Denver."

The name of her father's private car was also somewhat esoteric. It was called Atalanta. One day Helen explained patiently to the porter that in Greek mythology Atalanta was the daughter of Iasius, the King of Arcadia. Atalanta was extremely fleet of foot but very proud. She had vowed that she would marry a man only if he could beat her in a foot race, but if he lost, he would have to forfeit his life. The porter listened patiently, and when she finished he said drily: "I'm glad you told me that, Miss Gould. I always thought 'Atlanta' was a city in Georgia." For some reason Jay Gould was fascinated by this legend. And when he bought a spacious sea-going yacht, he also named it the *Atalanta*. So if he said he was leaving on the *Atalanta* for an extended trip, he would often be asked: "By land or by sea, Jay?"

Mrs. Shepard was an excellent traveler, and petty inconveniences never ruffled her temper. Little delays, dust storms, floods, or weather were all in the game, and she never uttered a word of complaint. The only thing that bothered her sometimes was her inability to keep a clear geographical perspective. Once going through a western state, she said: "I do think the Missouri Pacific is such a fine railroad—there's hardly any bumping on it at all." She had to be told politely that at the moment she was not riding on the Missouri Pacific lines but on the Iron Mountain. Actually, it was difficult to know where one left off and the other began.

Helen Gould's favorite line was the Denver and Rio Grande. The scenery there was "so wonderful," and the Colorado River ran alongside the tracks almost the whole way.

One year, long after her father died, an important official of the Missouri Pacific, Finley Shepard, was in charge of the expedition. It was his laborious duty to arrange every detail of Miss Gould's itinerary from the choice of a chef to the last coffee spoon. It was a laborious task, and he did the best he could. He prepared diligently for everything—except a train wreck.

When it occurred, and he heard the grinding of steel and the hiss of steam, he ran frantically to Miss Gould's stateroom, but she was not there. She was nowhere to be found. What could have happened? Where could she be? He ran up and down the car calling her name, tearing aside pieces of wreckage, searching everywhere. At last he found her.

She was outside on the tracks attending to the injured and comforting the frightened. She was helping with a tourniquet here, a bandage there, or a kind word. And now in the night, by the light of acetylene torches, she and Finley Shepard worked together side by side. His surprise turned to wonder, his wonder to admiration, and in time to love. One year later they were married.

"Your father didn't marry the boss' daughter," I said. "He married the boss."

"Exactly," Louis replied, "and there was no doubt that Father was well cast for the part. He was the son of a minister, and he combined a knowledge of the Bible with a sound understanding of railroads and double-entry bookkeeping. He helped Helen Gould with her good works, and while he couldn't quite stop her from giving away more than she could afford, at least he curbed her a bit."

Their marriage was an ideal arrangement. Helen Gould at last found someone to lean on, and Mr. Shepard found someone to take care of. It was a unique union that was blessed by everyone—big business, the church, and by society—and by the Bowery Mission, the Y.M.C.A. and the United States Army, Navy and Marines.

8

Lyndhurst

Mrs. Shepard enjoyed the four seasons—especially spring. She looked forward to it each year with trembling excitement: The March winds, the first dogwood blossom, the first swallow, her first spring hat. While her suits were always the essence of simplicity, she did indulge herself a bit with her hats. She would add to their natural design, imitations of the season's perennials. Her friends regarded her hats as a kind of monthly calendar. In March, a few hepaticas. In April, the golden marigolds. In May, the modest buttercup. Mrs. Shepard was a great deal more interested in keeping up with Nature, than with the times.

Shortly after buttercups appeared on her hat, Mrs. Shepard transferred her entire household, including Chinky, to Lyndhurst, her country home at Irvington-on-Hudson.

Mrs. Shepard inherited Lyndhurst from her father, and there she tended her gardens, supervised the trimming of each little hedge, and arranged for the feeding of migratory birds. Unfortunately, before she could go there, she always had to undergo a cardiogram and a visit to her dentist. The cardiogram didn't hurt, and the doctor's advice was easy to ignore, but the session at the dentist was another matter; it was a catastrophe. Mrs. Shepard's reaction to the sound of the drill was traumatic. Her body stiffened. She closed her eyes, clenched her tiny fists, and whimpered: "I can't stand this ... I shall go mad."

Miss Stebbins, standing faithfully by her side, muttered platitudes of encouragement: "This too shall pass, Mrs. Shepard ... only a little longer ... courage." The torturous hour was finally over, and after pain came the pleasure of anticipation: She could now go to Lyndhurst.

When Mrs. Shepard arrived at Lyndhurst she did not forget those she left behind. She wrote informative little notes to all her friends and relatives. One day I received a rather disturbing tidbit: "Dear Celeste: We are all comfortable and in good health except two of our horse-chestnut trees have come down with the blight. Everything possible is being done ... "

A few weeks later a happier message came: "Dear Celeste: Good news indeed! The surgeon thinks he can save our beautiful trees, though we must be patient. What a worry off my mind! Now, I would be so happy if we could share some of the glorious weeks of June together. Perhaps the week after Louis' examinations? We would find so many things to do and talk about—perhaps even have a glimpse of the night-blooming cereus. Affectionately, Helen Gould Shepard." My letter of acceptance was in the next mail.

Louis and I motored up to Lyndhurst one hot sultry afternoon. He had said farewell to Princeton a week before and we were looking forward to a few cool restful days in the country. After that I would join my mother at Lake Placid. A few miles past Irvington, named in honor of Washington Irving, we came around a long sloping curve and turned into a private driveway barricaded by a gate. I thought we were going through it, but Louis jammed on the brakes and stopped less than a foot away. Beyond the gate half hidden in a clump of birch trees was a two-story English graystone cottage.

"What a charming place, Louis! What a change from 579!"

"That's the gatekeeper's house, but I guess he's out to lunch. Anyway, here's Mr. Allan, the superintendent. He'll let us in."

Louis called out: "Hello, Mr. Allan," and a pleasant looking, middle-aged gentleman in a tweed jacket and gray-flannel slacks walked briskly over and greeted us in a thick Scotch burr:

"Hello, Muster Louis. I maun say yer lookin' braw the noo. Yer puir mither is aw a dither o'er the wee blawsoms cornin' oot the nicht. The cereus, ye ken."

I could hardly distinguish a word of what he said, but Louis answered as if it were his mother tongue: "Happens every year, Mr. Allan. We'll go right up. Thanks a lot." As the spiked barricade was slowly opened, I said: "Louis! What did Mr. Allan say?"

"He said I am looking fine and Mother is in a dither about the night-blooming cereus."

As we drove into the estate, I saw endless vistas of immaculately tailored lawns and gardens. The gravel driveway was lined with graceful elms, and here and there, in intimate groups, stood beautiful old Linden trees in whose honor Mrs. Shepard had named her little valley of tenderness and grace. After we had gone at least a quarter of a mile, we went over a little crest in the road, and there, in the full light of the sun, was a Gothic castle. "Here we are," Louis said.

Helen Gould Shepard

Jay Gould

Falk

The Shepard family: Olivia, Mrs. Shepard, Finley Jay, Louis, Mr. Shepard, and Helen Anna

Views of Lyndhurst, Mrs. Shepard's country home at Irvington-on-Hudson

Gardening at Lyndhurst

The Shepard family at Lyndhurst

The children with Mrs. Shepard: Louis, Olivia, Finley Jay, and Helen Anna

Swimming in the pool at Lyndhurst

(Underwood &Underwood)

**Mr. and Mrs. Shepard on their
twenty-fifth wedding anniversary**

"Louis," I gasped. "It's *bigger* than your house in New York!"

He was grinning like the Cheshire cat. "Don't be frightened, dear. It's only got forty rooms!"

"It has ramparts! And a bell tower! It looks like Elsinore."

"But not as draughty," Louis said.

As we approached, I thought how overpowering and medieval it was. This castle didn't belong on the Hudson. It belonged in Denmark, or maybe in Xanadu. It was so baronial that I half expected a flurry of trumpets and a corps of page boys to rush out under the porte-cochere and grab our suitcases. Instead, only Miss Stebbins opened the huge oak door and said in her loud hearty voice: "Welcome to Lyndhurst."

On her heels followed the reception committee — a swarm of dogs of all shapes and sizes who pounced eagerly upon us.

I felt more like a fox at the end of the hunt than a house guest. Miss Stebbins came to my rescue just as a big Chesapeake retriever was getting a bit *too* affectionate.

"Away with you, away with all of you," she shouted. "Scoot! Scatter! Vamoose!"

The dogs ran off barking in all directions. Miss Stebbins sighed as she watched them disappear. "Such an infernal nuisance, but I love them all—all ten of them."

The front door opened again and Miss Davis ran down the marble steps screaming in a high-pitched falsetto, "Quiet! Quiet! What on earth is happening? Mrs. Shepard and Chinky are napping." Then she saw us, and her little pique modulated to an ecstasy of greeting, "Welcome to Lyndhurst. We are all so happy to see you. You've arrived not a day too soon, and do you know why?" she added, as she lowered her voice confidentially. "Mrs. Shepard thinks that any evening now we may see the night-blooming cereus."

"I do hope so," I said. "I've never seen it."

"But now you must be tired," Miss Stebbins said. "Come, I'll show you to your room."

As we entered the castle, I was aware of high ceilings, groined arches, dark corners and endless space. I followed Miss Stebbins up a turning flight of marble stairs and down a long, gloomy corridor with small rectangular windows. After many turns and twists, I thought we had surely crossed the state line.

Finally we stopped before an open door. Miss Stebbins said, "You live here. I know you'd like to rest awhile. Dinner is at seven."

I asked rather pathetically, "Will I ever see Louis again?"

Miss Stebbins said reassuringly, "Don't be afraid, my dear. We lost Miss Davis once for five hours, but the dogs found her. Toodle-oo." And she closed the door.

The first thing I did was to pull back the curtains and open the window. Louis' family seemed to bear some kind of grudge against sunlight. Shades were invariably down, curtains drawn, and rare was the lamp that ever held a Mazda bulb over forty watts. I suppose the shadows and the half-light gave Mrs. Shepard a feeling of security and privacy. Although she was forever doing things in the public interest, she spurned the public eye with the bitterest disdain. Even her name in the most innocuous headline in a society page would set off a trembling fit of disapproval. She remembered how often as a young girl she had seen her father's name in the newspapers. His name and deeds had made the most sensational newspaper copy for two generations:

"Jay Gould controls stock of Erie Railroad!" "Jay Gould held in contempt of court!"

"Jay Gould bribes government officials..."

Mrs. Shepard wished no part of such a life. With her the pendulum had swung from garish notoriety to anonymity, and the simple, peaceful virtues.

I finished unpacking and looked at my watch. It was five-thirty. I had nothing to do until seven o'clock. I could take a nap, but I wasn't sleepy. Anyway, the lawn mower beneath my window was making too much noise. I might play solitaire, but I had no cards. Mrs. Shepard called them the devil's books. If only I had a book! Any kind of a book to read and pass the time. Oh—there was a book! I hadn't seen it half hidden on the bottom shelf of the little, white table by the bed. It was a slim, black volume embossed with gold lettering:

       Bible Verses to Memorize
       Selected by Helen Miller Gould Shepard

I started thumbing through it. There were one hundred and thirty-one pages, including a foreword. I began reading. It was a generous tribute by Mrs. Shepard to the American Tract Society for distributing her verses. They were issued, it said, ". . . in Arabic, Armenian, Armeno-Turkish, in Bengali and Hindi of India, in Bohemian, Danish, Dutch, Finnish, French, German, Modem Greek, Hebrew, Hungarian, Italian, Japanese, Latvian, in Mandarin and Cantonese of China, in Polish, Portuguese, Norwegian, Roumanian, Russian, Modem Russian, Ruthenian, Spanish, Swedish, and Yiddish."

I read on. This was very interesting. It said "... the verses were also published in England, Bulgaria, Egypt, Korea, India, Burma, Siam, Africa, and Persia."

This was excellent distribution, but I couldn't help hoping that someday the Eskimos would be included.

Just then I heard the ringing of the telephone beside the bed. I picked it up and it was Mr. Allan, the superintendent. I couldn't imagine what he wanted and I couldn't understand enough of what he said to find out: "Anoo, Mum, will ye hae the kindness tae direct yer laundry lasses tae use the proper path and no a shortcut tae the laundry house. Their muckle shoon hae trompled a foorow across the bock lawn."

I thought for a moment what to reply; then I said:

"Sorry, wrong number," and hung up.

The telephone had a row of buttons beside it, and a list of places about the estate you might get in touch with:

Gatehouse
Butler's Pantry
Garage
Bowling Alley

Laundry
Greenhouse
Superintendent's House
Swimming Pool
Yacht Landing
Tower House

Well, I thought, I'd do a little telephoning myself. First, I was tempted to get in touch with the yacht landing, but if someone answered, what could I say: "Are there any spare yachts today?" No, I'd try the greenhouse. I could always inquire about the *Rosa spinosissima*. I pressed the little black button, and a familiar voice answered the phone: "The greenhouse—Sitwell speaking."

"Sitwell," I cried, "it's Celeste Andrews."

"How do you do," he replied cordially. "I heard you were coming. Is there anything I can do for you? I have a bottle of . . ."

"No, no, no, Sitwell, but thanks anyway. How's everything in the greenhouse?"

"Splendid, Miss Andrews. Everyone is getting everything ready for the night-blooming cereus. We feel it's almost time."

"I hope everything will go off smoothly," I said.

"We trust so," Sitwell said dolefully.

I said goodbye and hung up. I'd killed thirty seconds.

I looked at the buttons again. How about trying the tower house. I buzzed—no answer. What next? The swimming pool! I buzzed, and the soft voice of a young woman answered, "Yes?"

"Hello," I said, "who is this?"

"Olivia." It was Louis' married sister whom I had never met.

"Olivia, this is Celeste."

"Celeste! You're here! Where are you? What are you doing?"

"Nothing."

"Come down to the pool and have a swim. Bring your suit."

"I'd love to."

I ran downstairs and across the lawn, following little hand-printed signs which read, "Swimming pool . . . use gravel path." In the center of a grove of cedar trees I came upon a large red brick building with Doric columns flanking the portico. It was an uneasy mixture of New England and ancient Greece. I opened the door and went in.

Immediately inside was a foyer with dressing rooms on either side . . . Men on the right . . . Ladies to the left. Straight ahead was the swimming pool. I had expected to see something more elaborate than "the old swimming hole," but not the largest indoor body of water in the United States! I wondered if it was high or low tide?

Immense columns surrounding the pool upheld a skylighted ceiling. The lower half of the columns were painted cinnamon red; the rest was pure white. Between the columns were pots of tall tropical palms and life preservers were carefully hung at equal intervals around the pool.

Far out in the middle of this great expanse of water was a lifeboat, and resting on the oars was a good-looking, blonde young man. His occupation was stamped in large block letters across his jersey: "Lifeguard." He was passing the time of day throwing a rubber ball to half a dozen dogs who frantically swam after it. "The cocker spaniel always gets it," he yelled, as he heaved it again halfway down the pool.

While I was watching the aquatics, the door of the

ladies' dressing room opened and a young, fair-haired girl walked rapidly toward me. It was Olivia. She was wearing a tight-fitting one-piece bathing suit, and to my surprise, a pair of black stockings. She put one arm around me and kissed me. She was just my height, attractive, dignified, and I thought she resembled Mrs. Shepard. She had an air of self-assurance and quiet poise that would have seemed more natural for an older woman. She wasted no time on small talk and idle formalities. She took me for granted—we were soon to be sisters of a kind, and that was all there was to it.

"It's good to see you, Celeste," she said. "I'll bet you're dying for a swim in this heat."

"I certainly am," I replied. "I'll run in and change." The ladies' dressing room was of Pompeian design. I wondered what the men's room was like—possibly Egyptian? I came out a moment later, and was about to plunge in when Olivia cried: "Celeste —wait a moment, please. You have no stockings on." I turned around a little bewildered.

"Mother never lets us go in without stockings," Olivia said.

"Without stockings!" I said incredulously.

"Yes, it's an absolute rule."

"I'm sorry. I didn't know. It seems rather old fashioned."

"It's from the Bible," Olivia explained. "Some chapter in Deuteronomy, I think. But don't worry, I have an extra pair. I'll get them for you."

She ran back for a pair of black cotton stockings which I put on. We went in for a dip, splashed about a bit, and after a few minutes climbed out and sat by the edge of the pool. In my stockings I felt more like dancing the cancan than swimming or talking.

But Olivia was very earnest about herself, life, and at the

moment Lyndhurst. She remembered the date Jay Gould built the castle, the fact that the greenhouse was over two hundred yards long, the date the corner stone was laid for the laundry building, and the time Mrs. Shepard bought twenty frying pans for the cooking school.

It seems that Olivia's mother had once conducted weekly classes for under-privileged children in the neighborhood. It was nicknamed "The Escoffier School for Young Girls." Yes, here at Lyndhurst, and not far from where we now sat, dripping wet, many a young lady had fried her first egg.

Olivia was quite a historian, but she enjoyed the present, too. She told me all about her husband, John Burr, who was away on a business trip with Mr. Shepard, and how disappointed she was that I could not meet him. I remembered what Helen Anna had told me and wondered how Olivia had ever *met* him!

And where was Helen Anna? And Finley Jay? Well, I wouldn't ask. By this time, I had learned that questions were often not the quickest way to an answer.

Olivia was just explaining the trouble they had getting the tennis court built when the lifeguard rowed his boat over to us and said, "Excuse me, Mrs. Burr. I'll have to close the pool now. It's six-thirty."

"All right. Come on, Celeste. I'll race you back across the pool."

We got up, dove in, and the cocker spaniel followed us. It was a close race all the way, and Olivia just managed to win. The spaniel was second. I was third. As we were leaving, I saw the lifeguard tying up the boat for the night. "Olivia," I said, "is that lifeguard necessary?"

"He certainly is!" Olivia said. "If he hadn't been here one day there might have been a tragedy. At least for Mother."

"What happened? Who was rescued?"

"Chinky!"

I started to laugh as Olivia hustled me out of the swimming pool. Dinner was at seven sharp and it was a long walk back to the castle.

9

The Rites of Spring

AT FIVE MINUTES of seven, Olivia tapped on my door and said: "Mother is waiting on the sun porch."

We went downstairs and started through the long, main hallway which served as sort of an auxiliary art gallery to the large one on the second floor. On its walls, hung in the most haphazard fashion, were a few oil paintings, prints and lithographs. An Italian primitive hung next to a Chinese scroll. A fourteenth-century Madonna was alongside a faded photograph of Jay Gould. He looked old and tired, and his beard was almost gray.

There was also one modern picture: A charcoal drawing of a huge spider dedicated and signed by the artist — "To Mother — Love from Finley Jay Shepard, 1918."

The grand salon at the end of the hall held a few surprises of its own. It appeared to be a combination living room and museum. Against the walls were wooden cabinets crowded with curios and souvenirs. A Buddha carved in green jade sat with arms akimbo beside an ordinary piece of sandstone; a priceless Chinese T'ang horse posed gracefully in front of a clam shell. These objets d'art were gifts accumulated over a lifetime, and Mrs. Shepard could never bring herself to part with the most trivial item. About the room were remembrances of more substantial size: Trophies of the hunt presented by explorers and missionaries from the Veldt, the Congo and the Nile. The glass eyes of a tiger, a lion and an alligator followed me from behind Louis Quinze chairs and a Lombardy desk.

Going through the salon was like going to the sun porch by way of darkest Africa. Once there however the atmosphere was refreshingly innocent. It had two dominant motifs: Bright gay chintz and Mrs. Shepard's smile. She toddled across the room with arms outstretched and kissed me on the cheek: "Celeste—my dear Celeste—how sweet of you to come."

"How pleasant to be here," I stammered.

"I'm sorry I was unable to greet you," she said, "but I understand Miss Stebbins and Miss Davis had the pleasure," and she looked at her two social secretaries seated together under a huge philodendron, who smiled affirmatively together.

"Please sit down," she continued. "We will have dinner any moment now—immediately after the whippoorwill calls."

I sat down, and Mrs. Shepard continued in her jumpy little sentences: "I hope you had a pleasant journey. I see that you and Olivia are already acquainted."

"We are," I said.

"How nice!" Then she paused for a moment to find a new topic. Suddenly her face became animated: "Do you like Olivia?"

I felt myself go crimson at the direct question, but I answered without hesitating: "Yes, I do. Very much indeed."

"I'm so glad. Finley Jay and Helen Anna will not arrive until next week, so you two and Louis will have to get along as best you can."

Louis came in from the salon and said as he entered: "Has the whippoorwill gone off yet?"

"Not yet," Miss Stebbins said, "but it will."

"Where've you been, Louis?" I asked. "I haven't seen you since we arrived."

"I've been bowling."

"Bowling!"

"I didn't call you. I thought you'd be resting."

"No, I went swimming with Olivia."

"I wish someone would teach me to swim," Miss Stebbins exclaimed pathetically. "All I can do is float."

Miss Davis said wistfully: "It's better than wading. That's all I can do."

Just then, from a clump of bushes near the house, I heard Nature's dinner bell: "Whip-poor-will, whip-poor-will, whip-poor-will."

Almost immediately Sitwell appeared and formally confirmed it: "Dinner is served."

The dining room was the only room in the whole castle which approached simplicity. It was a large and airy room with an immense fireplace. A huge crystal chandelier hung down over the table. The furniture was Victorian Gothic, and French windows framed a flamboyant sunset which flooded the room with fiery crimson. This evening the sun disappeared earlier than usual. Sitwell came in and drew the curtains.

In each of three corners there was a niche holding a sculptured head on a black marble base. I squinted at the one nearest me. Yes, I'd recognize that face anywhere. It was Louis—cast in bronze. I looked at the head in the next niche—it was Finley Jay. The next, Olivia. The last niche, however, was empty. I stared at it until Miss Stebbins explained: "Helen Anna goes in there if Signor Paulo ever gets her to sit still long enough."

Mrs. Shepard started conversation at once: "Do you like it here. Celeste?"

"It's wonderful," I answered. "Why, when I was walking back from the swimming pool..."

As I was talking, I felt my foot step on something soft, and a terrifying yip came from under the table. Apparently, I had stepped on Chinky, Mrs. Shepard's Pekingese dog. I bent down to see if I had hurt him, but Louis was already there picking up the little beast. Under his breath he said, "You stepped on the Chinese cockroach!"

"Give Chinky to me," Mrs. Shepard cried, and her loving arms went out to receive him. "Did they hurt you, Chinky? Did they step on your little toes?" She cooed as she fondled him with exaggerated caresses.

"I'm so sorry, Mrs. Shepard," I said. "I had no idea he was right under my foot."

"It's not your fault, Celeste. He knows he shouldn't get off his chair." Then she started to give her pet a variety of things from the table that would have made an animal breeder shudder in horror. She was *murdering* the dog—not *feeding* him. I said, "I haven't seen Chinky since the first time I came to tea in New York."

"No, Celeste dear. I think you must be mistaken."

I was positive I had seen him. I knew a Pekingese when I saw one. But I was wrong.

"You met Chinky number five," Mrs. Shepard explained. "This is Chinky number six."

I began to understand. As fast as Mrs. Shepard fed her pets to death, they were replaced by others. The dogs passed away happily, one by one, as the years went by, but the name "Chinky" was immortal.

"Now, where were we, Celeste?" Mrs. Shepard went on after giving Chinky a large mouthful of chutney.

"Just outside the swimming pool," I said.

"Oh, yes."

"I saw a hummingbird."

"A hummingbird," Miss Stebbins repeated enthusiastically. "Wherever was it?"

"On a honeysuckle vine."

"I love that buzzing noise they make," Miss Stebbins said.

"I love them best when they fly backwards," Miss Davis said.

"What kind of a hummingbird was it?" Mrs. Shepard asked.

"I don't know. It had a little red patch around its throat."

"That's the ruby-throated hummingbird. *Archilochus colubris*. They are very common. You'll see many birds here, Celeste, if you keep a sharp eye. Watching and identifying them is a rewarding pastime. No wonder they inspired poets like Shelley, and Keats, and William Cullen Bryant!"

"Didn't Bryant write the 'Ode to the Ruffed Grouse'?" Louis said slyly.

"No, Louis. It was 'To a Waterfowl':

> *'Whither, 'midst falling dew,*
> *While glow the heavens with the last steps*
> *of day,*
> *Far, through their rosy depths, dost thou*
> *pursue,*
> *Thy solitary way!'"*

Mrs. Shepard was voluble on any subject to do with nature—at times, even lyrical. This was so different from her limited conversation in the city. On almost every subject at 579 she talked in isolated words and phrases. With people, even with her own immediate family, she often seemed a stranger; but at Lyndhurst among the birds and the flowers, she was always at home.

"Of course, Celeste," she went bubbling on, "you know what we are all waiting for?"

"I think so — the night-blooming cereus."

"Exactly, my dear, the *Hylocereus undatus*"

"Last year the blossoms were rather small," Louis said. "Yes," she said, "but they did their best."

Louis apologized, "I meant no offense."

"Of course you didn't, but we shouldn't talk about our flowers without thinking, should we?"

"No, we should not," Miss Stebbins agreed emphatically. "Into every life a little rain must fall."

If Miss Stebbins' tongue was in her cheek, she paid for it a few moments later. She caught a piece of endive salad in her throat and began to cough; it developed alarmingly into a little spasm. Mrs. Shepard got up quickly, toddled over, and patted her secretary on the back.

"Are you all right, my dear? Mercy me, are you all right?"

Miss Stebbins recovered slowly: "Yes, I'm quite all right, thank you," and she added rather gruffly, "It must have gone down the wrong way."

After dinner on the way out of the dining room Mrs. Shepard asked me if I hadn't forgotten something; and I replied: "I don't think so, but I'll go back in the dining room and look."

"I mean dear," she said, '"have you signed the guest book?"

"No," I answered, "but I will immediately," and I went over to the desk and signed in. Then we sauntered back to the sun porch to have coffee and look for the evening star. Miss Davis discovered it first in the western sky: "There! There's Venus!"

"It seems so close!" Miss Stebbins said.

"It is," Louis said. "Only forty million miles away." There wasn't much to do at Lyndhurst at night, so bedtime was early. At ten o'clock, we all kissed Mrs. Shepard goodnight ceremoniously and went up to our rooms. From my window I looked far out over the countryside. It was a beautiful, still night. There was a three-quarter moon, and its light sparkled on the Hudson.

I looked at the Great Dipper and followed the ladle up to the North Star. North, for all that it mattered, was just a little to the left of the laundry building. I did my best to think profound thoughts in the mystery and quiet of the hour, but try as I might, all I could think of was Miss Stebbins' choking on a piece of endive. Once I jumped as I heard an automobile horn far away on the main road; in this ivory tower normal sounds seemed strange and intrusive.

Then I undressed and went to bed and soon I was fast asleep. I dreamed that I was walking in a great garden, and the garden was filled with monstrous honeysuckle vines. The smell of the honeysuckle was sweet and cloying, and I could hardly breathe. Feeding on the honeysuckle were thousands and thousands of ruby-throated hummingbirds sucking the nectar from the flowers. They were making a terrible humming noise, and as soon as they saw me, they flew at me from all sides, and I felt that I would die of suffocation. *"Archilochus colubris, Archilochus colubris,"* they seemed to say, as they relentlessly attacked me. "Buzz! — buzz! — buzz!" I tried to scare them off — to break free — to escape, but I was helpless.

The dream ended abruptly, and I awoke with a start. I was frightened and exhausted, and in my half daze I still heard the echo—the awful buzzing of the birds, but as my head cleared, I realized it was really the telephone. I reached over wearily and lifted the receiver. It was Louis: "Celeste," he said excitedly, "are you awake?"

"Kind of," I said. "What's the matter?"

"The night-blooming cereus—it's blooming! Hurry up! Throw on anything. Meet us downstairs in front. We're all going over to the greenhouse."

"All right, Louis. I'll try." I put the phone down as he urged: "As quickly as possible."

Then instinctively I looked at the clock. It was three-thirty—really! Suddenly the bells in the tower began to ring like an alarm in the dead of the night. I dashed some cold water over my face, threw on a coat over my nightgown, and started downstairs. Every light in the castle had been turned on, and from all directions I heard the patter of slippers against marble. I ran through the main hall into the foyer and out the front door to the porte-cochere. Louis was already there with Olivia. They were both in dressing gowns, and there was excitement written plainly on their faces.

"The time has come," Louis said. "They phoned Mother from the greenhouse. They're beginning to blossom."

"Isn't it exciting?" Olivia said. "I had a feeling it would happen tonight."

The door opened and out stumbled Miss Stebbins still in the process of wrapping a huge blanket around her, and muttering: "These flowers perform at the most inconvenient times. We'll all catch pneumonia."

And then we heard Mrs. Shepard's voice inside: "At last! At last! Isn't it thrilling? Isn't it wonderful," and she toddled through the door looking like an apparition. She wore a white, woolly bathrobe, and on her head at an angle a lace night cap. To help guide her through the night, she carried an enormous flashlight.

"There is not a moment to lose," she cried. "Follow me. We must all hurry down the path to the greenhouse."

The streetlamps along the cinder paths had been lit, and it was as bright as day. We hurried along after Mrs. Shepard who trotted as fast as her little feet could carry her. We made a strange ghostlike procession hastening to our destination. When we approached the entrance to the greenhouse, a shrill piercing voice—half alto and half scream—cut through the night: "Wait for me. Heaven-a-day, wait for me."

It was Miss Davis, whom we had all forgotten in the excitement. "Wait for me," she cried, and she ran up wheezing and out of breath. "I didn't hear the bells," she gasped. "Thank heavens, I'm here on time."

"Don't worry, there is time," Miss Stebbins said putting her arm around her companion for support.

We all quieted down when Mrs. Shepard opened the door to the greenhouse, turned, faced us, and said solemnly:

"Now we will enter and proceed quietly and orderly to the south wing."

The greenhouse was a long building subdivided into many sections. In some were coffee and cinnamon plants, in others roses and lilies. One contained endless varieties of ferns, elephant ear, and other tropical plants. In another were tier upon tier of orchids, and I recognized an old friend—*Cattleya trianae*. Finally, we arrived at the last section. Mrs. Shepard hesitated a moment—then quickly opened the door and looked in. Her expression told us we were not to be disappointed.

"How beautiful! How divine!" she said.

We walked inside. The entire end wall of the greenhouse was a foam of white. Hundreds of white flowers were born and being born. Hundreds of white flowers were unfurling and unfurling. This was the night-blooming cereus in its white radiant glory. This is what made Mrs. Shepard say: "How beautiful! How divine!" This was the white vision that rang the bells in the ivory tower.

No one spoke. Sitwell and the gardeners stood off quietly to one side. Soon the other servants in the house began to arrive in little groups and took their places along the edge of the wall. It was a strange, unearthly, predawn gathering. I looked at Mrs. Shepard.

Her face was fatigued. There were lines of anguish in it. Tears were streaming down her face. She made no attempt to hide them. Suddenly she perked her head up, straightened her bent figure, and said loud enough for everyone to hear: "Thank you — thank you all very much." Then she left hurriedly by herself.

Soon the rest of us followed, and we walked slowly and silently back to the castle. As we started up the marble steps to the door I glanced back over my shoulder. One by one the little lights on the cinder path to the greenhouse were slowly blinking off.

10

Plan of Battle

THIRTY-FIVE ACRES OF the estate at Lyndhurst had been cleared to accommodate a huge vegetable garden. All vegetables and fruits common to the temperate zone were cultivated, and there was always such an abundance of produce that only on rare occasions was anything but meat and staples bought at a store. "We will eat off the land," Mrs. Shepard had said, "and besides, it cuts down expenses."

Since the time Louis, Finley Jay, Helen Anna, and Olivia were able to lift a spading fork, they were given a thorough education in the care and raising of garden staples. Text-books on the planning, growing, care and preservation of vegetables, fruits and berries were required reading.

"The children may never learn mathematics," Mrs. Shepard once proclaimed, "but they will certainly know how to bring a potato into the world."

Practice never lagged behind theory; small plots of ground were staked out, and each child was responsible for his own cultivating. To avoid specialization, assignments were constantly varied. One year, Louis would be responsible for onions; the next year he would be assigned to summer squash, and Helen Anna would take over the onions. Mrs. Shepard believed in the rotation of children as well as the rotation of crops.

To encourage interest and incentive, prizes were awarded annually. It didn't take long to find out where everybody stood. Finley Jay was acknowledged to have superior skill with fruit. He could do wonderful things with strawberries although it was difficult to keep him from eating his harvest on the spot. The girls were more at home with root vegetables like beets and carrots, and potherbs like spinach and mustard. Unfortunately, Louis' talents left a lot to be desired, although he did receive a prize for swiss chard in 1923.

Throughout the years the children had sown many crops of vegetables and memories. When they grew up, they left their gardens to other hands but never forgot the hard-won lessons of the vegetable patch. Any gardener at Lyndhurst could testify that working conditions were exacting; every member of the family was an expert.

On Monday it might be Olivia who would remark, "I don't think the rows of wonder beets are quite far enough apart," and on Tuesday the suggestion might come from Helen Anna, "I don't think the potatoes have been sprayed enough with Bordeaux mixture." Once a Japanese gardener sighed for his native land when Finley Jay snapped: "Osato, my good fellow, you must be more careful. There are lots of beetles in the asparagus patch. Kill them at once with calcium arsenate, but mind, if you see a big one, get him alive—I want him for my collection."

Nowadays, the four children were more interested in flowers, and indeed it must have been more satisfying to raise an orchid than a tomato—to bring forth a host of daffodils than to nurse along a muskmelon—unless, of course, you were hungry.

When I arrived at Lyndhurst, flowers had a stranglehold on the conversation as the annual flower show was only a few weeks away. Mrs. Shepard had always been extremely active in the local horticultural society. For years she had graced the institution with wonderful specimens from her greenhouse and large checks from her bank account. But when it came time for the flower show, she insisted that the awards must be made on pure merit and that her years of benefaction must in no way influence the decision of the judges.

And on merit alone, Mrs. Shepard had done extremely well. With the exception of 1929 which was a bad year all around, I don't believe that there was any show in which she did not receive at least one award. Although her flowers and plants had won fame and acclaim over all America, her zeal, ambition and strength were reserved for this amateur, almost neighborly competition. She set out each year to capture the silver loving cups that were awarded as prizes with a purpose as intense as though she were seeking the Holy Grail.

So, the flower show was the most important event on the June calendar, although Flag Day was not forgotten. Helen Anna and Finley Jay arrived from New York, bringing a new flag which Mr. Shepard had sent for the latter occasion. And early, before breakfast, on the morning of June 14th, we all stood at attention around the flagpole while the new flag was raised, and sang the National Anthem.

Miss Davis started us off: "In the key of E flat—E, B and A are flat—remember? Helen Anna! Finley Jay! Stop talking, please. Now—everybody ready!"

This little ceremony, though dutifully patriotic, was

simply infantile, but Mrs. Shepard would never forego it except for rain. For all her specialized knowledge, she clung to many of her favorite customs with unrelenting stubbornness.

After the national anthem, Mrs. Shepard left with Miss Davis for a meeting with the officials of the flower show to oversee final arrangements. A hundred and one details had to be attended to; there were eight auxiliary committees — Mrs. Shepard was on seven of them.

At Lyndhurst, lunch was served at twelve-thirty; however, if you said you had just come from the gardens or the greenhouse, no excuse for tardiness was necessary. It was the standard alibi, and Mrs. Shepard never questioned its veracity. On Flag Day, however, an unusual thing happened. Mrs. Shepard, herself, was late, and while we were waiting the conversation drifted to the flower show.

"Personally," Helen Anna said, "I think the whole thing smells."

"Helen Anna!" we all exclaimed with shocked surprise.

"Treason," cried Miss Stebbins.

"No, I mean it," Helen continued. "I love the bees and the flowers, but what a bore! And the show is always on the hottest day of the year."

"We ought to have an insect show sometime," Finley Jay suggested.

"What a terrible thought!" Miss Stebbins said.

"There's a species of beetle, right here at Lyndhurst, that can run as fast as a man."

"Why don't you arrange a race?" Olivia dryly suggested.

"They won't run in a straight line," Finley said, winking at me.

Miss Stebbins abruptly changed the subject.

"I wonder where Mrs. Shepard is? She's never been late before. I'm worried."

"You won't have to fret any longer," Finley said, looking out the window. "Mother's here now," and we heard the big Locomobile come up the gravel driveway and stop under the porte-cochere. A moment later, Mrs. Shepard came skittering into the sun parlor with Miss Davis, and we rose to greet her.

"I'm so sorry," she cried. "You must forgive us for being late, but something terrible has happened. I don't know how to tell you."

"What happened?" we exclaimed in a chorus.

She paused a moment, and then said slowly: "I've been arrested."

It took a moment for this information to sink in. Louis was the first to recover. In a rather unsteady voice he asked for confirmation: "Did you say you were *arrested*, Mother?"

"Yes," she answered pathetically. "It's the truth, but do please sit down, and someone be kind enough to bring me a cup of tea."

Miss Stebbins flew out to the kitchen to get it.

"What were you arrested for, Mother?" Louis asked.

"For speeding," and as she said it, a sigh of relief went up to the ceiling. "It was a horrible experience," she continued. "It was along the Albany Post Road—just above the chicken farm."

"How fast was the car going?" Olivia said, with a practical turn of mind.

"Thirty miles an hour."

"Are you sure it was for speeding, Mother?"

"Yes, the speed limit there is twenty-five. Before I knew it, a policeman on a motorcycle stopped us, and he made us follow him down to the police station because we couldn't find the registration. Fortunately, an officer recognized us when we came in."

"What were the damages?" Finley Jay asked. I beg your pardon, dear?"

"How much was the fine?"

"Oh, it was ten dollars."

Miss Stebbins came running back with a cup of tea, and after Mrs. Shepard had recovered some of her strength, we learned more about the details and were able to understand what had happened.

When Mrs. Shepard entered the police station and the clerk of the court recognized her, it was most embarrassing. He recalled how generously she had subscribed to the Policemen's Ball last year; she had bought twenty tickets. The situation clearly called for leniency, but Mrs. Shepard wanted no favors. She insisted on paying the fine, and gave her promise that in the future her Locomobile would be driven more carefully. As long as she was in the car, the speedometer would never see thirty again. It was like owning a racehorse and never allowing it to trot.

On the way out of the police station, Mrs. Shepard witnessed a little drama in the courtroom across the corridor. A trial was nearing its climax. A man in a ragged suit and three-days' growth of beard pleaded guilty to killing a young deer out of season. The fine was one hundred dollars or ten days in jail. The man had no money, and as sentence was about to be pronounced, Mrs. Shepard interrupted. To the amazement of the court, she insisted on paying the fine. All she wanted from the defendant was his promise that he would never harm another animal. "Have you ever looked into the eyes of a fawn?" she said. "Do so, and you will never kill one again."

And there was something else on her mind. She could

not get over how dirty and rundown the police station was.

"That police station is the most depressing place in the world. You sit on a little wooden bench, and there are absolutely no decorations on the wall. Louis, I think it would be nice if we did something about that."

Louis raised his head quizzically. "What do you mean, Mother?"

"Would you bring them down something they can hang on the walls? That room is a disgrace to this town."

"I think some Chinese scrolls would be nice," Helen Anna suggested.

I bit my tongue to keep from laughing, but Mrs. Shepard didn't flick an eyelash.

"An excellent idea, Helen Anna. Would you help Louis select some nice ones — and take them down; and also, if you could find a small Oriental rug we're not using."

"There are two in the tower," Olivia said. "A Boukhara and a Kazak,"

"The Kazak, would be better," Mrs. Shepard decided. "It's a wonderful bright red and the geometric designs are most effective. I think it would improve the sergeant's office. I don't remember his name.'[5]

"It's Clancy," Helen Anna said.

Miss Stebbins suggested that perhaps now Mrs. Shepard should have something to eat. Mrs. Shepard said that she couldn't eat any lunch and felt the need of a short rest. But she asked the whole family to meet in the sun parlor for a discussion of the flower show at three o'clock sharp. I went in to lunch thinking how Chinese scrolls and Oriental rugs would look in Sergeant Clancy's office. "East is East and West is West . . ." but Mrs. Shepard had arranged that the twain would meet in the local police station.

At three o'clock sharp we assembled in the sun parlor

and Mrs. Shepard outlined the master plan for the flower show. Awards would be given for garden varieties, hybrids, arrangements, stands, potted plants, foliage and hot-house specimens including rare tropical plants, though Mrs. Shepard, herself, was concerned with displaying only garden and hybrid varieties.

This year, for example, she thought it would be a happy idea if she displayed the new Coolidge Rose, which she assumed we all knew was a hybrid. Personally, I didn't know a Coolidge Rose from a rambler. Mrs. Shepard had explicit reasons for her choice. The rose was the New York state flower, and besides, her husband had once voted for Calvin Coolidge as president. She regretted that Mr. Shepard was still away on business, but we would have to get along as best we could, without his guidance. She asked us if we all approved of her choice. We did — unanimously.

"Remember," she cautioned, "you must speak frankly if you do not agree with my suggestions. The flowers should represent *all* of us. If we win, we share the victory together — if we lose, we share the disappointment." All of us agreed that united we would stand, modest in victory — gracious in defeat. Mrs. Shepard elaborated her plans — like a general preparing for a campaign:

"I think, in addition to roses, sweet peas would be nice. I have never displayed our sweet peas, and I'd like to give them a chance to show what they can do. This year they are blooming exceptionally well. Don't you think so?"

Olivia was enthusiastic. "Sweet peas would be wonderful, Mother! Last year they were a little sun scorched, but this year they're perfect."

"Do they have any insect injuries?" Finley Jay asked. "No," replied Olivia, "no blemishes of any kind."

"Then if no one has any further comments," Mrs.

Shepard said, "I think we will show the sweet peas. Agreed?"

"God bless them," Miss Stebbins said.

Then Mrs. Shepard sighed deeply as she went on to a more complicated problem: "Now about the Delphinium divaricatum—you know, we have shown them before, but they have never won. Do you frankly feel we should give them another chance?"

"I don't," Louis said emphatically. "I just don't think they have the will to win. They've been in every flower show since I can remember, and they've done nothing except take up space."

Helen Anna waved her hand furiously, and Mrs. Shepard nodded for her to take the floor.

"I disagree absolutely with Louis," she said. "I don't think the fault is with the delphiniums. I think the fault is ours. I'm positive the fertilizer we've used is wrong. Possibly too much super-phosphate. Besides, we have never achieved the proper balance between stem and flower. Why, last year somebody cut the stems so short they looked stunted. Furthermore, we had so many blossoms of different sizes that the balance—well, well, it just plain stank."

"Helen Anna!" Mrs. Shepard exclaimed in horror. "What a thing to say about a delphinium!"

"Well, it's true, Mother."

"All Helen means," Olivia said, coming to the rescue, "is that we may not have given the delphiniums enough attention. Helen Anna just puts things a little bluntly sometimes."

Mrs. Shepard meditated. After a little while she spoke her mind: "I personally think the delphiniums should be given another chance. Does anyone disagree?" The silence indicated complete agreement.

"And our fourth exhibit, I think, should be rubrum lilies with contrasting foliage — possibly caladium leaves or maidenhair fern."

For some reason at the mention of the kinds of foliage bedlam broke loose. Everybody started talking at once. Louis jumped to his feet. "Mother," he said, "you surely can't mean caladium."

"Why not?" interjected Finley Jay.

"But it's from the greenhouse," Louis pleaded. "Can we seriously think of blending a garden flower with hothouse foliage? I think it's wrong, and it's against tradition. The lilies should be blended with maidenhair. It is a natural fern; it grows out of doors like our lilies—in the same soil—under the same sun. The only way you will mix caladium and lilies will be over my dead body." Then he sat down—a little pale, I thought.

"I agree with you, Louis," Helen Anna cried.

"Bless you, child, so do I," Miss Stebbins said.

Olivia got up to present the case for caladium. "I would like to mention," she said, "that all flowers and ferns are neighbors whether they grow in greenhouses or in the fields. Personally, I think caladium and especially caladium bicolor, makes a finer ornament than maidenhair; it makes the lilies much more beautiful, and besides it's more original. No one likes maidenhair better than I do, but in this case, I honestly believe caladium would be the better choice."

"Hurrah for caladium!" Finley Jay bellowed. "Three cheers for caladium."

Mrs. Shepard seemed a little annoyed and spoke a bit sharply: "I know you all have very strong feelings about this, but please, children, do not make a Tower of Babel out of the sun porch. I suggest we avoid further discussion and put it to a vote.

"First," Mrs. Shepard said, "those who favor maidenhair will kindly raise their hands." Hands went up: Louis', Helen Anna's, and Miss Stebbins'. "Now those in favor of caladium," Mrs. Shepard said, and Olivia, Finley Jay and Miss Davis raised their hands.

I saw to my horror that it was a tie—three and three. From the expression on Mrs. Shepard's face, I could see she was in a dilemma. She said: "Will anyone reconsider?" There was no answer. "Will anyone abstain?" No one would budge an inch. This was, indeed, a greenhouse divided against itself. Then a smile crossed Mrs. Shepard's face. She looked at me. "Celeste," she said, "you have not voted. You can solve the problem for us."

I took refuge in honesty. "Mrs. Shepard," I said, "I don't think I should vote. I know what maidenhair fern is, but I have never seen a caladium. It wouldn't be fair."

"Of course not," she replied, attempting to conceal her disappointment. "Then there is only one way out. I will have to telephone Mr. Shepard in Chicago. Excuse me." She got up, toddled out of the room, and we waited for the decision.

After a little while, Mrs. Shepard came back. "I have talked to your father in Chicago. We will abide by his decision. Three of you will be happy; three of you will be disappointed." Then she proclaimed the victor: "Caladium."

The final word was spoken. The die was cast! Long live caladium! The meeting was over.

I went up to Olivia and said: "Don't you think you had better take me down and show me what a caladium is?"

"I certainly do," she replied emphatically. "Come with me. I will introduce you immediately to them. At

Lyndhurst they're something every young girl should know." We walked rapidly down to the greenhouse and in a few moments stood before a caladium bicolor. It was a striking plant with large, almost heart-shaped leaves, delicately veined in rose and green.

"There you are, Celeste," Olivia said, "that's what caused all the trouble."

"It's beautiful. I would have voted for it."

"You don't understand botanists," Olivia explained. "They feel very strongly about their pets—particularly at election time."

"Nevertheless, I'm glad it won, and thanks so much for the introduction."

We started back. Before we came to the door, Olivia stopped before a small bulletin board. There were several things tacked up, but she seemed particularly interested in one.

"Read this, Celeste," she said. "I don't know who could have put it up—Finley Jay, probably."

I came closer and read it.

THE GARDENER'S PRAYER

O Lord, grant that in some way it may rain every day, say from about midnight until three o'clock in the morning, but you see, it must be gentle and warm, so that it can soak in; grant that at the same time it would not rain on Campion, Alyssum, Helianthemum, Lavender, and the others which you in Your Infinite wisdom know are drought-loving plants — I will write their names on a bit of paper if You like — and grant that the sun may shine the whole day long, but not everywhere (not, for instance, on Spirea, or on Gentian, Plantain-lily, and Rhododendron), and not too much; that there be plenty of dew and little wind, enough worms, no plant-lice and snails, no mildew, and that once a week thin liquid manure and guano may fall from heaven. – Amen.

—Karel Capek

When I finished, we both looked at each other, grinning from ear to ear.

"I think we'd better take it down," Olivia said. "I rather doubt that Mother would approve."

11

Le Grand Prix

THE NEXT FEW days were spent in frenzied preparation. The flower show was to be held in a week, and there were endless tasks to do before then. The flowers had to be watched, cleaned, examined for blemishes, prepared for cutting, and given a good talking to.

Because I could not contribute anything of a technical nature, I tried at least to lend moral support by exhorting everyone on to victory. A hundred times I said that the flowers were the most breathtaking, the most exquisite I had ever seen and that the caladium leaves so enhanced the beauty of the lilies that the combination defied description. "Solomon in all his glory," I vowed, "was not arrayed like one of these."

Every time I saw a shooting star, I wished on it; every time I saw a toad, I wished on it; in fact I wished for victory on every talisman I could think of, including the wishbone in the Sunday turkey.

But for a born naturalist like Mrs. Shepard, good wishes and good intentions were not enough. One afternoon, in greenhouse number three, while I was watching her clip the moss around some caladium pots, she put down her little gold scissors and said: "Celeste, my dear, you have been at Lyndhurst almost three weeks and I have been observing you very carefully."

I had no idea of what was coming, and I thought: "Now what have I done?" — but I could think of nothing in which I had been remiss. I had been on time to all meals. Helen Anna and I had not taken a single cocktail. I had always worn stockings when I went swimming with Olivia, and I was quite positive I had destroyed every cigarette butt in my room. But I did not have long to ponder, because Mrs. Shepard came quickly to the point: "Celeste, my dear," she said, "I have thought for a long time that you should be better equipped."

Equipped for what? I thought. I certainly brought enough clothes with me, including four tea gowns and a pair of blue jeans. "Equipped for what, Mrs. Shepard?" I asked plaintively.

"To fully appreciate the world of nature," she said.

"Oh yes, Mrs. Shepard," I said, "I realize I am not very well equipped."

"I don't think it's too late," she added encouragingly. "Oh, Mrs. Shepard, I'm so glad of that."

"You will realize more and more," she said, "that as you grow older you will discover most things made by man are fleeting, but the creations of God are eternal. The more we learn, the fuller and more rounded our life becomes if we recognize and understand His handiwork."

"I agree, Mrs. Shepard," I said, "and I'm very sorry that I know so little. I would like to know a great deal more."

"You may, my dear, if you wish to. I learned about flowers from my father. He brought many of them to this greenhouse from South America and India. Even from beyond the Trebizond. At one time he had a collection of eight thousand orchids, and two thousand azaleas. I have always thought that flowers were his closest friends."

"He had a lot of friends, Mrs. Shepard," I said politely, though I fear my mind was on the Trebizond. Where could it be? The name certainly had a fascinating ring!

Mrs. Shepard seldom mentioned her father but whenever she did she pictured him in her own image; tender, and innocent, and good.

Then she continued:

"Celeste, I have a book with me you might like to read." She turned and pointed to it on the work table beside the caladium plants. "It is called *Plant Ecology*, by Coulter, Barnes and Cowles."

"Oh, thank you very much, Mrs. Shepard!"

She picked up the book and carefully, almost ceremoniously, handed it to me. I was impressed immediately by one thing—its weight. I opened the flyleaf. There was an inscription: "Souvenir of Lyndhurst, with affectionate love, Helen Gould Shepard."

"After you have had time to read it, we'll have some nice long talks, and let me suggest—don't neglect the footnotes."

I assured her I would not. Then Mrs. Shepard went back to her work. But as I opened the door of the greenhouse to leave, she called after me: "Perhaps after a little while, Celeste, we can learn something about birds, too. After all," she said, "are not the lilac bushes more enchanting when the vireos nest in them—and the orchards more friendly when the bluebirds come?"

"I would love to learn about the birds," I said as I closed the door and started walking up the path toward the castle. I met Olivia running down. She stopped abruptly and looking suspiciously at the book under my arm asked:

"What have you got there?"

"A book."

"Oh, I know," she said. "*Plant Ecology*. We've all had to read it and there're *two* more after that." Then she was off to the greenhouse.

As I entered the front door Miss Stebbins walked out carrying an armful of empty flower pots: "Busy days! Busy days!" she said, and then she saw my burden. "That looks familiar."

"Souvenir," and I held it up.

"Thought so. And it's only the beginning. Good for the soul," and she was off post haste with her flower pots. Everybody was in such a hurry!

I went upstairs to my room, sat down on the edge of my bed, opened my book, thumbed through it, looked at the photographs, and read a bit here and there. I came to one paragraph which described how the cactus plant, over a period of time, had adapted itself to the desert; how now, due to its elaborate root system, it could live under the most arid conditions. Well, if the cactus could adapt itself to the desert, I certainly should be able to adapt myself to Mrs. Shepard! But on page seventeen I fell asleep over a footnote.

The day for the opening of the flower show finally came, and the entire household was up with the sun. Immediately after breakfast we all got into the big Locomobile and started off. Mrs. Shepard sat pale and tense under a large, pink maline hat harboring a row of satin roses. I felt that if our exhibits didn't win a prize, the hat would. She did not speak except to give an occasional warning for the chauffeur to drive more slowly. Eventually we arrived — all safe but a little late. It was a glorious day- clear and bright with enough scattered clouds to keep the sunlight from flattening out the colors of the outdoor displays.

Crowds of people had already arrived, and we followed Mrs. Shepard up a small roped-off pathway which wound its way through endless displays of beautiful flowers. I saw one group of sweet peas that looked to me even better than ours, and Mrs. Shepard thought so too, for she whispered confidentially, "I'm terribly afraid of Mrs. Eliot."

Mrs. Eliot was an apple-cheeked fat lady who greeted us lustily: "Good morning, to you and yours, Mrs. Shepard. I have seen your exhibit up ahead. It's delectable, and your sweet peas, especially."

"Thank you so much," Mrs. Shepard said meekly, "but they're not nearly as lovely as yours."

"Indeed, you're wrong," Mrs. Eliot continued as she shooed away a butterfly which was trespassing around her flowers.

"I don't think so," Mrs. Shepard contradicted.

"Well, time alone will tell," Mrs. Eliot concluded, "and may the best sweet peas win."

We arrived at our exhibit—truly, a breathtaking sight. Mrs. Shepard had arranged her flowers skillfully, and she had added a coy but novel touch—a little handwritten card was clipped to each group: "We are delphiniums," one said; "We are sweet peas"—another. "We are lilies." "We are roses." A larger plaque thumbtacked to a small stake supplied additional information:

Exhibited by Mrs. Finley J. Shepard and her family.
Gardener: James McGovern Osato (Assistant)

The festivities were a four-day affair so the results of the competition would not be known immediately. There was plenty of time to realize you might have done better and to discover that your neighbors could raise flowers as well as you. Yes—there was plenty of time for comparison, regrets and remorse. By the end of the third day, Mrs. Shepard was in such a state of apprehension and nerves, I didn't think she would ever last through the show. "We haven't a chance," she kept repeating. "I have not done my best. I have not worked hard enough." Finally, the afternoon of the fourth day came—the day of botanical judgment. The judges were ready to award the prizes and everyone assembled on the lawn in front of a little wooden platform.

Mrs. Thackeray, serving her fourteenth year as Chairman of the Horticultural Society, brought everyone to attention with an authoritative cough and a small gavel. After a brief introductory speech, she started to give out the prizes. Cups, ribbons and plaques were awarded for innumerable classifications of flowers and plants. Then came the moment we had all been waiting for. Mrs. Thackeray said: "And now the award for roses. Can you all hear me?"

I glanced down our row. Everyone was paying attention except Finley Jay who was taking a cat nap and Helen Anna who was daydreaming over a paper cup of orangeade. Mrs. Shepard was sitting tense and upright on the edge of her chair as if she were about to hear the sentence of her life or death pronounced upon her. There was not long to wait.

Mrs. Thackeray's voice rang out loud and clear: "For the finest display of hybrid roses—to our good friend and neighbor—Mrs. Finley Shepard."

Mrs. Shepard stood up proudly, toddled to the platform, and received her silver loving cup with trembling hands. Her face beamed in embarrassed triumph. She turned to face the audience and in her little high-pitched voice acknowledged the tribute: "Thank you—each and every one," and toddled back to her seat, clutching her trophy tightly to her breast.

Her moment of triumph was exalting, but it was short lived, for when the awards for the sweet peas were announced, her name was not included. Mrs. Eliot won, and she strode boldly forward to receive her prize. As was the custom, she too made a speech of acceptance: "I won't hide it from anyone; this is a great day for me."

Soon came the award for the lilies. It was a happy pronouncement. Mrs. Shepard won again and she rose in a little spasm of happiness, and another loving cup was hers. She turned again to the audience and said: "Dear friends, I really don't deserve this, though I thank you just the same from the very bottom of my heart and it's going awfully, awfully fast." The applause was loud and spontaneous. We hadn't done badly so far—two prizes out of three.

There was one final decision we impatiently awaited: "For the finest array of delphiniums," but alas it was unhappy tidings. Our delphiniums were not mentioned—not even honorable mention. We all sat in gloomy silence. It was the delphiniums that Mrs. Shepard had really hoped would win. The sweet peas had won in other years, but the delphiniums had never received anything but common courtesy. Louis whispered to Finley Jay: "I said they couldn't win—remember?"

Miss Davis looked the picture of extreme dejection, and I thought she might cry. Miss Stebbins patted her on the back and mused philosophically, "We did everything that was humanly possible."

However, Mrs. Shepard insisted on assuming complete responsibility. She said, "It was all *my* fault. I have never been able to achieve the proper fragrance. But I did so want them to win! And they are your father's favorite flower. In a way I'm glad he wasn't here; he would have been *so* disappointed."

The afternoon was slipping into twilight, and the show was over. Everyone said his goodbyes, and started home. But Mrs. Shepard had a sentimental suggestion: "Before we leave, let us all walk back and see our flowers for the last time."

We threaded our way through the dwindling crowd and stood silently in front of our offering. It was as if we were applauding the victors and consoling the vanquished. In the lengthening shadows the sweet peas and the delphiniums seemed to droop their heads as if they realized they were doomed to end their short, beautiful lives defeated, unheralded, and unsung.

Mrs. Shepard looked at them wistfully and said, "Farewell, my flowers—farewell, my gentle friends."

12

Seven Days Shalt Thou Labor

IT HAD BEEN a long, tiring week, and when the flower show was finally over, I was happier than anyone in Lyndhurst except possibly the flowers. Tomorrow was Sunday, and I looked forward to sleeping late and breakfast in bed. There would be no chores nor problems. Nothing to do — A holiday.

I slept Saturday night through in an instant. And now somebody was knocking at my door! My eyes opened, and the hands of the clock on the bed table came slowly into focus: Ten minutes past seven. As the knocking continued, I said, "Come in," thinking what in Heaven's name is *blooming* now? The door opened. Mrs. Shepard was blooming — in a pink moire kimono and lavender night cap. She rustled toward my bed, chirping gaily, "Good morning, Celeste dear, *good* morning!" and pertly tilted her cheek for a kiss. "It's a heavenly day. Celeste," she bubbled on: "Not a cloud in the sky, and do you hear the robins out getting their breakfast?"

The robins are doing a lot better than I am, I thought gloomily as I started to reach for my dressing gown.

"Don't disturb yourself, Celeste. I'll get it for you."

"I can get it all right," I said weakly.

"No," she insisted, "don't trouble yourself," and she took it off the chair, helped me into it, and, in motherly fashion, deftly tidied the covers and arranged the pillows neatly at my back. Then she sat down on the edge of the bed.

In my half-somnolent state, I couldn't imagine the reason for this call. But when I saw tucked under her arm a familiar black book, *Bible Verses to Memorize*, I became suspicious.

"It is my custom," Mrs. Shepard explained, "to drop into the children's rooms on Sunday to read a few verses before breakfast. I am sorry I have not been able to visit you before."

Then asking the most rhetorical of questions, "Shall we begin?" she opened the book to a page marked by a thin, black ribbon and started to read:

Blessed are the poor in spirit: for theirs is the kingdom of heaven.

Blessed are they that mourn: for they shall be comforted.

Blessed are the meek: for they shall inherit the earth.

Blessed are they which do hunger and thirst after righteousness: for they shall be filled.

Blessed are the . . . .

Then she paused and looked up at me to complete the verse. I was silent. I remembered my rendition of the Twenty-Third Psalm — this was no better.

She started to read the verse again, very slowly! "Blessed are the . . .," then stopped and tried to prompt me by forming the next word with her lips. I wasn't a lip reader, but I looked intently at her lips, and the only word that they suggested was m-onk-ey. Blessed are the monkeys — no, that couldn't be right. I managed a little delaying cough and added: "Now let me see," and knitted my face into a contorted agony of concentration. After an embarrassing silence, she finally prompted me: "Blessed are the merciful ..."

"I know, I know," I said, "'For they shall obtain mercy.'"

"Quite right, Celeste. Do you know what I am reading?"

"Yes," I answered, "the 'Beatitudes.'"

"Of course, my dear, the 'Beatitudes'—one of the most beautiful passages in the New Testament." Then coaxing me as she might a ten-year-old child, she said: "And they are from the Gospel according to . . . ?"

I knew they were either from Matthew, Mark, Luke, or John, but which one I could not recall. Well, I had a four-to-one chance. Which one should I pick? Eeny, meeny, miney, mo—I picked John.

"No, dear," Mrs. Shepard said, "not quite."

"I mean Mark," I said quickly.

"No, dear, not Saint Mark, not quite."

"I give up," I said.

"It's Saint Matthew," she said in a manner that made me feel that I was the only Christian in the world who didn't know this. Then she read slowly through to the end of the lesson and after the "Amen," she said, "Now Celeste, I am going to Helen Anna's room, but I am planning to have breakfast with all of you at ten o'clock sharp."

There went my breakfast in bed! My happy idle hours! She kissed me benignly on the cheek, toddled to the door, opened it, turned, and repeated: "Now the 'Beatitudes' are from?"

"Saint Matthew," I said. She nodded and went out, leaving me somewhat purified, and very wide awake.

As I was getting dressed, I continued to recite the "Beatitudes" and to wonder about Mrs. Shepard. Helen

Anna told me that her most vivid childhood memory was of her mother standing beside her with a bowl of oatmeal in one hand and a Bible in the other. You might not always be hungry on time, but it you weren't, the punishment was prompt enough: Ten verses to learn by heart.

Louis said he always felt she adopted the children from a sense of sacred duty and reared them with her own exacting moral code. Their life was strict, unreal, and not much fun. Carefree moments came only with a governess, a butler, a maid, or with each other in a room in the attic, but even then one ear was always alert for intruding footsteps. The four youngsters learned about life from backstairs gossip, from smuggled literature, and from the window. The first cigarette, the first cocktail, the first kiss were the results of well-planned conspiracies. They plotted to find out about the pleasure of life: no one taught them.

Dear Mrs. Shepard! Generous, naive, and unreasonable, spending so much of her life trying to make her children something they would never be—little angels. You could spend your life reflecting about Mrs. Shepard, but *nothing* in this world would ever change her. And for all that, who would really want to?

At ten o'clock we assembled for breakfast like a wolf pack. We kissed Mrs. Shepard good morning and marched into the dining room. Someone had put a baseball cap on the bronze head of Louis, but Olivia snatched it off before her mother saw it. The menu, besides grace, included orange juice, cereals and scrambled eggs—a conventional breakfast—until you ate it. If the orange juice had been a degree colder, it would have become orange ice. The rolls, on the other hand, were so hot that it seemed they were baked in a blast furnace. The coffee was an unpleasant mean between the two extremes—lukewarm. But for Miss

Davis it was just right—she drank four cups of it.

When the preserves were brought in, they looked like a display at a county fair! There were twelve different kinds, if you counted the quince. They were placed on a lazy susan, and immediately Finley Jay spun it around shouting: "Place your bets, ladies and gentlemen, place your bets, and remember, if the orange marmalade stops in front of you, the house is the winner!"

Toward the end of the meal, Sitwell staggered in with a dozen Sunday newspapers and put them down by the window. I was dying to see if a special sale of Princess Eugenie hats had begun at Saks Fifth Avenue, but, at the moment no one showed the slightest interest in the morning's news.

After breakfast all of us, somehow, found places in the big Locomobile and started out for Saint Barnabas' Church in the village. I had no idea who Saint Barnabas was so I asked Miss Stebbins. She was the handiest person to question as she was sitting on my lap.

"Saint Barnabas was one of the twelve Apostles," she explained, "and do you know, Celeste, that Saint Barnaby Day used to coincide with the summer solstice? I remember a little rhyme about it: 'Barnaby-bright, the longest day and the shortest night.'" Then she added a postscript: "Am I too heavy for you?" She was, but I did not want to offend her. The discomfort was a fair price to pay for: "Barnaby-bright, the longest day and the shortest night."

A half block from church we stopped, parked the car, and scrambled out. Bunched together we looked like a Macedonian phalanx. In front of the church we broke ranks because the door was not wide enough to accommodate eight people abreast. Suddenly a bird flew out of a pine tree, and I thought it was going to go through the front door, but at the last second it swerved and sailed straight up toward the sky. Mrs. Shepard identified it immediately: "Hairy woodpecker—male—and it's going to Heaven the most direct way."

Church services in the country were a great deal shorter than in the city, but Mrs. Shepard made up for this difference by a very simple arrangement. She went to church *twice*. At five o'clock that afternoon we would return for vesper service.

On the way back from our morning devotions we ran into a thunder shower: Although we were only about three minutes from Lyndhurst, Mrs. Shepard insisted that we stop and put up the top. We all pitched in—some with willing hands, others with advice.

Although we had a crew of eight and the chauffeur, it would have been easier to raise the mainsail on a schooner. Finley Jay shouted: "Shove it—harder, harder." Miss Stebbins, holding a newspaper over Mrs. Shepard's head, kept screaming: "It will never go up if you *force* it." Helen Anna's contribution was a poem: "Rain, rain go away—come again some other day," while Olivia looked on the brighter side of things: "Surely there'll be a rainbow," she said, searching the skies.

Finally, after many experiments and after we got Miss Davis' wrist out of the crossbar, the top went up. At precisely that moment, it stopped raining, and we had to go through the same process in reverse. By the time we pulled up in front of the castle, we looked more like survivors of the storm than defenders of the faith. Sunday was taking more out of me than Saturday.

During lunch, I noticed the twelve newspapers still reposing untouched by the window. No one had yet rustled a page. I did so want to see about those hats!

And I was about to take a copy when Mrs. Shepard said: "Are we all ready now for the weeding?" At the sound of her voice I jumped back. Did she say "wedding?" What wedding? I turned to Louis and said: "Are we getting *married* today?" Louis looked blank, and I added: "Didn't Mrs. Shepard say something about a *wedding?*'

Louis burst out laughing, and said: "No, Celeste, not wedding; w-e-e-ding. Every Sunday afternoon we take the weeds out of the front lawn."

"I don't believe you!"

"Custom," Louis explained, "an old custom."

"But it would take a lifetime!"

"I know it. Come on, we have to put on some old clothes and get the tools."

"Louis," I asked plaintively, "when can we read the Sunday papers? There's something very important I have to find out."

"Monday," he said.

When we straggled out onto the lawn that glorious Sunday afternoon, we were a motley crew. Louis was carrying some sort of insidious, curved instrument that looked more like a cutlass than a weed puller. Finley Jay appeared with an old coonskin hat and a knife between his teeth.

"All right, Daniel Boone," Helen Anna said, "don't be such a show-off. You're going on twenty-three now!"

The girls had less lethal tools: small garden scissors honed to razor sharpness. I thought we would be able, if called upon, to give a pretty good account of ourselves in a street brawl. Miss Stebbins and Miss Davis were excluded from the front-line fighting. They pushed around small wheelbarrows to gather up the debris.

Louis and I were assigned to weed a portion of the lawn

that had been converted into a small practice golf course. I had never seen anyone use it, so I presumed it was there purely for decoration. Louis and I would have preferred to play it; instead we got down on our hands and knees and began to weed it. Once we started, we worked hard. Louis knew the enemy when he saw it, and he cursed the dandelions, the chickweed, and the sorrel as he violently uprooted them.

"If they sprayed the iron sulphate a little more generously around here," he said, "we wouldn't have to go through all this!"

"Anyway, Louis, it's a new experience. This is the first time I've ever started around a golf course on my hands and knees."

Once during our labors Miss Stebbins rolled up the wheelbarrow.

"Louis," she said enthusiastically, "look how much you've done!"

"Not so much," Louis replied acidly, "so far we're four dandelions under par."

Suddenly Finley Jay who was clipping some timothy grass nearby exploded: "A mole! a mole! Look, everybody, a mole!" and he pointed to little bumps of earth that were being pushed up as the rodent was making its way somewhere underground. "I'll get him—stand back," and with a few hasty turns of his knife, he uncovered the hideous little animal and held it up in his hands. It gave out frightened little squeaks until Finley twisted its neck, and its days were over. Although he was quite proud of his catch, I was revolted at the spectacle and Olivia looked as if she were going to throw up.

"What a joy you are," she muttered.

Finley defended himself as best he could: "Those things

ruin the lawn. They do more harm than weeds."

Mrs. Shepard didn't agree. She ran over screaming: "Don't ever do that again, Finley Jay, never again! Don't you realize how many insects those rodents eat?"

"Mother is right," Helen Anna said, "the moles are on our side."

"And another thing," Mrs. Shepard continued: "You have interfered with the balance of nature."

From the general consternation it seemed plain that Finley had not only interfered with the balance of nature, but that he had ruined it!

At four o'clock the weeding was over and it was time to get ready for vespers!

As I was scraping the dirt off my hands with pumice, I decided the weeding party had been one big flop. We had weeded only a few square yards. This was like taking water out of the ocean in a teacup, but it satisfied Mrs. Shepard's wish that no one should ever be idle. She was afraid of idleness as if it were the plague.

At five o'clock promptly we returned to church for vespers. Again, we were an octet. We sang hymns for one hour with great respect for God and little respect for music. On the way home, the seating arrangements were different. Now I sat on Miss Stebbins' lap and as soon as I was comfortably seated, I asked her, "Where is the Trebizond?"

"Gracious me," she answered, "I have no idea."

Sunday was finally finished, and so was I! I started up to bed with aching limbs. But first I made a little detour into the dining room to steal a Sunday paper. In vain — they were all gone!

Once in my room I undressed, jumped into bed, but I was too tired for sleep. Desperately I counted sheep; recited the "Beatitudes"; but it was useless. Between the hours of eleven and one I got up at least a half dozen times to get a glass of water. Finally, I thought of the ecology book Mrs. Shepard had given me. An inspiration! After three pages I was sound asleep. At last! Sweet dreams!

Not for long! I was awakened by a dog barking under my window. What an infernal nuisance! It stopped after a few minutes but left me wide awake. Well—back to plant ecology! It did the trick, and I fell asleep, but it wasn't long before I was awake again. The dog was yelping his head off. I was right back where I started from. The flora was putting me to sleep, the fauna was waking me up. The barking continued for a full quarter of an hour. You'd think in a big establishment like this somebody would do something about it!

Suddenly I heard two shots ring out. "My God," I thought, "somebody did!" I hoped the dog would bark again, but he was silent. Instead I heard voices—almost inaudible at first—then louder and louder. Someone screamed. I threw on my robe and ran downstairs.

Everybody was up and babbling hysterically on the sun porch. I ran to Louis' side and shouted above the noise: "What happened, Louis? What's the matter?"

"There's been a robbery!"

"A robbery—a thief?"

"Yes, he tried to get into the art gallery."

"Did he steal anything," I asked excitedly. "Was anyone hurt?"

"No, the night watchman shot at him, but he escaped." It was clear now why the dog was barking. I felt I should find him a bone and apologize, but my intention was distracted by Mrs. Shepard. She was sitting in a huge wicker chair, practically in a state of collapse. Miss Davis and Miss Stebbins were both holding a large bottle of smelling salts under her nose.

"Take deep breaths," Miss Stebbins urged frantically.

No, no," contradicted Miss Davis, "short breaths." When they put the bottle aside for a moment, I tested it for strength and thought the top of my head would come off. Miss Davis was right: "Short breaths, Mrs. Shepard," I advised.

After Mrs. Shepard recovered, somewhat, from the combined effects of the robbery and the smelling salts, she asked: "Why would anyone want to rob us? Please tell me why," and she looked pathetically at Helen Anna and then at Olivia.

Practically all of the vast estates along the Hudson had been subject to thieves and prowlers at one time or another, and it was a wonder it had not happened at Lyndhurst before. Mrs. Shepard would never comprehend that evil could ever be directed toward her.

Suddenly we heard the lugubrious wail of a siren from the driveway, and in a few moments we were confronted by the law itself—the well-tailored but confused presence of Sergeant Clancy. He removed his hat, walked across the sun parlor, and after an awkward bow before Mrs. Shepard said: "Your watchman telephoned. I am sorry to hear about the disturbance, Mrs. Shepard."

The Sergeant was ill at ease, and I sensed he felt that catching footpads was nothing compared to the ordeal of entering Mrs. Shepard's household, but after he took out his notebook and started asking official questions, he was more self-possessed: "And now if someone will please give me the details!"

He got them all at once and no two versions alike. Olivia heard the dog barking; she was sure, about eleven-thirty. Louis said it was exactly midnight. Helen Anna didn't think it was a dog at all; she thought it was a wolf. There was equal disagreement about the shots. Miss Davis said she heard them at exactly twelve o'clock. Miss Stebbins said, "No," she heard the shots at one o'clock. Finley Jay was positive he didn't hear anything.

Sergeant Clancy was off to a poor start, and things were going to get worse before they got better.

Miss Davis swore by Saint Peter that she heard two shots fired, and Miss Stebbins swore by Saint Barnabas that she heard five. She was also sure she heard footsteps right outside her bedroom.

"That was me," Louis said. "I was looking for the Sunday papers."

"Did you find them, Louis," I asked eagerly.

"No."

"Say, I was looking for those papers myself," Finley Jay said. "Who took them anyway? There's a thief in this house!"

"What would you like me to find around here," Sergeant Clancy said somewhat exasperated, "the Sunday papers or—"

"I think I can help you about the shots," the watchman interrupted, as he ran in from the sun porch. "Here's my gun. See! There're only two used cartridges," and he pulled it out of his pocket.

"Put that thing away!" Miss Stebbins screamed.

"It's all right, lady, it's on safety."

"I don't care what it's on—take it out of here."

I thought that if Sergeant Clancy ever solved this case, he'd be made a commissioner. Mrs. Shepard evidently sensed herself that things were getting out of hand, for she came up with a sound suggestion: "Perhaps the sergeant would like a cup of hot coffee."

"I sure would, Ma'am. Thank you very much — black, please."

After Sergeant Clancy finished his refreshment, Mrs. Shepard started to ask a few questions of her own. She took over without his realizing it. "What are you planning to do?" she said quietly.

"Don't you worry, Mrs. Shepard, we'll find the thief — sooner or later we'll get him."

"And then what do you do?"

"He'll get a nice long jail sentence, if I'm any judge."

"That would be a pity," Mrs. Shepard commented, but the sergeant was oblivious to her sympathy.

"Why, we'll institute a state-wide search. We'll call out every available officer. We'll find our man if we have to search every acre in the state."

"A man hunt," Miss Stebbins cried gleefully.

"Exactly. Believe me, you may rest assured that justice will be done."

"What a poor, misguided soul he must be," Mrs. Shepard reflected.

Sergeant Clancy agreed: "He certainly is."

"What a pity he had to do such a thing," she added. "The thief is, indeed, his own worst enemy."

"You're right, Mrs. Shepard, and it's our responsibility. We'll catch up with him soon enough."

It was apparent that Sergeant Clancy was not quite catching the drift of Mrs. Shepard's conversation, but her next remark left no doubt as to what she was thinking: "You mustn't worry too much about it, my dear sergeant. God will punish him."

"What's that, ma'am?"

"God will punish him," she repeated. "He has broken one of the Ten Commandments."

"One of the most important ones," Miss Stebbins added. "Which one is that?" said the sergeant, looking a little puzzled.

"The eighth," Mrs. Shepard explained. " 'Thou shalt not steal,' " and she said that she was positive the man's own conscience would punish him. She, herself, would not for a moment think of lodging a formal complaint. Then she looked sweetly into his eyes and said: "Always remember, Sergeant Clancy, 'Forgive and ye shall be forgiven.' "

"Well, Mrs. Shepard," he said, "I'll have to consult my superiors about that. Usually when there's an attempted robbery we try and catch the robber. It's been that way ever since I've been in this country. However, if that's what you want, Mrs. Shepard . . ."

"That's what we all want, I think," and she looked around the room for acknowledgment, and everyone nodded in complete agreement. Divine law had spoken.

"I will do the best I can, Mrs. Shepard," Sergeant Clancy said, "but, possibly, to avoid similar incidents in the future, you'd better put on some extra watchmen at night."

"Or more dogs," Helen Anna said.

"We've got ten now, child," Miss Stebbins said testily, "not counting Chinky."

The sergeant's night was almost over. He walked slowly and disconsolately to the door, then stopped. There was still something weighing on his mind. He said slowly, "Mrs. Shepard, me and everybody down at headquarters want to thank you for those nice Chinese pictures and that carpet you sent us after we arrested you. They certainly make a difference! We are greatly obliged."

"How sweet," Mrs. Shepard said, "how charmingly sweet."

After the sergeant went out, Mrs. Shepard dolefully

shook her head: "I do hope they will not try to capture that poor, unfortunate man."

"I'm sure they won't," Louis said, "and don't worry, Mother dear, everything will be all right."

"Thank you, Louis, and now it's time we went back to bed, and tomorrow, I think, we should all sleep late and have breakfast in bed. Don't you agree?"

There was not a dissenter among us, and each stood in line, tenderly kissed Mrs. Shepard goodnight, and went his separate way.

On the way upstairs, something was still bothering me. I waited for Louis and said: "Where is the Trebizond?"

"I have no idea," he answered.

As soon as I got to my room, the dog started barking again, but this time *nothing* could keep me awake. Tomorrow was Monday, and I looked forward to sleeping late and breakfast in bed. There would be no chores nor problems. Nothing to do! A holiday!

13

The Wedding

I EXPECTED TO LEAVE Lyndhurst on Thursday to join my mother at Lake Placid. In her last letter, she said that she was anxious to get started on plans for my wedding. Though Louis and I were not going to be married until November, Mother never believed in putting things off until the last minute.

I had been at Lyndhurst now for over three weeks. It was already twelve days after Flag Day, or eight days before the Fourth of July. I would not have missed Flag Day nor the Flower Show for anything in the world, but there was no question that I should take my departure before the fireworks began. Leaving Lyndhurst however, proved to be a lot more difficult than getting there. Mrs. Shepard implored me to stay a little longer and suggested that I call my mother immediately on the telephone, send a telegram, or write her a little note by special delivery.

Finally, I said that I would love to stay until Friday, and Mrs. Shepard beamed with delight and immediately begged me to visit her again later in the summer. I hadn't yet finished my first visit, and here she was already extending an invitation for my second!

"I would love to come back here again," I said enthusiastically.

"That would be wonderful," she replied, "but we won't be here."

"Oh!" I replied a little flustered.

"We will be in Roxbury," she explained.

"Roxbury, Connecticut?"

"No, no, dear, Roxbury, New York."

Then I learned that Mrs. Shepard always moved her household to her home in the Catskills during the hot weather. "Though I wouldn't say it out loud," she confided, "I like it there even better than Lyndhurst." It was apparent that Mrs. Shepard did more than change her hats with the seasons—she changed her houses too.

Now, however, Mrs. Shepard said she was behind with her letters, excused herself, and went up to her room. This was the literal truth. She was prompt about every appointment in life, but always late in answering her correspondence. It would have been impossible to be otherwise because she kept in persistent touch with all her relatives, her many friends, and her countless acquaintances at home and abroad. With the assistance of Miss Stebbins and Miss Davis, she wrote over a hundred letters a week. Louis said his mother spent more money each year on postage stamps than she did on her clothes.

I didn't see very much of my hostess for the rest of my visit and had no opportunity to talk with her. The events of the month had tired her, and she stayed close to her room, appearing only for meals. There was, however, one memorable exception. On Friday, my last day at Lyndhurst, Louis and I were looking at the pictures in the art gallery on the second floor. The gallery contained a heterogeneous collection, including two autumn scenes by

Corot, and "Dance of the Nymphs" by Bougereau, framed in gold. We were standing under the nymphs when all the trouble started. Louis kissed me.

Who would have thought that at that precise moment Mrs. Shepard would be standing — framed in the doorway! She walked slowly across the art gallery, and her usual bright little smile had changed to a foreboding frown. I thought to myself, I should have left on Thursday.

"Celeste and Louis," she said sharply, "will you please come with me?"

We followed Mrs. Shepard out of the art gallery, downstairs, and into the music room. I had never seen anyone use this room, but one thing was certain, we weren't going to sing love duets in it now! Mrs. Shepard closed the door and motioned to us to sit down on the large davenport against the wall. It was a very comfortable piece of furniture, but we felt very uncomfortable. Mrs. Shepard sat down in front of us on a small straight-backed chair.

"Louis and Celeste," she said sternly, "I wish to have a little talk with you."

It was easy to guess just about what was coming and I decided to say as little as possible, agree with everything she said, and promise never to get caught again.

The lecture began:

"Now children, I regret very much that I came to the art gallery when I did. What I found — well, I am afraid I must be truthful — was not a pretty picture."

Mrs. Shepard was at first hesitant and ill at ease, but it wasn't long before her moral convictions overcame her embarrassment.

"I am truly shocked," she said indignantly. "It is hard to believe that you and Celeste could behave in such a disgraceful way. You must realize that you have done something very wrong. I trust such unbecoming behavior has not been going on for long."

"'No, Mother, I assure you it hasn't,'" Louis said contritely.

"I should hope *not!* Here at Lyndhurst it is impossible to chaperone you every minute of the day but Louis, what could have come over you?"

"I lost my head, Mother."

"And you, Celeste?"

"Mine, too," I said.

"I hope and pray," she continued, "that in the future you will learn to control yourselves. To be able to control our minds and bodies raises us above the beasts of the field."

Mrs. Shepard embellished her little lecture on propriety with illustrations from both the Old and New Testament. She said that if we thought evil, we would do evil, because our actions were the mirror of our hearts.

"Remember the 'Beatitudes', " she said, " 'Blessed are the pure in heart: for they shall see God.' "

This was the only time that I had been really annoyed with my future mother-in-law. I was so mad I was about to stand up and defend my virtue. Fortunately, before I said anything tactless, Miss Stebbins knocked on the door and announced that Mr. Shepard was telephoning from New York. Immediately Mrs. Shepard popped up and started to leave, then paused, and said sweetly:

"I hope, children, we will never have to talk about anything like this again. Remember, it will not be very long until November. Soon you will be married."

Then she kissed us both affectionately on the cheek and went out.

"That was unfortunate," I said. "I feel like Hester in

Hawthorne's *Scarlet Letter*."

Louis and I sat for a long time in the music room and talked about Mrs. Shepard. It seemed that all her life she had fought a vigorous, but losing battle against sex. Though she was ever on the alert, every now and then, some simple manifestation of it was bound to appear—a dress too short, a neckline too low, a shoulder too exposed.

Louis went on to tell me, that his mother's naivete and misinformation on this subject were staggering to the human mind. One afternoon at tea she had rendered her guests speechless when her curiosity about the origin of the Centaur became too literal for comfort. Mrs. Shepard was full of paradoxes about "love, chivalry, and romance." She knew in detail many of the tortured and twisted relationships in Roman, Greek and Scandinavian mythologies. And although she violently disapproved of a boy and girl holding hands, she wasn't disturbed at all by the fact that Oedipus was passionately in love with his mother. Once, speaking of the affection that Siegmund had for his sister, Sieglinde, she said: "Wasn't it sweet that they had a baby —and named it Siegfried?"

Louis told me that Olivia's courtship with John Burr, a remote cousin of his mother's, was chaperoned from the day that he first entered 579. Some trustworthy person was always with the happy couple. "Two's company, three's a crowd," and Miss Stebbins was usually the crowd. The fact is that when John finally did propose he did it in writing— on a calling card, presented to Olivia on a silver tray by Sitwell.

Yes, in Mrs. Shepard's world, Pelleas might woo his Melisande to his heart's delight, and Tristan his Isolde, but never John his Olivia, nor Louis his Celeste.

The turnout for my departure from Lyndhurst Friday

morning was very gratifying but a little overwhelming. There were fifteen people, counting Mr. Allan and his family, and thirteen dogs, including an Airedale and her family. Mr. Allan's farewell was touching though obscure:

" 'Tis facheous ye maun gang awa sae soon. Muster Louis surely hae a guid ee frae a lass. May ye hae many a bonnie bairn."

"Thank you, Mr. Allan," I said, "and the same to you."

The morning was very confusing, and for a while I wasn't quite sure if I was coming or going. When I kissed Mrs. Shepard goodbye, she pinned a beautiful corsage of lilies-of-the-valley on my coat. As Louis and I drove off down the gravel road to a final fading chorus of farewells, I heard the loud, hearty voice of Miss Stebbins calling, "Aloha."

Louis headed down the Albany Post Road as if it were the Indianapolis Speedway, and after dinner he put me on the night train for Lake Placid. On the platform he kissed me goodbye but first looked around, almost unconsciously, to see if, by any chance, Mrs. Shepard might be watching. Just before the train pulled out of the terminal, he said that he had some very important information.

"What's that, Louis?" I said.

"The Trebizond was the Medieval Empire of the Byzantines."

"Oh Louis, it was sweet of you to go to all that trouble."

"No trouble, Olivia knew."

Twelve hours after I learned about the Trebizond, I was having breakfast with my mother in Moosewood Cottage. On the table was coffee, toast, orange juice, *The New York Times*, seven fashion magazines, and a copy of *Field and Stream*.

"Going fishing, Mother?" I said.

"No dear, I haven't fished since that summer on Lake Chipuineticook. That magazine was sent over by mistake."

Mother said that she had been working industriously on plans for my wedding and that she had asked a few of her friends for their opinions. What Mother meant was that practically the entire membership of the Lake Placid Club had been canvassed for advice—in strict confidence, of course. Should it be a small wedding or a large wedding? Personally, I thought it would have to be a large wedding, though I was fearful that the "friends" of the groom would outnumber the "friends" of the bride by, at least, three to one.

"No worry about that, dear," Mother said. "This is a wedding, not a battle. Besides I'm sure that practically all the Chase Bank will be there."

Father agreed. "As a matter of fact," he said, "I'm counting on the entire discount committee!"

There were endless decisions to make. Should the wedding be held at home or in a church? In the afternoon or at night? Would it be advisable to have police? If necessary, I thought, preferably on horseback. Where should the reception be held? Should champagne be served or would it offend Mrs. Shepard? Mother didn't think it would be practical to put ginger-ale labels on all the bottles. And how about dancing? Mother thought waltzes would be all right, but positively no fox trots, and no saxophones. "All the violins you want dear, but no noisy brass or that funny little thing that looks like a potato."

"An ocarina," I said.

"Yes, that."

Most of these weighty problems were finally resolved, at various times, and sometimes in odd places. One morning at the caddy house Mother said that she had decided what she would wear at my wedding: a blue velvet ensemble with a corsage of orchids. One evening on the way back from an Indian ceremony, which the club held every year to celebrate the founding of the Iroquois Confederacy, my wedding dress was decided upon: white crepe with a Queen Anne cap and a tulle veil, embroidered around the edge with mother-of-pearl calla lilies.

The question of the dresses for the bridesmaids and maid-of-honor defied solution. In July it looked as if the bridesmaids would wear blue moire dresses with picture hats and bouquets of cerise roses, and for the maid-of-honor, it was to be cerise moire with blue velvet trimmings and an electric blue turban.

But in August, influenced by the changing colors of the mountains, we decided the bridesmaids should wear lime- green taffeta dresses with matching hats, the maid-of- honor to wear emerald green, and they would carry sheaves of chrysanthemums in varying shades of yellow, ochre, and bronze.

In the cool September breezes Mother and I had a better idea. The bridesmaids would wear ice blue, and the maid-of-honor would wear pearl pink, and they would carry bouquets of white camellias and forget-me-nots. On first thought, this looked like the answer; on second thought, it didn't. The effect would be too pale, even a little sickly.

After summer was over and we returned to New York, the change of scene had a clarifying effect, for on Columbus Day we made our final and irrevocable decision: the bridesmaids and maid-of-honor would wear exactly what we had planned for them in July.

With the problem of the wedding costumes out of the way a girl feels pretty close to the altar. Somehow the other things will get done, and as long as you know what the bridal attendants will wear, you feel pretty secure. The last-minute invitations were finally mailed, the last rehearsal held in the church, the last dress finished at the dressmaker; the last party over. And then comes the final evening before you leave your parents' home forever.

On November 10, 1934, at four o'clock, the organist of St. Bartholomew's Church played "The Wedding March" from Lohengrin and three hundred people rose and half-turned their heads to the rear of the church to see me begin my long walk to the altar. I was trembling when I took my father's arm, and followed the ushers and bridesmaids slowly down the center aisle. Everything seemed distorted and unreal. The three hundred people in the church seemed like thousands, and there was such a profusion of flowers that it was almost like walking through Mrs. Shepard's greenhouse. I caught glimpses of people staring at me whom I had never seen before. The men had cold, stern faces, and the women seemed sad, and one little old lady could not hold back the tears — tears, perhaps, in memory of her own youth and beauty.

When we were half the distance to the altar, I realized that my anxiety about the number of the "friends" of the bride had been unfounded. Practically all the left-hand pews were filled. I whispered to my father:

"The entire discount committee must be here."

"Yes," he said, "and most of the foreign department." As we approached the front of the church, members of both families were looking at the bridal procession with loving eyes. Mrs. Shepard was standing on tip toes and nodding her head in time to the music. Mr. Shepard was standing by her side, proud and stately in his immaculately tailored cutaway. I recalled the afternoon at 579 when he had played the wedding march for me on the huge

Wurlitzer organ.

But there was no time now to think of the past—the present was upon me. I walked up the steps to the altar, and the Reverend Paul Sargent, with quiet solemnity, pronounced Louis and me "man and wife."

Then Louis kissed me, but this time there were no objections from anyone; the organ began to play Mendelssohn's "Wedding March," and we walked quickly up the center aisle. The ceremony was over.

Louis and I went out of the church, excited, happy and self-conscious. There were crowds of people lined up on both sides of the red carpet leading down the steps to a long, black limousine, complete with chauffeur, speaking tube and white-wall tires. Louis helped me in and shut the door; I waved to the crowd, and we were off.

It was good to sit back and rest for a moment. It was a luxurious car, and we could have motored to California quite comfortably, but almost before the car started, it stopped again. We had arrived at our destination! Sherry's was just one block south on the other side of Park Avenue from the church. Never were such extravagant preparations made for so short a journey.

Soon the bridal party arrived, and we stood in line to receive our guests. Mrs. Shepard came toddling over to take her place, threw her arms around me, kissed me, and said:

"God bless you, my child, and now you will call me Mother Shepard."

There were a great many people to welcome, and it took a long time. A lot of people kissed me that afternoon, including many I had never seen before. Cordiality on such a large scale was somewhat tiring. Mrs. Shepard must have thought so too. She looked a little pale, and I suggested that perhaps she should go in and sit down at her table. But she would not hear of it. She smiled and shook hands as sincerely with the last guest as she had with the first; not once did her smile lose its charm, not once did her little hand falter.

When the last guest had run the gantlet of the receiving line, we went into the ballroom to find our places. Louis and I sat in the center of the long wedding table with Olivia, Helen Anna, Finley Jay, and many of our friends. Mrs. Shepard sat at a small table close by with Mr. Shepard, my father and mother and Doctor Sargent. She looked over at us a little wistfully. I suppose she felt as if she were losing another of her children.

The orchestra began to play, and according to custom, Louis and I danced first, alone. The music was sweet and tuneful, and Louis led me gracefully around the floor until the number was finished, and everyone applauded. Then all the guests joined in the dancing. I am sure every man at the reception had kissed me; now they danced with me. There were tall ones, and short ones, and thin ones, and fat ones. One gentleman coyly asked where I was going for my honeymoon. I said it was a big secret, but I'd tell him if he'd promise not to tell.

"I promise," he said.

"We are going to the Trebizond—if we can get reservations."

Almost every dance was a waltz, and the orchestra played gaily and liltingly in the spirit of Old Vienna. The conductor was an elderly gentleman with sideburns and a long white mustache who looked vaguely like the Emperor Franz Joseph. Once Finley Jay danced "The Blue Danube" with Miss Stebbins, and Louis danced "The Tales of the Vienna Woods" with Miss Davis.

"Thank you so much," she said, as she sat down panting a little. "I don't think I kept time very well."

"You did fine," Louis said, "and when they play 'Die Fledermaus,' we'll try it again."

Louis and I danced so many waltzes that I was beginning to breathe in three-quarter time! To people listening outside, it must have sounded as if the wedding reception was a Strauss Festival. Once I saw the conductor pick up a piece of music, and I read over his shoulder: "Waltz by Glinkowitz."

"Who is Glinkowitz, Louis?" I said.

"He's a friend of Strauss."

After an hour of continuous dancing the music stopped. The lights were dimmed, candles were lit, and a five-tiered wedding cake was wheeled in and with a huge silver knife I broke the icing. Then the waiters came in with bottles of Pol Roger, and by and by they were popping all over the room. After everyone was served, the Reverend Mr. Sargent rose and tapped on a glass with his fork. The little ringing noise called everyone to attention, and there was quiet. In an oratorical voice, he said:

"A toast to the bride and groom."

Everyone stood up and tipped his glass, I looked across at Mrs. Shepard. She stood up with her glass in hand and seemed to hesitate. I knew that she was debating with her conscience if she should, for the first time in her life, allow her lips to touch liquor. At last she made her decision. She slowly raised her glass — but did not drink. Nothing would make her break her creed, not even for the beau geste!

Louis and I danced once more around the room, and Louis said it was getting late. Miss Stebbins, sensing that the time for our departure was near, ran up to us and presented Louis with a small Bible.

"A little gift from your mother before you leave."

Louis opened the Bible and saw an envelope peering out from between the pages of "Proverbs." It contained a check for a thousand dollars.

"Wouldn't you know Mother would do something like this?" Then he quoted a passage from Proverbs: "She looketh well to the ways of her household, and eateth not the bread of idleness. Her children rise up, and call her blessed."

Now it was time to leave. We went around the room quietly and bid adieu to our families and our friends. Louis' final kiss was for Mrs. Shepard. Bravely, but sadly, she said: "Goodbye. Goodbye, my dearest children."

Louis and I went out quietly through one of the side doors, but before we closed it, we looked back once more into the room. The music was still playing, the people were dancing, and there was laughter. Our gaze fell upon Mrs. Shepard. Miss Davis and Miss Stebbins had drawn their chairs a little closer around her. We lingered at the door. It was hard to leave even for our honeymoon because, yes — it was very plain to see — Mrs. Shepard had a tiny white handkerchief in her hand. She was crying.

14

The Catskills

AFTER OUR HONEYMOON we rented a small apartment on Central Park, and Louis started looking for a career. When it became apparent that he would have no success, he started looking for a *job*. Unfortunately, the depression showed few signs of letting up, and jobs were almost impossible to find. Reluctant to take advantage of any of his friends and family, Louis studied the want ads in the newspapers and called on every investment house in Wall Street, including the one that handled his own trust fund. But things were so difficult, he found he couldn't get work even if he paid his own salary!

My father was certain he could land Louis a job with the Chase Bank, and Mr. Shepard was very optimistic about a connection with the Missouri Pacific, but Louis politely refused assistance from either of them. He even discouraged Mrs. Shepard when she suggested "writing a sweet little note to Max Schling, the florist."

Personally, I didn't see why Louis had to be such a rugged individualist, and I urged him to reconsider the bank. It would be nice clean work and he didn't have to advertise the fact that he had succumbed to a little family assistance. However, Louis was adamant so we were faced with a problem in our marriage even before the rugs were down.

After Thanksgiving and Christmas went by and my energetic husband's only work consisted of carving the turkey and decorating the Christmas tree, his unemployment took on the aspects of a family tragedy. Mother called every day to see if her son-in-law might have "thought twice" about the Chase Bank, and Mrs. Shepard called every other day to remind us about Max Schling. Louis' predicament provided the main subject of conversation and speculation in all three households. One afternoon we called on Mrs. Shepard, and as Sitwell opened the door, he said:

"Any luck. Master Louis?"

"No luck."

"Don't worry, Master Louis — it's the times. It happened to me in the panic of 1908."

Olivia came running up, kissed us, and said: "I hear you can't find work. Aren't you lucky!"

After we were all seated comfortably around the refectory table in the living room, Louis told his mother that he had been studying the unemployment problem and thought that at last he had found the answer. This was indeed unexpected news, and we all leaned forward in our chairs to hear the happy details. Louis explained that he wanted to join a new company as a limited partner. It was a fine company, and he thought it had exceptionally good long-range possibilities; it would be necessary, however, to put up a certain amount of capital, and he was thinking of asking Mr. Shepard to underwrite him.

Mrs. Shepard replied enthusiastically that her husband was always interested in promising new business ventures, and every now and then, she was inclined to take a conservative risk herself.

"It sounds very interesting, Louis," she said, "what kind of a company is it?"

"I think, Mother dear, you could call it a manufacturing company," Louis replied rather cautiously.

"What does it manufacture, dear?"

"Thompson sub-machine guns."

Mrs. Shepard's reaction to this news was somewhat delayed. Then slowly from deep down in her throat I heard a series of half-articulate, choking sounds. Finally, she managed to say:

"Louis, what *can* you be thinking of! Do you really want to become a murderer?"

Her disapproval could not have been greater if Louis had said he was planning to run opium. He tried to mollify her by explaining that the guns would only be used for target practice. Also, he pointed out that Alfred Nobel, who had done so much for the cause of peace, had invented dynamite; and the Chinese, the most cultivated people in the world, had initiated gunpowder. Louis' arguments were logical enough, but trying to convince Mrs. Shepard that her family should make machine guns was as hopeless a task as trying to persuade Al Capone to join the Salvation Army.

All through tea and afterwards Louis was the picture of dejection. When we were leaving, Mrs. Shepard suggested Max Schling for the umptieth time, and for a moment I thought he was going to capitulate. But he was made of sterner stuff.

"Before I sell flowers, I'll sell *apples!*" he said. "And I'll stand on the steps of 579 to do it!"

Louis' next scheme had to do with machines for killing

time instead of people. One afternoon he tried to sell the Grand Central Station the idea of installing pin-ball games, in the waiting rooms. The official of the Grand Central, with whom Louis discussed this brilliant idea, admitted that the notion was not without imagination, but he made it very clear that his railroad was not interested. "However, you might try the Missouri Pacific," he said a little acidly.

After this Louis had one final flight of youthful fantasy. He became interested in a scheme to salvage gold from a ship that had struck a coral reef off a Polynesian atoll. This enthusiasm caused him to spend two whole nights on the bedroom floor of our apartment studying maps in a Rand McNally Atlas.

"Don't be absurd, Louis," I finally said. "Put the maps away and come to bed. It's three o'clock!"

Still Louis' unrelenting attempts to find work were not in vain. One grand morning he was offered the job of assistant personnel director for a New York relief organization, and he accepted it. My mother was so happy that she sent us down a bottle of champagne with a little card reading: "Good luck!"

Louis was afraid the job would not be so romantic as searching for sunken gold. He was wrong. His very first duty was to organize a fashion show to raise money for the needy. The models were the prettiest and most alluring girls I had ever seen, and Louis went about his work with such efficiency that I rather regretted I had been so quick to discourage him about Polynesia.

Now that Louis had a job, we could settle down a little more calmly to home life. There were lots of things we needed. This was apparent from the blank spaces on the walls and the wide open spaces in the living room. We needed pictures, furniture, lamps, ash trays, and encouragement. It was not long before I received them all in abundance—from Mrs. Shepard. She appointed herself my interior decorator.

Every few days packages arrived from the most expensive shops and department stores in town. As time went on, there was a curious continuity to the gifts. One week we would receive lamps, another week, tables, and another week, books. "Book week" was rather interesting. On Monday we received an exquisite set of Shakespeare. Two days later we received a leather-bound set of Charles Dickens. On Friday we received a copy of *Lady Chatterley's Lover*. I knew this must be a mistake, so I telephoned Brentano's. Yes, there *had* been a mistake. I should have received *The Letters of Lord Chesterfield*. When I told Louis about it, he said to call the bookstore back and tell them we would keep *Lady Chatterley's Lover*.

One weekend when Olivia came up from Philadelphia, she told me that soon after she was first married, gifts from Mrs. Shepard came regularly as rain, but she urged me not to discourage these rather embarrassing quantities of presents because the decorator role gave her mother a continued sense of usefulness and importance to her children.

"Anyway," Olivia said, "after about a year the gifts tend to slacken off."

Olivia's experience was comforting, though it was to be a long time before I noticed any appreciable letup in Mrs. Shepard's attentions. For example, one afternoon, while I was looking out of my front window at the magnolia trees blooming in the park, the house phone rang and the doorman said:

"Mrs. Shepard is calling. Shall I send her up?"

"Please do," I said.

I emptied the ash trays, straightened the sofa, hurried

into a tea gown, and I had just put some water on the stove to boil for tea, when the doorbell rang. I opened it, and Mrs. Shepard walked in followed by Miss Stebbins and Miss Davis, carrying an Audubon drawing of a cock pheasant. We spent the afternoon hanging the pheasant and never did a game bird receive so much attention out of season. We tried it on every wall in every room of the apartment and at every height. Miss Stebbins handled the hammer and nails, and Miss Davis was the expert on distance.

"A little to the left," she would say, "now a little more. Now just a little to the right. That's fine!"

On the horizontal alignment Miss Stebbins and Miss Davis worked well together — vertically they were impossible.

"Higher! Now lower! Lower than that. Go back the other way. Higher! Sorry, dear, it's too high."

Mrs. Shepard said sweetly, "It should be at eye level, you know."

"Of course," Miss Stebbins said. "When the eyes of that bird look into the eyes of Miss Davis, it's time to stop."

Finally, the pheasant was hung to everyone's satisfaction though I must say I would have preferred something else. Of course, Mrs. Shepard's love of nature was a beautiful thing, though at times it struck me as a little exaggerated. When Louis came home that night we took down the pheasant. Whenever Mrs. Shepard came to call, we hung it up. The poor bird went up and down so many times that the wire broke.

Before Mrs. Shepard went to Lyndhurst in April, we received a final expression of her generosity. One afternoon when she came to call the radio was on and Rubenstein was playing Chopin's "Second Sonata." During the funeral march, Mrs. Shepard asked me if I liked music. I said I loved music, but that lately I had not had time to go to many concerts.

"Do you play yourself, dear?" she asked.

"A few things, Mother Shepard, when I have the opportunity."

A week later opportunity knocked at my door, and four men carried a beautiful mahogany piano across my threshold. Although there was no card attached, I knew at once who had sent it. It was a munificent gift, which Louis and I were proud to own. And for a while Louis thought he might take up the music lessons, which he had abandoned at the age of eight. But after two lessons, he decided to stick to golf.

"*You* play it," he said generously. "After all it's *your* baby grand."

One afternoon soon after this Mrs. Shepard arrived with Miss Stebbins and Miss Davis because they were anxious to see how the piano was getting along. Miss Davis, who had perfect pitch, said it needed tuning. Mrs. Shepard admitted she didn't know since she was tone deaf but she suggested that I get in touch with Mr. Stronovitchenbach at Aeolian Hall. Then Mrs. Shepard had another idea. She thought it would be nice if I played a little piece just to show them how the instrument sounded.

"And I know you play beautifully, dear," she said.

"I play very badly," I replied truthfully.

"I'm sure you play well. Won't you give us just *one* little piece?"

"Please do," said Miss Stebbins. "Just any old thing."

"Please do," added Miss Davis.

I was not flattered by such encouragement, but if I didn't play, Mrs. Shepard would be offended. Now what piece did I know best? I had practiced "The Wild Horseman," except that I always stumbled on the last two measures. I could play "Old Black Joe," but I didn't think my audience would care for it. Then I had an inspiration! I would play "Nearer My God to Thee." Although I hadn't played it in ten years—perhaps my fingers would remember it. I sat down at the piano and began the famous hymn with little hope and a heavy touch.

Because I was so nervous it sounded more like a Sousa march than a hymn. But fortunately, Mrs. Shepard loved it, and clapped as heartily as she would have applauded Clara Schumann.

"How wonderful! You play beautifully, Celeste!"

"It was lovely," Miss Stebbins said.

"Quite nice," Miss Davis said, "but it's A flat, dear, not A natural."

"Yes," I said, with an embarrassed smile, "I'm terribly sorry."

"Never mind, child; it sounded very nice anyway."

The concert was over. It had been one of the shortest performances in the history of music—and no encores. Still Mrs. Shepard was pleased, and that was all that mattered. At least her gift would be used for more than just a piece of furniture. As I opened the door, I thanked her again, and kissed all three ladies goodbye. Miss Davis looked back over her shoulder and stared at the picture of the cock pheasant on the wall. With a little shake of her head, she said: "I still think it should be a little further to the left."

After my debut at the well-tempered clavier, Mrs. Shepard's gifts gradually became less frequent as Olivia had predicted. Geography was also a factor; Mrs. Shepard was now in Lyndhurst. Louis and I were asked regularly, once a week, to visit her, but he had to work practically every Saturday and Sunday so we could never get away.

However, during the summer his work slowed down considerably, and when his vacation rolled around, we were able to accept Mrs. Shepard's invitations. By this time she was in Roxbury, a little earlier than usual, and she wanted to have the whole family together on the Fourth of July.

Louis and I were unable to start the long trip until the late afternoon of the holiday. "We won't make it by dinner," Louis said, "but we'll eat along the way."

Roxbury is in the heart of the Catskill Mountains, and Mrs. Shepard's home is in the heart of Roxbury. It is roughly three hours from Times Square, if you drive at a steady pace of ninety miles an hour and don't stop for dinner.

Roxbury itself, hasn't changed much in a hundred years. It has one main street, a few stores, an old-fashioned inn, a gasoline station, and a bank. Mr. Fanning, who owns the drugstore, claims that even today more deer, skunks, and woodchucks use the road than people. The town is hardly known outside the county except by a few who remember it as the birthplace of two famous men: John Burroughs and Jay Gould. John Burroughs, born in 1837, loved the town and the lonely countryside and never left it. From the eastern slope of a windy hill his grave looks out over the land which once inspired him to write so poetically and tenderly about it. A verse is crudely carved on his headstone:

I stand amid the eternal ways And what is mine shall know my face.

Jay Gould, born in 1836, did not share this fine poetic

enthusiasm for Roxbury. Even as a boy in his teens he planned to escape to a more exciting world. He would revisit Roxbury once or twice in his lifetime, but he was not going to live in it—or die in it.

Because it was Jay Gould's birthplace Mrs. Shepard was sentimental about Roxbury even before she saw it. And shortly before she was married, she bought a house not far from where her father used to live as a boy. It was a small house, so she gradually enlarged it, but in contrast to 579 and Lyndhurst, it was simple and unpretentious, and she reveled in it. It was miles from any important town or resort, and they could live there "without fear or favor from the crowd."

As Mrs. Shepard expanded her house, wing upon wing, she did not forget the town. She loved Roxbury and did everything except legally adopt it. She enlarged its roads, put in flagstone walks, and installed granite curbings. Then she built a library, a Y.M.C.A. and when that was finished, she had plans drawn up for a church: The Jay Gould Memorial Church. She wished her father's name to be always remembered in the town where he was born.

When Louis and I arrived in Roxbury on the evening of July fourth we stopped to get a glass of beer at the inn, for even though repeal of the Eighteenth Amendment had been ratified by two-thirds of congress and three-fourths of the states, Mrs. Shepard was still holding out. While Louis was having his fourth beer to celebrate "The Fourth," he told me that after the Jay Gould Memorial Church was built, Mrs. Shepard named her house, Kirkside! He pronounced "Kirkside" with a faint suggestion of a Scotch burr and looked at me quizzically.

"I know what it means, Louis," I replied, " By the side of the church.' I'm a bright girl. Just because I couldn't understand Mr. Allan! Even his own wife..."

"I know, I know. Let's have another beer."

"No, let's not. We're late enough as it is."

As we stepped out into the street, I heard the hissing whine of a Roman candle rocketing over the elm trees.

"The fireworks!" Louis exclaimed. "They've started — let's hurry!"

Just as another Roman candle went off, we arrived at Kirkside. Louis took my arm, and we ran around to the vast lawn in back of the house. There were rows of chairs and campstools where the family and all the neighbors had gathered to watch the display. I ran up to Mrs. Shepard and kissed her.

Then Louis and I started down a narrow aisle, stumbling over everybody's feet, and I kissed in turn Mr. Shepard, Miss Stebbins, Miss Davis, Olivia, Helen Anna and a strange man whom I didn't recognize in the dark. When I kissed Finley Jay, he said, "You've been drinking!"

By the silver light of a few sparklers we found two empty seats and sat down to catch our breath and watch the spectacle. Giant firecrackers were exploding from all directions, and sky rockets ascended, shooting out balls of green and red which showered fanciful patterns in the sky.

I heard one old gentleman, sitting behind me, whisper to his wife that the pale green light reminded him of the star-shells at Chateau-Thierry.

After the firecrackers came lots of other kinds of fireworks: giant pin wheels of incandescent light and girandoles of vivid purple convoluted far above our heads. A diorama of Niagara Falls, and its glittering, cascading waters was so bright that it bathed the lawn in a white mist and hid the stars. For a vivid moment a mosaic of trees and ice-capped mountains washed out the silhouettes of the rocky crags at the end of the valley. In rapid succession came rosettes of flowers, playing fountains, and the American flag. Then suddenly, miraculously, the profiles of famous patriots looked down upon us: George Washington, Thomas Jefferson and John Paul Jones.

"I think Jay Gould comes next." Louis whispered.

All the colorful tableaux were greeted with applause and shouts of wonder. At times the light was so bright and dazzling that it must have been seen as far away as the Hudson River. I heard Finley Jay say, "Roxbury has never set the world on fire, but Mother is certainly doing her best to set fire to Roxbury."

At the end of almost two hours, the fireworks came to a dramatic end: A huge Liberty Bell, with the date "1776" superimposed over it, fit up half the southern sky. As it swayed, I half expected to hear it ring, but it merely evaporated rather tamely in the gentle breeze.

Everybody thanked Mrs. Shepard for a lovely evening. Louis and I started back towards Kirkside, got in fine, kissed Mr. and Mrs. Shepard, Miss Stebbins and Miss Davis goodnight, and went upstairs to our room. Tomorrow, we would see the gardens in a more natural light.

It had been an exciting evening. We had been part of a dazzling, fiery fairyland, and I was sorry that it was all over. I sat down by the window. A half-moon was starting its late journey across the Catskills. There was still the heavy smell of sulfur in the air, and I heard the voices of men cleaning up the lawn. While I was looking far out into space, I saw a shooting star and I followed it until it disappeared. This was an unusual sight because the Perseids do not appear until August, and then there would be shooting stars all over the heavens. I guess this one must have seen Mrs. Shepard's fireworks and thought the time had come.

15

Fancywork

WE WERE ALL up early the next day, and immediately after Louis finished his Shredded Wheat and I signed the guest book he showed me around Kirkside. Kirkside was a two-story, white colonial house with green shutters and four tall red brick chimneys. The pillars on the front porch supported a graceful balcony which extended half-way across the front of the house. That was about all anyone might remember about it, except for the large dormer and the extraordinary number of windows facing Main Street—twenty-four of them! There was nothing remarkable about Kirkside's architecture, its topography, or even its age. Nothing distinguished it from the other white frame buildings which dotted the nearby countryside—except its size. It was the largest private residence between the Ashokan Reservoir and the Indian Reservation at Tonawanda.

But as Louis had already told me Kirkside did not always have the distinction of size. When Mrs. Shepard bought it several years before she was married, it had seven rooms, a wood stove, and many drafts. Under her meticulous supervision, the house grew as consistently as the young pines she planted on the lawn, though not in the same direction. She elaborated on its width and breadth, but added nothing to its height. Kirkside expanded a little to the north, a little to the south, and considerably to the west.

According to Mr. Shepard's count in nineteen hundred and thirty, Kirkside had twenty-two bedrooms, fourteen baths, twelve maids' rooms, a half-dozen dens and offices, two dining rooms, living room, library, sewing room, silver room, housekeeper's room and a connecting corridor between the kitchen and dining porch called the "breezeway." These forty-odd rooms were connected with a labyrinth of confusing passageways and corridors. There were three different routes from my room to the front door, and until I became used to them, I felt like a rat taking an aptitude test. Louis drew a rough sketch to make the trip easier but suggested that, "in case of fire, it might be safer to jump."

Kirkside, for all its space, seemed congested. There was a higgledy-piggledy of couches, tables, wicker chaise-lounges, rockers, footstools, and ten foot rubber plants in Chinese jardinieres. There were student lamps on every desk and reading lamps behind each chair. If Mrs. Shepard ever needed an extra display for her fireworks, all she had to do was switch on all the lights.

The walls were decorated with Currier and Ives prints, samplers, shadow boxes containing specimens of butterflies and moths, and a few American primitives. There were three Audubon drawings of wild turkeys in the living room and a large picture of a hooded merganser in the dining room. Beneath the merganser was a chair whose design was vaguely derivative of Duncan Phyfe, but which turned out to be an early Louis Seton. He made it when he was twelve, and Mrs. Shepard was so proud of her son's handicraft that she had it varnished every five years to preserve it. She came into the room as Louis was telling me about its history and I'm afraid I was praising it too enthusiastically for my gushing gave my mother-in-law a very practical idea:

"Wouldn't you like to sit in it, Celeste?"

"Why yes. Mother Shepard," I replied, "I would love to sit in it."

"Go right ahead, dear."

The chair was small and didn't look very strong so I eased into it gingerly.

"Isn't it comfortable?" Mrs. Shepard said.

"Extremely comfortable," I answered, although it was cutting off my circulation.

"While I was struggling out of the clutches of Louis' chair, Mrs. Shepard was boasting that her boys had shown an aptitude for carpentry.

"One year Louis made a see-saw," she said, "out of spruce," and she beamed with admiration at my husband.

Louis, however, was amused at his mother's pride in this accomplishment for he remembered distinctly that the balance had never been right. The first time they tried it, Miss Davis was catapulted into a large clump of poison ivy. After a great deal of experimentation, it was discovered that if Miss Stebbins straddled one end of the see-saw and Miss Davis sat on the other with a large Webster's dictionary in her lap, it worked fairly well.

"Those were happy days," Mrs. Shepard said nostalgically.

Before she left to "go to her desk," she said that at two-thirty sharp she would conduct her fancywork class and hoped I would attend.

"I would love to, Mother Shepard," I said.

In the mean while there were other things around the house that piqued my curiosity. On the mantle in Mrs. Shepard's office, midway between a Seth Thomas clock and a miniature totem pole, stood a hand-carved, wooden knight in armor. The children used to love it because all the parts were movable. The visor went up and down, and one could take the tiny sword right out of its scabbard. Louis said there was considerable excitement one morning when the sword was missing. Everybody joined in an exhaustive, but needless search. The next day it was discovered back in its usual place. Finley Jay admitted that he had borrowed it to clean his fingernails.

"Use a paper clip," Helen Anna suggested.

The large attic at Kirkside contained among dozens of packing boxes and trunks four items of mild historical interest: A cradle, a spinning wheel, an old-fashioned bed, and a pump organ. Miss Stebbins used to demonstrate how the early settlers used the spinning wheel, but she gave this up when she thought it was aggravating her arthritis. The cradle served no purpose except to collect the dust of the ages, and the bed was equally without distinction. George Washington had never slept in it, though, on occasions, Finley Jay used it to take a cat nap. The organ was completely non-functional. Mrs. Shepard bought it at an auction, but it suffered the consequences of a rocky trip from Kingston; the ivories came off most of the keys, and the entire flute section was missing.

With all its oddities, incongruous furniture, and size, Kirkside was a happy, healthy, and cheerful place. The whole atmosphere was different from 579 or Lyndhurst, and I didn't feel that everybody was hiding from something. This was due partially to the sun. Far away from New

York, curiosity seekers and cranks, Mrs. Shepard never drew the curtains in her Arcady, and sunlight poured in from the multitude of windows. You could practically see the vitamins dancing on the sunbeams.

The territory around Kirkside consisted of 1,600 acres of first and second-growth forests, mountains, fertile valleys, and pastures. Much of the land was untouched, though, here and there, a few modern conveniences had been added: A baseball field, a nine-hole golf course, an artificial lake, a boat house equipped with canoes and two lifeguards. The estate also had a plant for refining maple syrup, and a bird bath. There were also several anachronistic touches: A life-size silhouette in white paint of Rip Van Winkle on a boulder near the summit of a mountain, an Indian tepee on the golf course, and two sundials. On one of the sundials, which could never indicate the hour because it stood under the shade of a tree, two verses from Robert Browning were chiseled around the Arabic numbers:

Grow old along with me
The best is yet to be.

The other sundial had plenty of sun but was more ambiguously inscribed:

Jay Gould – latitude 42 degrees.

The estate, though vast, was honeycombed with roads, and miles of wandering, winding trails which were blazed with little red arrows pointing discreetly in the proper direction. It was along these shaded pathways that Mrs. Shepard's children once learned the rudiments of woodcraft and forestry. They knew how to make a fire without a match, how to tell an edible mushroom from the deadly amanita, and, one year, Mrs. Shepard taught them how to cut a hole in a blanket and make smoke signals. But one piece of advice she drilled into them unceasingly: "If it starts to rain, come home at once."

Some evidence of the children's forestry lessons still remained. On the bark of a few trees were crudely carved their names: "Birch," "Hemlock," "Ash," and "Sycamore." The carving on one hickory tree went a little further than simple identification. It said: "Louis stinks." The author of this poetic reverie was "unknown," but at the time Louis suspected Finley Jay. Louis said that he in turn had whittled a compliment to his brother on the tall black walnut by the bridge.

After luncheon, everyone scattered to various parts of the house and I wandered alone into the library. Picking up a book at random: *Except Ye Repent*, by Harry A. Ironside, Litt.D., I read on the flyleaf that the author had been awarded a prize of a thousand dollars "by a friend." Undoubtedly the "friend" was Mrs. Shepard for she often disguised her endless "gifts" as awards and prizes.

I started to look for a book that would suit my tastes a little better. *New Bible Evidence* was the next title that caught my eye. No, that wouldn't do! Neither would *The Seven Deadly Sins*. I was about to give up the quest for suitable reading material when Mr. Shepard walked slowly into the library.

"Want something to read, Celeste?" he said cordially.

"Yes, I do," I answered, "something..."

"Something sort of light after a heavy meal? Well! Well! I think I know exactly what you're looking for," and he reached over, picked out a book, and blew the dust from it.

"You'll enjoy it after you get into it," he said. I glanced at the title: *Taxation: The People's Business,* by Andrew Mellon.

I was about to say that I thought I would find it most entertaining when Mr. Shepard began to chuckle. "As a matter of fact, Celeste," he said, "I don't think you'll find many books to your taste in this room. The other bookshelves in the living room are better." Then Mr. Shepard told me that he used to read a lot but didn't any more on account of his eyes, though he enjoyed being read aloud to.

"I'd love to read to you, Father Shepard—any time. Now, if you like."

"Thank you, Celeste, not right now. I have some important work to do outside. What are your plans for the afternoon?"

"I'm going to the fancywork class."

"Oh yes, oh yes! Perhaps you'd rather come with me? I'm going to supervise a little dynamiting."

I couldn't believe my ears, but I managed to say, "I would love to do a little dynamiting, but I promised Mother Shepard..."

"I understand. Well, if you change your mind, come out and join me."

Mr. Shepard went out the front door, and I stared after him not quite sure if he had been joking. I found out that this was no jest. Dynamite was often used to improve some portion of the grounds: To grade a road, reclaim a swamp, or destroy a cliff which obstructed a view. Louis said when the side of three mountains were blasted away to clear ground for the golf course, it sounded more like the last act of *Gotterdammerung.*

I would have preferred to learn the elementary principles of dynamiting rather than the advanced principles of fancywork, but Mrs. Shepard had not given me a choice for my afternoon's activities, and it would have seemed a little absurd to say, "Mother Shepard, would you mind if I did a little dynamiting instead?"

Fancywork class met once a week in the big living room. Everyone brought her work in a knitting bag and was eager to show how much she had accomplished during the week. The contestants, or rather the participants, were the ladies of the household and neighbors. This was not always true, because Louis and Finley were required to attend until they reached the shady side of fourteen. Louis had several beaded bags to his credit, and Finley Jay received a passing grade in doilies.

Miss Davis, Miss Stebbins, and Olivia sat in chairs, and Chinky went to sleep beside Mrs. Shepard. Helen Anna and I sat on the large window seat in the company of some fifty hymnals, piled in neat stacks of five. Just as we were comfortably organized, Mrs. Shepard toddled in with a lady in a dark blue traveling suit. I recognized her at once. It was Miss Quincy, from Chatham, whom I had met at that first Sunday dinner at 579.

"I have a happy surprise for all of you," Mrs. Shepard said. "Miss Quincy just arrived on the 2:19."

We all rose and shook hands with Miss Quincy, and then we all sat down again. Miss Quincy sat down beside me, and after a moment or two, said softly, "You're looking well—congratulations." I considered that she was looking well, too, though I didn't think well enough to merit congratulations.

"And how is your husband?" she added.

Now I understood why I was being congratulated. "He's fine, thank you," I said.

"He must be very tall now."

"No," I said, "just about the same."

"You seem taller," she added.

"It's just my hairdo," I explained.

As Miss Quincy and I digressed to other equally fascinating subjects, the telephone rang, and Miss Stebbins picked it up. We all stopped talking and listened.

"Yes, yes, yes, yes, yes," Miss Stebbins said. Then after a final "yes," she smiled, put down the phone, and announced jubilantly, "They're coming."

"How nice!" Mrs. Shepard said, "all the way from Siam."

I wondered *who* might be arriving from Siam, but nobody told us. Miss Quincy, however, contributed an interesting fact about her own journey. She said, "I have just come from Schroon Lake."

Then Mrs. Shepard stood up in the center of the room and made a little speech:

"For the benefit of those who have not attended our fancy work class before, perhaps I should explain. We all have our little projects. We do as much as we can during the week and meet here on Fridays to exchange ideas, and," she added with a smile, "sometimes—thread. Now, I believe Miss Stebbins has a project for Miss Quincy and Celeste."

Miss Stebbins started toward a small closet, but at that moment two middle-aged ladies rushed in, a little out of breath.

Miss Shepard greeted them ecstatically, "It was sweet of you to come. I have been looking forward to seeing you all day," and she kissed each of them affectionately.

"I hope we're not late,' one of them said.

"Just five minutes," Mrs. Shepard answered. "Now, I think you know everyone here today except Miss Quincy and my daughter-in-law, Celeste. This is Mrs. Dilling, and this is Mrs. Bronson."

We all rose for the introductions, and then we sat down

again. Mrs. Bronson sat in a slippery leather chair next to the fireplace, and I noticed that during the course of the afternoon she kept slipping lower and lower down. At times she would pull herself up, but then her slow inevitable descent would begin all over again.

Mrs. Dilling sat down next to me. The window seat was not slippery, but it was more crowded; it was beginning to look rather like a bus.

After Mrs. Dilling got settled, I said, "It seems incredible you've come all the way from Siam." I thought she looked a little sad as if the Far East held unpleasant memories for her.

"Where in Siam do you live," I said, "Bangkok?"

"No," she said, somewhat surprised. "I don't live in Siam. I live in the house across the street."

Once again Miss Stebbins started toward the closet and just about got her hand on the knob, when the telephone rang. Miss Stebbins was certainly having trouble opening that closet. She skipped back to the phone, and the conversation picked up exactly where it had left off.

"Yes, yes, yes," she said.

She hung up and explained to Mrs. Shepard, "They took the wrong road at the fish hatchery. They'll be a little late."

"What a pity!" Mrs. Shepard said.

Miss Stebbins edged toward the closet door, and this time nothing interfered. She was lost from view for a moment, darted rapidly out, came over to Miss Quincy, and handed her a spool of crochet thread, a large steel needle, and a pattern.

"You might like to start on an antimacassar."

"It seems easy enough," Miss Quincy said, and after a cursory look at the design, started her work so nimbly and expertly that, if there had been an Olympic team for crocheting, she certainly could have made it. I watched her fascinated by such dexterity. Miss Stebbins went back to the closet and returned with an armful of large yellow skeins of silk boucle.

"Just wind these into balls. Celeste, she said, "I'll be right back," and she ran hurriedly out of the room on another of her endless errands. I took one of the skeins, and with the help of Louis' little chair, started to wind it into a ball.

Everybody was now working away enthusiastically: Mrs. Shepard was making a new petit point covering for a footstool, while Mrs. Bronson, seated next to her, was pretty far along on her gros-point cover for a piano bench. Around three-thirty, she got into a little trouble when she thought she had used the wrong color wool, but Mrs. Shepard quickly came to the rescue: "Do use my color chart!" she said.

Helen Anna was making fair progress on a pullover sweater. Olivia was knitting a pair of argyle socks and Mrs. Dilling was persevering with an applique bedspread, although she did not always find it clear sailing. Once, she looked at Miss Stebbins rather pathetically. "I have just put on the last flower design. Now will you please help me with the French knots?"

"Of course, Mrs. Dilling. It just takes a little knack." I had almost finished winding my skein into a ball when Miss Stebbins returned briskly and said, "Celeste, you look as if you're ready to go to work." Then she handed me two typewritten sheets of onion-skin paper and four bone needles. "Just follow the instructions carefully, and if you need any help, I'll be back again," and she quickly stepped over to talk to Helen Anna.

I looked down at the instructions Miss Stebbins had given me:

Two Piece Boucle Suit with Raglan Sleeves
Materials: 18 skeins boucle
No. 3 round needle
Set No. 3 double point needles
Set No. 1 double point needles
Start at back of neck, using 2 of the No. 3 double point needles as a pair. Set up 38 stitches, purl one row, then knit as follows: 1st Row — Widen on the 1st stitch, K 1 stitch, throw the thread over needle, K 1 stitch, throw the thread, K 2 stitches, throw thread, K 1 stitch, throw thread, K 26 stitches, throw thread, K 1 stitch, throw thread, K 2 stitches, throw thread, K 1 stitch, throw thread, K 1 stitch, and widen on the last stitch, et cetera.

I had done a little knitting in my day and could do passably well on a sweater or a pair of plain socks, but a two-piece suit was beyond me. I might just as well have been assigned a Gobelin tapestry. Before I could take the first stitch I needed assistance and I was about to call Miss Stebbins when we heard a screech of brakes, and a car pulled up in front of Kirkside. In a moment a thin, bald-headed gentleman and a very tall lady appeared at the door, and Mrs. Shepard went quickly to greet them: "Mr. and Mrs. Tinsdale. It was sweet of you to come — all the way from Siam."

As the Tinsdales went upstairs, Mrs. Shepard made a little announcement. She said that Mr. and Mrs. Tinsdale were missionaries, and after he had unpacked and signed the guest book Mr. Tinsdale was going to tell us something of their work in Siam.

In a half hour Mr. Tinsdale returned, and greeted us with a clean shirt and an appropriate quotation: "She seeketh wool and flax, and worketh willingly with her hands."

Mrs. Shepard beamed with delight and said, "Now, Mr. Tinsdale, I think we're all ready to hear about Siam." Mr. Tinsdale nodded, walked slowly to the fireplace, took out a small red handkerchief, wiped his glasses, and began with a rather curious statement:

"I would like to take a moment to apologize for my wife."

I didn't think she was so bad, but I suppose he knew her better than I did. Then Mr. Tinsdale explained that his wife was very tired. She was going to refresh herself with a cold bath and a little nap, and hoped no one would mind.

"Not at all," Mrs. Shepard said, "though I'm sure there's plenty of hot water."

"She likes it cold," Mr. Tinsdale explained, and I saw Miss Davis give a little involuntary shudder.

Mr. Tinsdale folded his hands behind his back and began his lecture:

"Siam is composed of an area of about two hundred thousand square miles and has a growing population of about sixteen million persons. Its flag consists of a red, white, blue, white, and another red stripe, in that order." "Five stripes!" Mrs. Dilling said, without stopping her work.

"Yes," Mr. Tinsdale replied, "five stripes across. Siam, you may recall, was formerly called Thailand, or in the native language, 'Muang Thai.'"

I saw Miss Quincy pronounce this quietly to herself as if storing it away in her brain for some future use, but I was sure she said "Mug-wump." Well, if Miss Quincy wanted to change the ancient name of Siam, that was her business.

Mr. Tinsdale was talking louder now because the

click- clack of the needles and Chinky's snoring afforded healthy competition. He described the topography of Muang Thai, its location, the principal resources, the names of its rivers, its tributaries, and the tributaries of the tributaries.

All the ladies continued working, but their little exclamation of surprise and wonder at the encyclopedic information was proof of their rapt attention. But I found it impossible to concentrate on both Miss Stebbins' typewritten directions and Siamese statistics. The written and the spoken word were beginning to overlap into senseless, disjointed phrases:

"Siam is a constitutional monarchy, throw thread over K 1, teakwood is an important article of export, throw thread K 2, the monetary unit is the tical, widen on the last stitch."

It got worse and worse, and suddenly everything ran together and sounded like something out of Gertrude Stein:

"The principal crop in Siam is rice and K 5, there are also large quantities of rubber, tobacco, Englishmen, K 6, fighting fish, cotton, coconuts with raglan sleeves, and throw thread K 27 over King Prajadhipok."

It was no use. I had to choose. I had to knit *or* listen. But before 1 could make up my mind which to do, I had another problem: The ball of wool started to fall off my lap. I tried to grab it, but it was too late, and it bounced erratically across the room and rolled right up to Mr. Tinsdale's feet.

"Oh, I'm so sorry," I cried, and ran to retrieve it.

"Pythons are also very important," Mr. Tinsdale was saying, but he stopped abruptly, bent down, and handed me my elliptical ball. "Rapunzel's hair?" he inquired.

"No," I said, "mine."

I walked back to the window seat as quietly as I could, and Mr. Tinsdale resumed:

"My friends, I have lived in Siam for almost twenty years, and I have seen many extraordinary things happen there. Things that you would hardly believe," and he paused as if debating whether he should become more specific. While we waited in suspense, we heard in the distance a noise that sounded like a heavy explosion: "Boom! Boom! Boom!"

Everyone raised his head a little in surprise, but Mr. Tinsdale was so deep in thought that he didn't hear a thing. He said: "Yes, extraordinary things happen in Siam!"

Again, the explosions rumbled—closer and louder. "Boom, boom! Boom, boom! Boom, boom!" Mr. Tinsdale heard it this time, cocked his head, and walked a step or two toward the nearest window and reflected, "Sounds as if we're in for a bit of weather."

"No," Mrs. Shepard said sweetly, "that's just dynamite." Mr. Tinsdale did not answer. He stared blankly at Mrs. Shepard for a moment, went back before the fireplace, and continued his lecture in a more arithmetical style. He told us the number of temples in Siam, the number of monasteries, the number of monks in the monasteries, and finished with a few facts about the rainfall.

Then we all surrounded Mr. Tinsdale and thanked him for his fascinating talk. While he was answering a few questions, Mrs. Shepard called me over to one corner of the room.

"Here is a gift for you, Celeste, a little book."

"Oh, thank you, Mother Shepard," I said. I thought surely it was a text on fancywork, but I was mistaken. It was a book with which I already had a nodding acquaintance: *Except Ye Repent*, by Harry A. Ironside, Litt.D. On the flyleaf was inscribed in ink: "To Celeste Seton, love from Mother Shepard, Souvenir—Kirkside Fancywork Class."

"Oh, Mother Shepard," I said, "this is so sweet of you." As she bent her head forward to kiss me, I heard another series of detonations—Boom! Boom! Boom! Boom! Boom! Mrs. Shepard listened, nodded her head approvingly, as though she were in silent communication with her husband, and said, "Each to his taste, my dear, each to his own."

16

Fore!

THE HOUSEHOLD GODS of Kirkside were the clocks and the chronometers. Events and activities followed a precise schedule from the hour of rising to bedtime. Only an Act of God could change the lunch hour or the swimming period, the two-thirty afternoon drive, the five o'clock nap, or the game period immediately after dinner.

There was, however, one hour in the day that was left to chance. Between ten and eleven o'clock each morning, Mrs. Shepard was "at her desk," and permanent and itinerant guests were left, more or less, on their own. A few days after I had arrived at Kirkside, I was day-dreaming away this idle hour in one of the large leather chairs in a corner of the living room, when a Japanese gentleman peeked cautiously around the door. Apparently satisfied that it was all right, he came in boldly and walked around examining the various appointments, but he stopped abruptly when he saw the Audubon drawings of the turkeys: "Three very pretty birds," he said.

I had not expected to see an Oriental enter the living

room this morning, but, somehow, I was not surprised. From experience I knew that one might turn any corner in Kirkside and bump into a Hindu, a Lithuanian, or an Egyptian. And if Sitwell had interrupted Mrs. Shepard at her desk some morning and announced: "Mrs. Shepard, there is a Ubangi on the lawn," I am sure she would have answered, "Thank you, Sitwell; just tell him to wait."

During the summer, missionaries, friends of missionaries, and Bible readers found their way to Kirkside from the North Pole, the South Seas, and "East of Suez." Some stopped off for tea, some for a day, others stayed endless weekends, and a few stayed weeks on end. If there was no room at Kirkside, they were put up at Mrs. Shepard's expense at the Roxbury Inn, a little way down the street. If there was no room at the inn, they were put up at the Roxbury Hotel, a little further down the street. All Mrs. Shepard required of her guests was that they observe the customs of her household and give a lecture about the country from which they came. During the month of July, 1934, I learned, in addition to Siam, a good deal about Lima, French Equatorial Africa, Samarkand, and now it appeared that I was going to learn something about the Land of the Rising Sun.

But while these thoughts had been flitting through my mind, the Japanese gentleman had transferred his attention from the turkey pictures to Mr. Shepard's golf trophies. There were silver golf balls, paperweights, miniature silver golf clubs, and cigarette boxes given him by friends in memory of old times and good fellowship. There was such an extraordinary collection of "free silver" that William Jennings Bryan would have felt quite at home there.

Now the Japanese picked up a small replica of a golf player and examined it closely. Then he started to polish it furiously with his sleeve. His intentions were good, but Mr. Shepard kept these mementos spotless, and if there was a bit of tarnish on this particular figure, no silken sleeve could help where silicon polish had failed.

After watching this activity for a few minutes, I felt I should restrain the man's useless exertions. So I stood up slowly in order not to frighten him and said, "Excuse me!" I had spoken softly, but he jumped like a hare.

"Oh! Oh! So sorry, excuse please," he stammered in embarrassment, and his face became crimson.

Obviously, it was up to me to make him feel at home. "I am Celeste Seton," I said, "Mrs. Shepard's daughter-in-law."

After these simple words he recovered his composure, bowed low, and said: "I am Mr. Ito."

"Are you waiting for Mrs. Shepard," I asked.

"No, thank you," he said politely.

"For Mr. Shepard?"

"No, thank you."

"For Miss Stebbins?"

"No, thank you."

Enough was enough. Mr. Ito wasn't going to volunteer any information, and I wasn't going to drag it out of him. So switching to more general conversation, I talked about the golf trophies and told him that Mr. Shepard was an excellent golfer. I explained that he was almost seventy but that he played in the low eighties.

Mr. Ito seemed very interested, and, in no time at all, we were hitting it off splendidly.

"Golf is a most fascinating game," he said.

"Do you play golf, Mr. Ito?" I asked.

"No, I play tennis. All year around."

"In Japan?"

"No, in San Diego. I am second generation."

"You must be a very good player," I said.

"I have a wicked chop," he said, and proceeded to demonstrate how he held his racquet.

There were two tennis courts at Kirkside, and they were kept in perfect condition. They were rolled every morning, and new lime was applied to the lines. The courts were alike as two twins, with one exception. On one of them, just a few feet behind the base line, a giant apple tree grew in conspicuous splendor. Everyone affectionately called it "the umpire." No one would think of cutting the tree down, for the balm of its shade offset the inconvenience of its location. Besides, in case anyone ran into it, the point was always played over.

I suggested to Mr. Ito that he might like to play tennis, but he sadly confessed that he had not brought a racquet. "Just sneakers."

While I was wondering where to find him a racquet, Miss Davis came into the living room, and it was immediately obvious that my initial interrogation of Mr. Ito had stopped one question too soon. He had been waiting for Miss Davis! They greeted each other enthusiastically, and I thought I was watching an affectionate reunion of old friends, but it developed that Miss Davis had never seen Mr. Ito in her life. She had, however, known his brother for many years. "Your brother wrote me," she said, "that you were coming and that you were a wonderful tennis player."

"Mr. Ito would like to play," I explained, "but he has no racquet."

"Just sneakers," Mr. Ito said.

"There're plenty of racquets and balls in the chest outside

the housekeeper's room," Miss Davis told us. "Why don't you show Mr. Ito where they are, and I'll scurry around for a partner."

Mr. Ito and I started expectantly down the long hall to the housekeeper's room. Opposite her door was a large Benjamin Franklin treasure chest. I opened it, and there were fifteen or twenty racquets of assorted models, weights, and sizes. That chest contained the history of American lawn tennis. Some of the racquets looked as if they had been made before the Spanish-American War. One must have been invented by Benjamin Franklin. Others were the latest models, but whatever their vintage, all of them had one thing in common—they were warped. They were so twisted and bent by age, travel, and the heat of an adjacent radiator that they resembled lacrosse sticks. The balls were equally mellow. They were so dead and lifeless that I felt it would be an act of kindness to bury them before the dogs found them.

I felt sorry for Mr. Ito. He had walked down the corridor with such happy anticipation, and now he was the picture of dejection. I attempted a weak smile and said that even though the racquets were warped, everyone used them and had a lot of fun.

"It's very different in San Diego," he said sadly.

When we returned to the living room, it was crowded with people: Mrs. Shepard, Mr. and Mrs. Tinsdale, Miss Quincy, Louis, Helen Anna, Olivia, Finley Jay, Miss Davis, Miss Stebbins, and a few strangers. It looked like a meeting of some kind, but the only significance was one of time. It was eleven o'clock, and the formal activities of the day were about to begin. While Mr. Ito was being introduced, Mr. Shepard walked in, dressed in a pair of old-fashioned golfing knickers, and held up a box of repainted golf balls.

He announced enthusiastically:

"Golf lessons on the flats in five minutes. Come one, come all; the more the merrier."

Immediately Louis, Finley Jay, Helen Anna, and Olivia stood up, excused themselves, and filed out after their father. Mr. Shepard certainly had his children's confidence, but I learned it was more than just the appeal of the game. For the girls, it was the appeal of tobacco; Mr. Shepard occasionally allowed them to smoke, a tremendous secret that was diligently kept from Mrs. Shepard all her life. For the boys, golf lessons were simply an escape from the ladies.

When they had left, Mrs. Shepard evidently did not feel that the response to her husband's invitation had been too overwhelming and tried to drum up a few more customers. She said no one should feel modest or timid about taking lessons because Mr. Shepard had a lot of time and the patience of Job. "He's particularly good with beginners."

"Mrs. Shepard is right," Miss Stebbins said. "When I took my first lesson, I didn't know an andiron from a putter."

For a moment I didn't think anyone else would volunteer, but suddenly without warning Mr. Ito stood up and said with simple dignity: "Excuse me, please. I would like to try golf, but I have no clubs. Just sneakers."

"There are plenty of clubs," Mrs. Shepard said sweetly.

"Then I will try, thank you," and he went out after a long bow that looked like an exercise in calisthenics.

"Wonderful opportunities here," Mr. Tinsdale commented expansively. "Wonderful opportunities."

"Why don't you take a lesson?" Mrs. Shepard said.

"No, thank you, Mrs. Shepard," he replied, "you can't teach an old dog new tricks."

"We taught the setter to carry the morning paper," Miss Davis insisted.

"You really should take a lesson," Mrs. Shepard said. "It's such a wonderful day."

"You'll never regret it," Miss Stebbins added.

I don't know what Mr. Tinsdale *intended* to do for the rest of the morning, but I knew he was going to take a golf lesson. Resistance in the face of such overwhelming odds was futile. He must have felt so, too, for he said with just a touch of bitterness, "Very well, Mrs. Shepard, I accept your invitation, but I assume no responsibility for any contingency."

"There will be no contingency," Miss Stebbins said. "Just keep your eye on the ball and a stiff left arm."

After we lost Mr. Tinsdale, Mrs. Shepard said it was now time for the *ladies* to play golf. She was going to have a friendly game with Miss Davis, Miss Stebbins, and Mrs. Tinsdale and hoped that I would join them. I explained that I was having trouble with my sacroiliac, and besides she already had a foursome.

I learned, however, that such a detail made no difference and that a five-some was very common at Kirkside. Occasionally, there were ladies' six-somes, and one gala weekend, they played a nine-some. Mr. Shepard was heard to remark that this was the largest concentration of women ever seen on a golf course since the year fourteen ninety-one, when James the Fourth of England banned the game for constituting a public nuisance.

After considerable hurly-burly, we all found places in the Locomobile, although the first time I sat down, Mrs. Shepard said, "Not there, Celeste; that's Chinky's place." Chinky knew it, too, for he snuggled down to continue his endless nap.

"That pooch," Miss Stebbins said, "eats four hours a day and sleeps twenty."

The golf bags were strapped into racks built over the front fenders of the car. Each bag carried the full legal complement of fourteen clubs, in addition to golf balls, sunglasses, gloves, first-aid kits, rain jackets, sweaters, rubbers, umbrellas, and shooting sticks.

We drove out across the flats, and approached the practice tee. Mr. Shepard's students were standing around him in a semi-circle listening to words of wisdom on the ancient game. When we drove past, the lesson was momentarily interrupted as we all waved enthusiastically.

We continued alongside the tracks of the Ulster and Delaware Railroad, and started up a winding mountain road which Mr. Shepard had constructed. This road was one of his earliest engineering feats and he was very proud of it. The surfacing was of stone locally quarried, and crushed in Mr. Shepard's dynamite plant. The sharp turns were banked, and the road was smooth. On the summit, we had an inspiring and uninterrupted view up and down the whole valley.

When we arrived at the golf course, an enthusiastic gallery was patiently waiting. Word of the event had evidently gone from house to house, for the gallery included neighbors, missionaries, and Bible readers who gave Mrs. Shepard an ovation befitting a champion.

We grouped ourselves around the first tee, and the caddies handed the ladies their drivers; they took a few practice swings. Since I would not be playing Mrs. Shepard asked me if I would like to keep score, and I said, "Of course, Mrs. Shepard." She gave me a score card, and I retired a safe distance to read it:

No.	Yds.	Par	Hdcp		Self	P.	Op.	Self	P.	Op
1	465	5	2	Elephant Back						
2	229	3	9	The Dip						
3	139	3	10	O'er the Loch						
4	558	6	*1-6	Long Pull						
5	330	4	8	The Shelf						
6	425	4	5	Oh Boy						
7	350	5	3	Up-e-nuf						
8	400	4	7	'Aper-chur"						
9	353	4	4	Ruff Stuff						
Out	3249	38								
Self Out										
Partner Total										
Opponent Hdp.										
Partner Net										
*Means 2 strokes, 1 and 6								See Rules on Opposite Side		
REPLACE TURF										

I asked one of the caddies what "Aper-cher" meant, and he looked blank. "I don't know, lady; I don't know what any of it means. I'll go over and ask Joe." But I never found out Joe's opinion because Mrs. Shepard gave the signal for play to begin:

"Are we all ready?"

Everyone stopped talking, and Mrs. Shepard approached the first tee in absolute silence. After her caddy teed up her ball, she raised her index finger to see which way the wind was blowing and took her stance. She made no perceptible movement. The seconds ticked away and the suspense was mounting. Then it happened: With a sway and a slow backswing that can only be described as resembling the letter "Z" and a low downswing resembling the letter "Y," she hit her ball a resounding "ping" straight down the fairway for sixty yards. It seemed a short drive after such a long preparation, and I felt rather sorry for her. I was about to say, "Too bad, Mrs. Shepard," but everyone enthusiastically applauded and exclaimed, "Good shot, Mrs. Shepard! Good shot! An excellent drive!" Even her caddy stopped chewing his gum long enough to say, "Swell."

I looked around to see who was going to drive next, but no one came forward. Mrs. Shepard's caddy was teeing up another ball, and after identical preparations, she drove again. The shot was no better, but the applause seemed louder. Once again, for the third time, she drove—and I was beginning to wonder what the ground rules were and how I was going to keep score.

At Kirkside, however, there were special rules for ladies: Regardless of age or skill, each contestant had three drives off the first tee, willy-nilly. It was a sort of "double-mulligan." I looked down the fairway at Mrs. Shepard's three balls. They were grouped together scarcely a yard from each other, a static tableau of patience and futility.

It was Miss Stebbins' turn next. She approached the tee with long, confident strides and, without breaking her rhythm, pulled her club back, yelled "fore," and let it rip. It was a beautiful swing full of power and grace, and the follow-through was classic perfection. As far as I could see she did only one thing wrong—she missed the ball.

"Oh fudge!" she said bitterly. "Head down," Mrs. Shepard suggested.

"I put it down, but it keeps coming up."

Miss Stebbins tried again: "Fore!" The same graceful rhythm, the same perfect wrist action, the same easy follow-through. This time the results were better. Not good, but an improvement, for the ball did trickle a few feet off the tee.

"I nicked it anyway," she said.

Miss Stebbins shouted "fore" twice more and twice more did no better. I thought it might be the "fore" that was causing the trouble, because she shouted it during her downswing. In any case, it was a redundant warning for no one else was playing anywhere on the course.

Miss Davis was next. She teed up her ball several times before she was satisfied. Finally, it suited her, and she took her stance. It was really more of a crouch, for her body was bent almost double. I thought she was going to pick up the ball and throw it, but apparently this was just her personal style. She drew her club back lazily, tapped her ball, and drove it almost one hundred and fifty yards. It was the best shot of the day, and the gallery responded enthusiastically.

"Beautiful drive," Mrs. Shepard said.

"Lovely," added Miss Stebbins.

"What a sock!" said a caddy.

After Miss Davis' two extra drives, which were no less spectacular, though they showed a tendency to fade, Mrs. Tinsdale was ready: What she lacked in style, she made up by brute strength. Although she was tall and thin, she had the forearms of a man and swung her club over her head like an axe and hit her ball so hard, that I thought she had taken the cover off. The ball sliced out at a few degrees less than a right angle, almost hit a Bible reader, and disappeared into a pinewoods.

"*Auf Wiedersehen*" Miss Stebbins said.

"Very nice!' Mrs. Shepard said, "but I don't think you swung from the inside out."

"You're right," Mrs. Tinsdale said. "I swung from the outside in."

Mrs. Tinsdale's second shot hooked off the roof of a

rain shelter, and on the third shot she was back to the slice and into the pine woods. She shook her head:

"Before I went to Siam, I didn't have that awful slice. The hook, yes, but not the slice."

The foursome was finally off the first tee, and each player went her separate way. The golf balls lay in such divergent directions that I wondered whether we would meet again before lunch, but Mrs. Shepard was optimistic.

"We'll all gather on the first green. Good luck."

I followed Mrs. Shepard. Surprisingly enough, the game was now played as if it were the National Open; the correct clubs were used, the balls were never moved to more favorable lies, and all shots were meticulously counted. Mrs. Shepard counted her score by a mechanical gadget she wore on her wrist. It worked on a punch-dial system; one button jumped the hand from number to number, another button moved the hand back to zero. Though Mrs. Shepard's golf score was always astronomical, it was certainly accurate.

Along the fairway, the ladies seemed to do better, but on the first green everything was back to normal. After her fifth putt, Miss Stebbins threw in the sponge. "I give up," she said. "Give me an X for this hole, Celeste."

"No, my dear," Mrs. Shepard said, "we must sink them all. That is the rule."

"All right, but I'm wearing out the ball."

After three more tries from a distance of six inches, the ball spun around the rim of the cup and dropped out of sight. Miss Stebbins sighed. "It's only the first hole and I've already got a blister!"

After all the putts were sunk, it was my grim duty to enter the scores for the first hole. Miss Davis had an eight; Miss Stebbins had a nine; Mrs. Shepard's calculator registered eleven; and Mrs. Tinsdale was still counting. "Let's see, now," she said, "one drive, and two iron shots; that makes three; over to that tree makes four; then I hit the boulder and lost the ball; then I hit another ball on the road; another shot in the ditch; then on the green, and seven putts. — Call it sixteen."

"Sweet sixteen," Mrs. Shepard said brightly.

"I don't think so," Mrs. Tinsdale replied, "but it could be worse. Can you imagine what would happen to me if there were *sand traps* on this course?"

The second hole was played without incident or improvement, but there was a flourish of activity on the third hole. It was the water hole, and everyone changed her golf ball.

"Would you care for a Dolly Dimple?" Miss Davis asked Mrs. Tinsdale.

"I'm not sure. What are they?"

"They're floaters," Miss Davis explained. "We all use them."

I thought floating golf balls were as extinct as the great auk, but Mrs. Shepard had bought a limitless supply of Dolly Dimples many years ago before they became obsolete. Unfortunately, instead of lessening the mental hazard of the water, they only seemed to increase it. "Plop! Plop! Plop!" the balls splashed into the pond, and a pair of mallards took off in terror. Miss Davis and Mrs. Tinsdale, on their second attempts, managed to carry diagonally across, but Miss Stebbins never made it.

"I'd as soon drive across Lake Erie," she said.

Only Mrs. Shepard was not distracted by the rippling surface. She didn't play "O'er the Loch"; she played around it — through a swamp. Her drive landed in a heavy growth of saw grass, and after she put on her rubbers, she and her caddy went doggedly after it. She disappeared for over a quarter of an hour, but when she finally emerged through the cattails, she had the same ball she started with, although she was now punching "nine" on her mechanical scorekeeper.

Mrs. Tinsdale was concerned about the Dolly Dimples which were bobbing on the surface. Miss Davis said not to worry:

"Before sundown, one of the lifeguards from the lake comes down and swims out after them."

The fourth hole was a surprise. The Locomobile was waiting for us on the dirt road that paralleled the course, and everyone got in without a word of explanation. I thought the game was over, but Miss Davis whispered that on account of Mrs. Shepard's heart, the doctor had forbidden her to play either the fourth hole or the seventh.

"What shall I put down on the score card," I said, "Par?"

"No, dear, just an X," Miss Davis said.

While we were playing the fifth hole, a gray fox in molt joined the gallery, but loped away when Mrs. Tinsdale whiffed an approach shot. After the sixth hole, we had another little ride in the Locomobile. In this game, the gallery of about twenty people covered more distance than the players. The gallery walked the entire nine holes, and never tired of applauding the most awkward shots, the widest hooks, and three-inch putts. All contestants played under the most ideal conditions of absolute approval and unflagging admiration. A morning golf at Kirkside was an excellent tonic for the ego.

After we got out of the car and approached the eighth tee. Miss Davis held up the game for ten minutes while she put on an extra sweater:

"That north wind can get a little chilly," she said, looking toward the south.

On the ninth green, Mrs. Shepard finished in a blaze of glory: She holed out a two-foot putt, and the gallery applauded enthusiastically. The game was over, but not the suspense: Who had won? To find out required a lot of addition. When I finished my tally, Mrs. Tinsdale double-checked it for accuracy, the gallery gathered around the green, and I announced the scores:

"Miss Davis fifty-nine; Miss Stebbins sixty-nine; Mrs. Shepard seventy-three; and Mrs. Tinsdale eighty-one. The winner, Miss Davis!" After this verdict, a friend of one of the caddies who had been waiting near the green, came over and said, "Pretty good scores for women." "Pretty good," the caddy replied, "—for *seven holes!*' Everyone was now crowding around Miss Davis to congratulate her.

"I was just lucky," she said modestly.

But luck was not in Mrs. Shepard's vocabulary. "You played beautifully!" she said. "You deserved to win."

"Your driving did it," Miss Stebbins said.

"And your putting," Mrs. Tinsdale added.

Miss Davis beamed in triumph and we started toward the car, for the return trip to Kirkside. I handed Mrs. Shepard the score card.

"Here is the score card, Mother Shepard. I'm sure you want it."

"No, Celeste dear," she said. "I have no use for it. I think Miss Davis should have it— After all, she won! This is her day. *She* is the champion."

17

Picnic Without Ants

THE ONLY THING that I missed at Kirkside, and could seldom find, was solitude. I found fellowship, brotherhood, and sisterhood, but solitude eluded me like the will- o'-the-wisp. A leisurely stroll in the country, a walk through the village, or a few moments alone with my thoughts were attained only after the most careful planning. The one certain way to find peace and quiet was to rise at dawn with the Rhode Island Reds, but it made the days uncomfortably long and tiring. At Kirkside individualism had long since rolled over on its side and died.

Helen Anna was a daring exception. She had persuaded Mrs. Shepard to buy her a horse, a beautiful young chestnut gelding called Romeo. Romeo received her undivided attention, and so permitted her to escape many compulsory activities. Helen Anna was constantly having to feed Romeo, curry him, exercise him, talk to him, and brush his teeth. Mrs. Shepard never guessed her daughter's real motives, but Mr. Shepard had his suspicions. During a backgammon game, he said offhandedly: "Helen Anna, you seem to spend most of your time at the barn these days!"

"Horses are just like babies, father, they need a lot of attention."

"So it appears," Mr. Shepard said as he threw double sixes, "so it appears."

With the exception of Helen Anna's solo activity, social life was conducted in groups of five, seven, nine, or more. Mrs. Shepard was gregarious, and it was common to hear expressions like "Mrs. Shepard's clique," "Mrs. Shepard's class," "Mrs. Shepard's circle," or "Mrs. Shepard's party." Whenever Mrs. Shepard said that she had been somewhere "alone," she really meant that she had been out with Miss Stebbins and Miss Davis.

Group life of this kind had charm, love, and security. It also had limitations. The groups, large or small, thought alike, acted alike, and felt alike. I was constantly required to change my opinions, accept on faith the most unusual hypotheses, guard my conversation, and conform to an ideal of conduct which was beyond me. True, I acquired a knowledge of fancywork, zoology, and parlor games, but that wasn't a fair exchange for complete conformity.

During my "assimilation period" I was aware that I gave the group something it unconsciously lacked—a new student. Mrs. Shepard's children had, in a sense, long been graduated, and now the teacher had no pupil. I fitted this role to perfection for I was ignorant of many things that Mrs. Shepard was interested in. She was constantly giving me oral examinations on her favorite subjects, including the names of the wildflowers, and the names of her neighbors:

"What was the name of the lady who came to dinner the other evening, Celeste?" she would ask me.

"That was Mrs. Mary More."

"And what is the name of the most common flower

along the road to the golf course?"

"The black-eyed Susan."

"Yes, dear, and do remember the St.-John's-wort."

The questions often varied from something a child could answer to a query that might perplex a Ph.D. In one breath. Mother Shepard would ask me the name of a mountain which I had heard a thousand times, and in the next, she would request the Latin name for the nighthawk.

For some reason, she often quizzed me on the names of dogs that members of the family had bought, adopted, or found. Mr. Shepard had an ancient Irish setter, Helen Anna had a Scotty and a white Sealyham, Olivia had a cocker spaniel, and Miss Stebbins had a Boston bull, which had been born in Philadelphia.

"What is the name of Olivia's dog?" Mrs. Shepard would ask.

"Spick.

"No, Celeste, Spick belongs to Helen Anna."

"Then its Span."

"No, his name is Sandy."

Spick, Span, and Sandy were a triumvirate that was easy to confuse, but a little rhyme helped me to remember two of them:

"Spick and Span to Helen Ann."

Everything possible was done to make the dogs happy, but pets of bygone days were not forgotten and lived in beloved memory: Holly, Rags, Jackie, Buddy, and two faithful German shepherds, called Caesar and Brutus. Mrs. Shepard told me that one of her saddest memories was the death of a beautiful collie, which Evangeline Booth had given her. He went to sleep at her feet and never awakened.

"May Remus rest in peace," Miss Stebbins said.

The dogs were a natural complement to the group

system at Kirkside. One, two, or even three dogs were not enough. There had to be a pack. Everybody loved them, even when the puppies felt the need of extra nourishment and nibbled the fringes of a Persian rug or Miss Davis' satin bedroom slippers. Once, when Spick added a bite of one of Mr. Shepard's dynamite sticks to his diet, there was an uneasy moment. Fortunately, nothing happened, though for days Spick wasn't allowed in the house when anyone was smoking.

The dogs were permitted to roam at will and were included in every social event. Often during Mrs. Shepard's afternoon motor trips, you couldn't see the people for the dogs. On one occasion, a gentleman walked along Main Street saw the Locomobile go by and said to his wife:

"Elsie, which one of those dogs do you suppose does the driving?"

A week after Louis and I arrived at Kirkside, Miss Stebbins said she had an idea that there was going to be a picnic. Miss Davis said she thought so, too, but cautioned everyone not to let the dogs know: They would go wild. Sitwell said he thought a picnic was imminent, and the chauffeur and the cook agreed. I don't know who started the rumor, but everyone felt something was in the wind, and a little fever of excitement ran through the house.

Two days after the rumor started, it was confirmed. Mrs. Shepard, with the gravity of a public official proclaiming a new national holiday, said there would be a picnic the following evening.

"A picnic—what fun!" said Miss Davis. "We mustn't forget to tell our neighbor, Mrs. Dilling."

"I hope it doesn't rain," cried Miss Stebbins and ran to the paper to look at the weather map. She found it and read aloud: "'A warm front is descending from the western portion of the quadrant through the isotopic layer, followed by warm up-drafts of rarified ozone.'" Then Miss Stebbins translated: "It will be a glorious day."

The light-hearted enthusiasm for the picnic was tempered somewhat by an unexpected development: Mr. and Mrs. Tinsdale had to leave the morning before the gay event. We all stood around their Chevrolet and said goodbye. Mr. Tinsdale issued a standing invitation to any of us who might come to Bangkok. He and Mrs. Tinsdale lived on Silom Road, just a few blocks from the big sitting Buddha and the Y.M.C.A. "You can't miss it," he said. As a parting gesture of friendship, he gave us each a Siamese coin for good luck, and soon the Chevrolet started slowly down the road for Siam. But Miss Stebbins cried out a word of warning:

"Don't forget! Turn left at the fish hatcheries!"

When the Chevrolet was out of sight, Miss Quincy thought it was the appropriate time to tell us that she had to leave too, "on the six forty-four train, Eastern Daylight Saving Time."

"What a pity!" Mrs. Shepard said, "such unhappy news!"

"But at least I'll have half a picnic," Miss Quincy said philosophically.

"And half a picnic is better than none," Miss Stebbins paraphrased.

The picnic was scheduled for five-thirty sharp, but pandemonium started at three. Everybody ran up and downstairs, back and forth to the pantry, and doors opened and closed all over the house. It would take a strong hand to get this picnic underway, and at five o'clock Mr. Shepard supplied it. "Everyone please get into the automobiles," he said with quiet authority, and after this was finally accomplished, he shouted, "Damn the torpedoes, full speed ahead," and the convoy moved off.

On this trip I was sitting between Louis and Mrs. Shepard's new trained nurse. Her name was Miss Gordine, "with an e," she always said. Miss Gordine kept pretty much to herself though she invariably knew what was going on. At the slightest cough she would appear from nowhere with a thermometer, thrust it into your mouth, and if it registered a fifth of a degree over 98.6, she treated you for pneumonia. When Finley Jay came down with a little rash between his fingers, she ordered such a variety of ointments that the local druggist was alarmed: "Must be some sort of epidemic up at Kirkside," he said. Helen Anna was less inclined to take the rash seriously:

"Just put some talcum powder on it," she advised.

As we were riding along to the picnic grounds, the route looked familiar, and I asked Louis if we weren't heading in the direction of the golf course.

"That's right," he said.

"I thought we were going on a picnic!"

"We are."

I felt cheated! I had looked forward to a chicken sandwich by a woodland stream or to a hard-boiled egg on the top of some high hill. A forlorn hope! The cars pulled up near the summer house between the seventh and eighth holes.

Everybody got out, and started to admire the scenery and the thousands of evergreen trees which Mr. Shepard had transplanted many years ago. While I was looking at them, he walked up beside me.

"Once, Celeste, they were only three feet high," he said. "How they have thrived!"

"They are beautiful, Father Shepard."

"Most of them were brought all the way from Manitoba. Some day when I'm too old for golf, I expect to start an evergreen nursery."

"I'm sure it would give you great satisfaction."

Mr. Shepard was silent for a moment and then said, "Perhaps one of these days, Celeste, you'll have a nursery of your own?"

I started to blush and was fumbling for an answer when a black Buick rolled up, and Sitwell, a footman, and three maids jumped out and began unloading a varied cargo: thermos bottles, wicker baskets, card tables, folding chairs, and queer-looking oilskin bags that resembled giant hot water bottles. I asked Mr. Shepard what the bags contained. He gave me a very warm smile and said, "Ice — for the iced tea."

Efficiently and quietly the card tables were set up in the rough back of the eighth tee, and covered with small Irish-linen table cloths. Then the tables were laid with Wedgwood plates, Georgian silver, and Bristol glasses.

During these elegant preparations everyone took constitutionals toward the seventh green, played with the dogs, looked for lost golf balls in the woods, or sought the shade of the summer house. I chose the summer house and found that the main topic of conversation there was the view:

"A beautiful vista," Miss Stebbins said.

"Breath-taking," said Miss Davis. "You can see for miles."

"I never tire of it," added Mrs. Dilling who was preoccupied with her fancywork.

Mr. Ito was sitting next to Miss Quincy. They were a little apart from the others and were staring intently into each other's faces, but they were not saying a word. I thought this silence might be a symptom of shyness, so I walked over and made what I thought was a safe observation:

"It's a lovely panorama to the east."

Miss Quincy shook her head.

I tried again: "It's a lovely panorama to the west," but Miss Quincy put her finger to her mouth in a gesture of silence. I said nothing more, but I couldn't figure out what was going on. They were either hypnotizing each other or falling in love. In either case, I wasn't wanted so I thought I'd chase Spic and Span for exercise, when Miss Quincy cried out:

"You win, Mr. Ito, you win!"

"It takes practice, that's all," Mr. Ito said, "I've been doing it for years."

I still didn't know what they were talking about until Mr. Ito explained that they had been playing a game. They looked straight into each other's eyes, and whoever blinked first, lost.

"Would you like to play blink?" Mr. Ito said, "the best two out of three?"

"No, thank you," I replied, "not on an empty stomach." Out of the corner of my eye I saw Mrs. Shepard coming our way and I hoped Mr. Ito wasn't going to ask her to join him in a game of blink. As a matter of fact, Mrs. Shepard was a little upset. She had not resigned herself to Miss Quincy's leaving so soon and was still trying to dissuade her from taking the six forty-four.

"I hate to have you miss dessert, Miss Quincy. Couldn't you possibly take the eight o'clock train?"

Miss Quincy consulted her timetable. "I would love to take the eight o'clock train," she said, "but it goes the wrong way."

At five-thirty sharp, Sitwell, immaculate in a gray

alpaca jacket, delivered himself of a short edict: "Supper is served."

Response was immediate: Every dog on the fairway began to bark. The dogs were good linguists. In addition to fundamental phrases such as "go," "stop," "down," and "stop chewing that napkin," they knew instinctively what Sitwell meant when he announced meals. If instead of "supper is served" Sitwell had said, "Mrs. Shepard, it's time to tie on the feed bag," the barking would have been just as spontaneous.

One evening by way of an experiment Mr. Shepard announced dinner in Greek: "rcepaaire, xapaxaXw,Tpaxet."

It fooled the dogs completely. It also fooled the people. Not a creature nor a person stirred, except the nurse who looked as though she thought something was the matter with Mr. Shepard's voice.

But now after a little shuffling everybody found his place-card on the card tables and when Mr. Shepard said grace, we all sat down. There were four people to each table, but the dogs were migratory and shuttled from table to table sniffing, begging, and committing petty larceny.

I was part of a quartet which included Mr. Ito, Miss Quincy, and the nurse, Miss Gordine. Our table was sagging on the bias, and Mr. Ito tried to fix it, but there didn't seem to be any way to keep it level. In desperation he said, "I have a suggestion: I'll put my toe under the wobbly leg."

When the food was served it was delicious, though hardly the stuff of which picnics are made: it included chicken a la king, green peas, buttered beets, tossed green salad, iced tea, and hot buttered rolls. We ate ravenously, and there was little conversation, but for Miss Gordine.

She kept up a nervous monologue which consisted principally of identifying the food while she ate it:

"Uh huh, garlic in the salad!"

"Uh huh, sweet butter!"

"Uh huh, pimiento!"

When she said, "Uh huh, potatoes, two hundred and fifty calories," Miss Quincy put hers down as if it were poison.

During the entree Finley Jay went from table to table taking pictures with his candid camera. Everybody, except Miss Quincy, wanted to be in the family album, and Finley Jay had a hard time keeping up with the demand. He took a picture of his mother, his father, all the guests except Miss Quincy, the dogs, and a still life of a plate of stewed tomatoes.

After the photography, Miss Quincy looked at her watch and said it was time to leave. She just had time to finish her iced tea. We escorted her to the car which was to drive her to the station. As she was getting in Mrs. Shepard presented her with a small white box.

"Miss Quincy, here is your dessert. You can eat it on the train."

"It's a Napoleon," Miss Stebbins said.

"Four hundred, fifty calories," the nurse said dolefully. Finley Jay joined the throng and hoped Miss Quincy would reconsider having her picture taken. "Not alone," she pleaded, and she looked imploringly at me.

I stepped beside her, put my arm around her waist and said, "Smile —now, Miss Quincy! Let's look at the birdie! Hold your breath!"

"I'll try," she said.

Finley Jay focused the camera. A pause—a click—and the agony was over.

"Please send me the picture," she said. "A negative will do."

Finley said that he would, but he never kept his promise. When the picture was developed it was remarkably clear, the composition was excellent, and a little cumulus cloud in the background lent a charming delicate touch, but there was one thing amiss — Miss Quincy had no head.

After she left, we went back to our places and soon had our Napoleons. The entire meal had been served exactly as if we had dined at Kirkside. The only difference was that we were on the golf course and a bright blue sky was overhead. After coffee, the men lit up their pipes and cigarettes, and a mood of relaxation and repose settled over the picnickers. Streaks of pink and crimson were coloring the west, and a hawk circled lazily above us.

I saw Mrs. Shepard, who was seated two tables away, follow the flight of the bird, and after it disappeared beyond some evergreens she stood up, and I thought the outing would be formally declared over. I was wrong.

"Now we will toast the marshmallows," Mrs. Shepard announced, "and I hope you will all help by gathering wood for the fire."

"And a few pine cones and spruce needles for kindling," added Miss Stebbins.

We walked over to the little woods bordering the fairway, and in a short time collected enough wood to last the whole winter. We stacked it neatly in piles next to a little circular clearing that Sitwell had bordered with stones. When everything was ready, Mrs. Shepard called upon her husband:

"Would you light it, Finley dear?"

"With pleasure," he said, and striking a match, he soon had a fire going, and everyone paid it more compliments than the sunset.

"How brightly it burns!"
"A wonderful blaze!"
"Listen to it crackle!"

Now everything was ready for the first marshmallow to be burned at the stake. Mrs. Shepard impaled one of the fluffy things on the end of a long stick and held it gingerly over the flame. When it was baked a nice brown color she gave it to Mrs. Dilling, who started to eat it too quickly and burned her tongue. "Ouch," she cried.

"Blow on it," Miss Davis advised.

The second marshmallow burned to a crisp, and it looked like a piece of charcoal. Mrs. Shepard was about to throw it away when Mr. Ito said, "I'd like that, please, if you don't mind." He ate it and smacked his lips. "Delicious," he said. Mr. Ito liked marshmallows very much— especially burnt ones. During the next hour he ate fifteen. He must have thought it was a contest.

"Mr. Ito," I said, "you certainly love marshmallows."

"I do," he answered, "better than chicken."

Just before the sun went down, a marshmallow caught fire and fell off the end of Mrs. Shepard's stick into the pile of spruce needles. The needles caught fire immediately and blazed into a flaming torch.

"Fire! Fire!" shouted Olivia.

"Don't let it spread!" warned Miss Davis.

"What can we do?" wailed Mrs. Dilling.

"Call the fire department!" yelled Finley Jay.

A feeling of panic seized the group, and no one moved. Everyone seemed to be momentarily paralyzed. The fire began to singe the dry grass, and there was danger that it would fan out and cause serious damage. I was wondering what I could do in this emergency when Mrs. Shepard took command of the situation.

"Will someone please bring me a pitcher of iced tea?" she said calmly.

I obeyed immediately and handed her a pitcher of iced tea and a glass.

"I won't need the glass, dear," she said sweetly as she poured the iced tea onto the flames.

"More iced tea," she said. "More iced tea! Quickly! Everyone!"

A bucket brigade was formed, and pitcher after pitcher of iced tea was emptied onto the burning pine needles. After ten pitchers of iced tea, the fire was brought under control, and the fire fighters sat down exhausted.

"Thank Heavens," Miss Stebbins said, "we saved the golf course!"

Mrs. Dilling swallowed some smoke, and Olivia's eyes were smarting, but there was no real harm done. Everyone helped stamp out the embers and there was nothing left to do but wait for Sitwell to fold up the card tables and then we would all go home.

As we were walking back to the road, we heard the melancholy whistle of a train in the distance. Mr. Shepard looked at his watch and said: "The six forty-four train is an hour late again. It's really a shame — Miss Quincy could have eaten her Napoleon with us."

18

Swordfish

WHEN LOUIS AND I returned to New York the third week in July, the weather was stifling hot and sticky. From the Battery to the Bronx there wasn't a breath of fresh air. The smells of the city were pungent, and a dense mist of smoke hung motionless in the sky. The water in Central Park was so low that there was barely enough for the children to launch their sailboats, and there was brisk trading on the New York Stock Exchange in the securities of companies who made ice cream, soft drinks, and popsicles. The newspapers said that unless rain fell soon, we would have a real drought.

Our apartment felt like a hothouse, in spite of six electric fans that Louis kept going at full speed. I felt uncomfortable, wet, listless, and thirsty. Louis thought the heat had gone to my head when I suggested that we split a tank of oxygen between us.

"Stick with Coca-Cola," he said.

"Be it ever so humid, there's no place like home," and the thin cloud of dust that permeated the apartment had a silver lining. Tomorrow I could do exactly what I wanted! And the next day! And the next day! I could continue my fancywork, but I wouldn't have to attend class on Friday. I could get up in the morning when I wanted to, go to bed when I wanted to, and ignore my neighbors. Though the sun might beat down on me relentlessly, I could walk down Fifth Avenue *alone,* read *alone,* and eat *alone.* Wonderful luxurious solitude!

I didn't see Mrs. Shepard again for the rest of the summer, although we were in constant communication. Letters arrived regularly. I was informed about every event, the names of all the guests, the first and last symptom of every cold, the progress that Mrs. Dilling was making on her applique bedspread, and the debut of each wildflower: Indian Pipe, dewdrop, wintergreen, the white woodland aster, and the white baneberry.

During the first week in September two items of general interest to sport fans arrived in the mail. While playing golf. Miss Stebbins turned her ankle when she inadvertently stepped into the cup on the fifth green. And Mr. Ito was finally persuaded to play tennis with Finley Jay. They played five sets, and Mr. Ito won: Six-love, six-love, six-love, six-love and six-one. Mrs. Shepard thought Finley Jay improved remarkably in the last set, and Mr. Ito had exceptional endurance for such a small man. There was no doubt about Mr. Ito's stamina; he had stayed at Kirkside since the middle of July.

Louis said he'd bet Mr. Ito would be there after the frost was on the pumpkin. Louis was right; Mr. Ito stayed far into September. He left for San Diego an hour before Kirkside was closed and the last Locomobile left for New York with Mrs. Shepard, Miss Davis and Miss Stebbins.

When Mrs. Shepard returned to 579, we were immediately invited to church and Sunday dinner. This was the beginning of a continuous stream of invitations to participate in Mrs. Shepard's busy and fruitful town life. During a single week, Louis and I were asked to attend a Bible class, an auction at the Anderson Galleries, a lecture entitled "Do Young Married Couples Need God?" and a performance of *Madame Butterfly*. I simply could not offend Mrs. Shepard and refuse all four invitations. I told Louis that we had to accept at least one.

"Well, you decide," Louis said.

"No, you decide; it's all the same to me."

"Let's hear Madame Butterfly."

"It suits me, except it means a top hat for you."

I accepted the invitation to *Madame Butterfly*, and we dined first at 579. While we were sipping our demitasses, Mrs. Shepard read us the entire libretto of the opera, and consequently we missed the first act. But it was a most enjoyable evening once we arrived at the Metropolitan Opera House. Miss Davis hummed all the arias during the performance, and Mr. Shepard hummed all the arias in the car as we were returning home.

In front of our apartment house, we kissed everybody goodnight and went inside, but we did not ride up in the elevator. We waited until the limousine turned the corner and then sneaked out cautiously to Fay and Dario's, now a legitimate bar, for an hour. We went for *one* hour, but stayed for *three*. The next morning when Louis went to work, he didn't look very chipper.

"I think we should have accepted the invitation to the auction," he said ruefully.

No matter how many invitations from Mrs. Shepard I refused, the quantity never lessened. At first, I gave my answers a lot of thought, and signed my name to little white lies only after careful deliberation, but gradually my notes of regret became shorter and less imaginative. Fortunately, Mrs. Shepard never noticed the gradual deterioration of my ingenuity. She said to me many times: "Your last letter was so sweet, Celeste, and your penmanship is very legible."

An extraordinary amount of ink and writing paper was consumed in our house. Louis used to say, "What shall I bring home tonight, dear—the evening paper or some more writing paper?"

Miss Stebbins told me that all of my letters were saved, dated, important passages underlined, and filed. Mrs. Shepard never destroyed a sheet of correspondence from anyone, and the number of letters acquired over a lifetime took up more closet space than her clothing. Mrs. Shepard felt that if you destroyed a letter, you destroyed a sentiment.

Once, thinking that she had torn up a receipt for a pepper mill, she destroyed by mistake a letter from a missionary in Pago Pago. By coincidence, she never heard from him again, and she sadly quoted a line from Robert Louis Stevenson:

> *The black arrow flyeth nevermore,*
> *The fellowship is broken.*

I told Miss Davis that I felt bad because I had to refuse so many of Mrs. Shepard's invitations, but she reassured me that the number of invitations I accepted or refused made no difference. It was just Mrs. Shepard's way of "keeping in touch." She urged me to write a little note occasionally about our activities because it made Mrs. Shepard happy to know that her children were thinking of her.

One night in April, after Louis and I had returned from

the movies, I sat down at my desk to compose a note to Mrs. Shepard. Louis wanted to know what I was going to say.

"You're not going to tell Mother we just saw *The Sin of Madelon Claudet!*"

"No, Louis," I said. "It's about something else. Perhaps you'll help me. I do need your help with this one!"

"Well, I'm a little tired, but I'll try. What do you want to say?"

"I have a little news—I know you'll be interested too. I want to tell your mother that I'm going to have a baby." Louis stood transfixed, then slowly he recovered his sense of speech.

"That's wonderful! It's simply wonderful," and he kissed me tenderly. "Congratulations!"

"Same to you," I said.

"But what a way to tell me!"

We were both happy about the baby, and Louis immediately assumed a fatherly air. He started to plan his son's education, beginning with kindergarten and continuing through grammar school, college, congress and the presidency of the United States.

"Louis, suppose it's a girl!"

"We'll cross that bridge when we come to it."

In the excitement, the letter to Mrs. Shepard was never composed. The next day I told my father and mother and we celebrated with a bottle of Cordon Rouge and decided to keep the news a secret among ourselves. Mother said, "Our lips are sealed. Wild horses couldn't drag it out of me."

The first telephone call the following morning was from a friend of mine who jubilantly said, "Celeste, darling, isn't it wonderful that you're going to have a baby!"

"Yes," I answered, somewhat surprised. "I've only just found out myself."

There had been a leak somewhere. Louis swore he hadn't mentioned it to a soul. "Nor I," said Mother. "Nor I," said Father.

By the end of the week, the news had spread far and wide, and by the end of the month I had received congratulations from every friend and relative I knew, including a cousin from Shreveport. I never found out who broke the vow of silence, but I suspected Father had let a Western Union operator in on the secret, or perhaps after all it was those wild horses on Park Avenue.

Anyhow, one fact was clear. Everybody, except Mrs. Shepard, knew I was going to have a baby. It was important that we tell her at once before someone else did. Louis agreed with me perfectly, but we did not agree on how it should be done. I thought the natural thing was to have tea at 579 and say, "Mother Shepard, I'm going to have a baby."

Louis was horrified at the thought of such a direct approach and said a more subtle way would have to be found.

"How about finishing the letter I started?"

"No, that's not the way."

"How about telephoning?"

"Worse yet. Too impersonal."

"What then, Louis? I have an open mind, and it's open for suggestions."

"I don't know. I'll spend all day at the office thinking about it."

Making such a problem of telling Mrs. Shepard that I was going to have a baby seemed absurd, but Louis tried to explain that it was a serious matter, far more important than, perhaps, I realized.

Mrs. Shepard loved babies, and had given large amounts of money to child nurseries and baby hospitals, but she completely blinded herself to the physiological facts of conception and pregnancy. She knew that not all babies came from the State Charities Aid, but she wanted so much to believe that they did.

Louis and I were concerned. If Mrs. Shepard heard the news from someone else, she would be offended—and unless we told her soon, it might be embarrassing.

We decided the best approach would be to accept the next invitation that came from 579, preferably for dinner or tea; then we would break the news. Louis said that if his mother were eating something, the food might cushion the shock.

This seemed like sound strategy, but it didn't work. No invitation was forthcoming. A week went by, then another, and no word from 579. I couldn't imagine what was wrong! Perhaps she had heard the "news" and was already offended! I decided to write Mrs. Shepard myself:

Dear Mother Shepard,

I do hope you have been feeling well. I am worried because I have not heard from you. Louis and I have been quite busy. Saturday we went to the Museum of Natural History and looked at the skeleton of a sperm whale. We also spent an hour in the Indian Village on the second floor.

I do hope you and Miss Stebbins and Miss Davis will be able to come to tea this week. Any afternoon is convenient.

Affectionately,
Celeste

Two days went by, and a letter finally arrived. Mrs. Shepard was going out of town to a Bible Conference, and she had been so busy making preparations that she had not been able to spend any time at her desk. Would we forgive her for not writing?

When Mrs. Shepard returned in early May, we were invited to attend church and Sunday dinner. At last, after all this time, we would be able to tell her the news. Before we entered the Collegiate Church, I asked Louis when he thought I should announce the glad tidings. Did he think the best time would be at the beginning of dinner? Perhaps during the soup course?

"I don't know," he said. "You'll have to sense the psychological moment. I remember that Olivia told Mother about her first baby one Sunday at dinner, while Sitwell was passing the swordfish."

"What did she say?"

"Mother didn't understand at first. She said, 'Don't eat it, dear, until the sauce comes.' "

After church was over, Louis and I walked back to 579 and sat in the living room with Mr. and Mrs. Shepard, Miss Stebbins, Miss Davis, and Helen Anna. Everybody was waiting for dinner to be announced, and I was waiting to announce that I was going to have a baby. I was nervous and self-conscious.

Because I couldn't sit still, I crossed the room and went over to Mr. Shepard who was working on another gigantic jigsaw puzzle. This time it was a New England farm scene, and he had finished a section that showed a mare and her young colt drinking from a watering trough, while a group of farm hands watched them intently.

Perhaps it was auto-suggestion, but suddenly I had the feeling that everybody was watching me! No, I was being silly! It must be my nerves, and I was just dramatizing the situation. My imagination was running away with me. Nevertheless, it was true! Everybody *was* staring at me. I wouldn't stand this any longer—I couldn't. I was about to stand up and say: "Ladies and gentlemen, I have been pregnant for two months, and I'm proud of it," when Sitwell opened the sliding doors to the dining room and said:

"Dinner is served!"

As we were going into the dining room. Miss Stebbins said in a quizzical manner, "Celeste, why were you staring at me so intently just now?"

"Why, Miss Stebbins! I wasn't staring at *you!* You were staring at me/"

"No, child, you were staring at me. Well, I don't know. It must be the bad light. Besides, I'm hungry."

"So am I."

"Good, I think we're having swordfish."

We sat down and Mr. Shepard said grace. While I was eating, I was aware that the dining room was different; something was missing. Oh yes, the two large oil paintings of Jay Gould and the Guernsey cow were gone. I inquired about them.

"Jay Gould is getting a new frame," Mr. Shepard explained, "and the cow is being cleaned. Be back Tuesday. I hope Finley Jay will be home then, too."

After the noodle soup Mrs. Shepard turned her attention to me.

"Celeste," she said, "you look very well."

"I'm feeling fine, Mother Shepard."

"It's been a long time since we have seen each other, and I'm sure you have many interesting things to tell us. Haven't you, dear?"

Mrs. Shepard was giving me a perfect opportunity to say what I had wanted to say for three weeks, but before I could reply, Miss Davis changed the conversation. "Don't you think Celeste has gained a little weight?"

"I have, too," Helen Anna said, "five pounds."

"It's cream," Miss Stebbins explained, "and French pastry."

Before I could return to Mrs. Shepard's original question, Mr. Shepard said in a loud voice: "Ah! At last the swordfish!" and Sitwell began to pass around a huge silver platter. While he was serving it, Mr. Shepard carried on an informative commentary on the life and habits of the main course: Its size, weight, and the fact that many of them were caught near Tocopilla, Chile.

"Fancy that!" said Miss Davis.

Everybody enjoyed eating the swordfish, and Mr. Shepard enjoyed talking about it. "The swordfish has no ventral fins," he remarked. Then he added with a smile, "And never forget it."

As I nibbled my food I was trying to come to a decision. If Olivia had told her family about her baby at Sunday dinner, I would do the same. What Olivia had done, I could do. I put down my knife and fork and decided I would get the agony over with immediately, once and for all:

"Mother Shepard," I said loudly and clearly, "I have something important to say."

"Yes, Celeste dear, what is it?"

"This summer during fancywork class, do you think you could teach me how to make some little bootees?"

"Of course," Mrs. Shepard replied. "I would be delighted, but how far away the summer is now. How far away!"

I had tried to break the news gently, but I had been too gentle. I would have to be more obvious. "Mrs. Shepard,"

I said in an unsteady voice, "would you like to be a grandmother?"

"Why, Celeste dear," she answered sweetly, "I *am* a grandmother,—you know, Olivia made me one—and I regret Olivia and John aren't with us today."

I had failed again.

No one at the table changed his expression except Louis who was smiling slyly at my discomfort.

It was difficult for me to continue eating. I had to try once more and do it correctly.

"Don't you like your fish, dear," Mrs. Shepard said. "If not, we can get you something else."

"Yes, Mother Shepard," I replied, "it's delicious, but before I have any more, I think you should know that I'm going to have a baby."

For a moment, the only sound was the resonant squeak of the swinging door to the pantry when Sitwell pushed it to or fro. Miss Stebbins was the first to respond. She put down her knife and fork and cried:

"A blessed event! Celeste, how wonderful! I knew you had something to tell us!"

"How happy you must be!" said Miss Davis.

Mrs. Shepard got up from her chair, came over, put her arms around me and kissed me on the forehead. We were both blushing like school girls.

"How sweet! How very sweet," she said. "That is the most wonderful news you could possibly tell me!" She went back to her place, sat down, and gazed at me in a kind of innocent wonderment. There was no doubt that Miss Stebbins now was staring at me, and so was everyone else.

After Miss Davis finally thought of congratulating Louis, Mr. Shepard asked for more specific information. "Celeste, my dear, when may we expect the heir?"

"In November," I said, "if all goes well."

"All will go well," he said reassuringly, "I know it will."

Our baby girl was born in the French Hospital at 2:30 a.m. on November 23, 1936. She weighed six pounds three ounces, had blue eyes, and we named her Gael after nobody. In all respects she was a normal infant, and the hospital staff considered her cute and adorable, though not unusual. A healthy baby in a maternity ward has no more prestige than an angel in heaven; there are too many of them.

Louis and I didn't feel that way, nor did my mother, my father, Mr. and Mrs. Shepard, Miss Davis, Miss Stebbins, Olivia, Helen Anna, Finley Jay, nor Sitwell. Both families collaborated in showering me with so much attention that the lady across the hall inquired if I had had quintuplets.

Everyone naturally wanted to see the baby and, in time, each one was conducted to the room at the end of the corridor where the newborn infants were kept in cribs behind a large pane of glass.

Mrs. Shepard tiptoed down with Miss Stebbins and Miss Davis, and the nurse on the other side of the glass mechanically held up "Baby Seton."

"What a beautiful little girl!" Miss Stebbins said.

Mrs. Shepard was ecstatic: "It's the prettiest baby there, and she's smiling!" Unfortunately, at that moment the baby began to cry; and Mrs. Shepard became alarmed: "Is anything the matter?"

"It's nothing," Miss Davis assured her, "just gas—all babies have it."

When my father returned from *his* tour of inspection, he said he didn't like seeing all the babies in "escrow." "Be sure you pay your bill, Celeste, so that you get your baby out when you are ready to go home."

Pretty soon life was almost back to normal, and there were fewer visitors. The novelty was wearing off for most of my family and friends at the time my own responsibility was just beginning.

But Mrs. Shepard always came to the hospital laden with gifts. My room was filled with flowers, sent down daily from the greenhouses at Lyndhurst, and my bed was piled high with enough tiny garments for the entire maternity ward.

One afternoon when Mrs. Shepard arrived, she sat down by the edge of my bed. "Celeste," she said, "I have brought you a little gift," and she handed me a small oblong box. It contained a beautiful gold and pearl heart locket with Gael's initials on one side and Mr. and Mrs. Shepard's initials on the other.

"Oh, thank you. Mother Shepard, that is extremely kind of you."

"And I have brought something else," she added, as she reached into her purse and took out a small Bible embossed in gold. "This is for Gael, too," she said.

"She will love to have it," I said. I opened the Bible at the page where the bookmark was inserted, and there was a check for Gael.

"Oh Mother Shepard," I said, "this is terribly generous of you. How can I ever thank you?"

"Do not try," Mrs. Shepard replied kindly. "It is a privilege. It is a great privilege." And then she looked over at Gael's tiny dresses and said:

> *Suffer the little children to come unto me,*
> *and forbid them not:*
>
> *For of such is the kingdom of Heaven.*

19

Southward Bound

JANUARY WAS ALWAYS an important and symbolic month for Mrs. Shepard. It was the beginning of the new year, the season of new hopes, plans, and resolutions. It was the time for Mrs. Shepard's rededication to Almighty God, the reaffirmation of faith in the destiny of her country, the time for restatement of her belief in the ideals of mankind, and the time to begin arrangements for her annual trip to Atlantic City.

The trip to Atlantic City was not taken to escape the wintry blasts of New York for, often as not, the seashore was colder. The journey had a more sentimental motive: to celebrate her wedding anniversary on January twenty-second. The twenty-second of January was also the anniversary of her mother's wedding, and as the date moved apace, a parade of memories passed before her. She took out the family album and looked lovingly on the fading pictures of her mother.

"My mother was a wonderful and beautiful woman," she said, "and just think, she had six children! Finley and I have only four."

A few times since their marriage in 1913, Mr. and Mrs.

Shepard had gone to more southerly resorts, but Mrs. Shepard didn't like them as well as Atlantic City. She thought there was something unnatural about seeing palm trees and wearing summer dresses in the middle of winter. Mrs. Shepard was never one to flee before nature, and until the vernal equinox, she preferred the icy chill of a northeaster to the tepid breezes of the Gulf of Mexico.

Atlantic City was patronized in the winter not only by conventions and business men, but by a host of lovers and honeymooners. The bleak skies and stormy weather brought the young couples together, and they strolled hand-in-hand along the shores of the ocean—two against the world. It was a little different with Mr. and Mrs. Shepard: Including Miss Davis, Miss Stebbins, Helen Anna, the maid, and the nurse, it was seven against the world, and if you counted the current Chinky, it was eight.

As the day approached for Mrs. Shepard to leave for her annual trip to Atlantic City, she thought that I should go with her. Each time she came to tea, she would stand by Gael's crib, appraise her carefully, then turn and look at me as if doubting that the rigors of childbirth could have left me so well and strong. I couldn't imagine what torture she thought I had endured, but whatever it was she was convinced I was still weak and fragile. Although she suggested calcium tablets, vitamin pills, liver and iron tonic, and sent me two pamphlets on the care of young mothers, she thought that a vacation trip was essential for complete recovery.

"Celeste," she said, "Atlantic City will do you a world of good."

"All the salt-water taffy you can eat and miles of board-walk," Miss Stebbins said.

I didn't want to leave the baby, but Louis was sure that

he and the nurse could take care of everything. I couldn't make up my mind, but after Mr. Shepard, Miss Davis, and Miss Stebbins urged me to come, and my father and mother urged me to go, I started to pack my suitcase.

"If the baby gets a sniffle," Louis promised, "I'll telephone."

We left for Atlantic City on January 17th, which Mrs. Shepard reminded us was the anniversary of Benjamin Franklin's birthday. Reservations had been made on the eleven o'clock train in the morning, and we would leave 579 promptly at ten. When I arrived at nine, I counted twenty suitcases lined up in the foyer. It looked as if the family were moving to Atlantic City permanently instead of just visiting there. I asked Miss Stebbins how long we would be away, but her answer was sketchy: "It all depends," she said.

Sitwell was busy putting tags on the luggage, and Miss Davis was preoccupied watching him do it. When he finished tagging one huge piece of luggage, he smacked it on the side as if he were patting an old dog and said affectionately: "Good Old Faithful." "Old Faithful" was smaller than a wardrobe trunk but larger than a steamer trunk, and I didn't see how anyone could possibly lift it single-handed. Out of curiosity I tried it, and to my surprise, found it as light as a feather. Miss Davis saw the puzzled look on my face.

"That's the empty, Celeste."

"The empty?"

"Yes. it's to carry back the salt-water taffy."

At a quarter of ten Mr. and Mrs. Shepard and Helen Anna came downstairs, and I kissed them good morning.

"I'm so happy to be going to Atlantic City."

"It's so nice to have your company," Mrs. Shepard said.

"You look better already."

Standing behind Mrs. Shepard was Selma, her personal maid, and a lady I had never before seen. Mrs. Shepard started to introduce me. "Celeste," she said, "I would like you to meet Mrs. . . .," but she never finished the introduction and looked imploringly at her husband.

"Mrs. Dodge," Mr. Shepard said.

"Yes, Mrs. Dodge, my new nurse," Mrs. Shepard explained.

Mrs. Shepard had no trouble remembering that the Latin name for the nurse's corsage of flowers was *Camellia japonica*, but she couldn't remember the name of the nurse herself. But there was nothing personal in this. She couldn't remember the name of any of her nurses whether it was Smith or Smolwitz.

This was different from her relations with the regular servants of her household. She knew their first, middle and last names and never forgot them. She regarded them all as her friends, and their jobs were as secure as the rock of Gibraltar. Often Mrs. Shepard would engage an entire family. The husband might be the chauffeur, his wife the cook, the daughter the parlor maid, and the son an assistant butler.

Mrs. Shepard did not like change and hated to have anyone leave her service. She always wanted to see the same faces in the kitchen, the same butler in the dining room, and the same maid in her bedroom. But with trained nurses it was a different matter; they were expendable, and she took rather a delight in dismissing them. It was her only revenge on the doctors who tried to curtail her activities, restrict her diet, and keep her from running up and downstairs.

Mrs. Shepard particularly resented the elevators when

they were installed in 579, Lyndhurst and Kirkside. Her life would end in God's good time, and no elevator nor nurse was going to interfere. She could discharge the nurses, but getting back at the elevators was difficult. Louis said he thought she withheld payment on the monthly maintenance bills, hoping that the Otis Elevator Company would take the elevators out, but they never did.

At ten minutes of ten we came down the front steps of 579 and were driven to the Pennsylvania Station. The footman put all the baggage in a taxi and followed closely behind the limousine. We rode down the whole way looking backward: We wanted to see if the cab with the luggage was still behind us. When our car turned into Seventh Avenue, a Budweiser beer truck came between the two cars, so we arrived at the station five minutes ahead of the luggage.

"Are we on time?" asked Miss Davis apprehensively.

"We have just a half hour," Mr. Shepard said. "We can make it if we don't stop to buy any magazines."

We all followed Mr. Shepard, and all the redcaps followed us. Like the porters in a safari, they labored under their loads of two or three suitcases apiece except the man who was carrying "Old Faithful." His fellow-workers looked at him with amazement, marveling at the ease with which he handled his burden. "Old Man River," one of them called him.

We found our parlor-car seats, the redcaps departed, and after an interminable wait we were finally on our way. Miss Davis' ears cracked while the train went through the tunnel under the Hudson River, and she was still distressed when the train stopped at Newark.

"Just yawn," Mrs. Dodge advised. "It releases the pressure on the ear drum."

"I'll try to yawn," she said, "but I'm not the least bit sleepy."

The parlor car had twelve chairs in it, and we had eight; four on each side of the aisle. At the beginning of the trip everybody stared out of the window admiring the New Jersey flats but Mrs. Shepard seemed moody and thoughtful. As she rested her head on the white antimacassar of her chair, I wondered what she was thinking about: the times when she traveled over her own great railroads, her anniversary, the passing of another year, or of her new grandchild? She adored Gael, but I am sure she realized her arrival meant the loosening of family ties. Of Mrs. Shepard's four children, only Helen Anna still lived at 579, but in time, she, too, would inevitably leave for a home of her own.

It was true, also, that Mother Shepard's philanthropic activities had been curtailed. She could not work twelve hours a day anymore, and the business depression had forced her to cut off funds to several institutions and charities that she had supported since her father died. Life was pleasant, but not quite as full as it used to be.

As the train rolled on, her mood passed. Mrs. Shepard sat up and her holiday spirit returned. She pointed out familiar landmarks and her talk sparkled with excitement. "We're coming into Elizabeth now," she announced. "It's a lovely town, but if I remember correctly, the road bed is a little uneven."

Mr. Shepard was more interested in the time. At each stop he would consult his watch, compare it with the timetable and inform us that the train was "ten minutes late at New Brunswick," or "right on schedule coming into Absecon-Pleasantville." Once when the train bucked a little, he said slyly, "This would never happen on the Missouri Pacific."

Periodically there was some light reading done. Between Burling and Palmyra Miss Davis read a chapter from the *Forsyte Saga,* and Mrs. Dodge finished a serial in the *Saturday Evening Post.* Then Helen Anna borrowed the magazine and began the story. Miss Stebbins slept most of the way and did nothing exciting except to take Chinky out to do his duty on the station platform at Trenton.

The train pulled into Atlantic City on time, and we took the hotel bus to the Marlborough-Blenheim on the boardwalk. Mr. Shepard entered eight names in the hotel register, and arranged for Chinky to have the best quarters in the dog kennel. "Will the Pekingese be on the American or Oriental Plan?" he asked.

After the suitcases were brought in seven bellboys and the manager conducted us to our rooms, which occupied an entire corridor. We changed to our tweed walking clothes, had a late lunch at a large circular table in a corner of the main dining room, and then we were ready to step out onto the boardwalk to explore Atlantic City. The holiday had officially begun!

It was a mild and gentle afternoon, and the twang of the salt air was immediately invigorating. The ocean was calm, and the waves broke gently on the miles of clean white beach. A few intrepid souls were bathing with the seagulls, and a lady in a fur coat was collecting seashells and bits of driftwood. Near a pier a group of fishermen were casting for sea bass, and two fat men were heaving a medicine ball at each other. A boy and a girl were riding horseback, and as the horses cantered up the beach, the girl's flaxen hair flew behind her like a pennant.

There were many activities to choose from, but Mrs. Shepard knew exactly what she wanted: "Wouldn't it be nice if we all took a ride in the rolling chairs?" she said.

Everyone was agreeable, though it was immediately apparent that there would be a slight problem of organization. The rolling chairs had different seating capacities: Some carried three people, and some of them two. We found two chairs that carried three people and one chair that carried two.

"I'll ride with Chinky in the double," Helen Anna said.

"There will be no discussion," Mr. Shepard said decisively. "The ladies should stick together. I will ride alone."

Mrs. Shepard, Helen Anna, and I stepped into one chair, and Miss Davis, Miss Stebbins, and Mrs. Dodge into another. The Negro pushers tucked the blankets around us and Mr. Shepard gave the signal for the caravan to start: "Westward Ho!"

"Please tell the chairmen not to go too fast, Finley," Mrs. Shepard called to her husband.

"Don't worry, my dear, there's no speed limit in the off-season."

Mrs. Shepard knew a great deal about Atlantic City and about rolling chairs as well. She told us that they were first used in Brighton, England, and one had been brought over to Atlantic City fifty years ago by a man who loved the sea but was unable to walk up and down the beach on account of his health. "Who would have thought," she said, "that one single chair from Brighton, England would be the beginning of a thriving business in Atlantic City?"

We rolled slowly up and down past the shops, the game concessions, and a restaurant which advertised itself as "the home of the purified lobster." Mrs. Shepard pointed out the various places of interest like a guide: The Hotel Claridge, the Hotel Traymore, the Steel Pier.

"Tomorrow," Mrs. Shepard said, "we will ride the other way. I'll show you Convention Hall. Inside there is an ice-skating rink. I used to skate a lot when I was a little girl. Would you believe it, Celeste, I could trace a figure eight!" When we approached a shooting gallery, Mr. Shepard stopped and asked if anyone would like to try his luck. Mrs. Dodge said she would, and Mr. Shepard escorted her to the firing range. Mrs. Dodge was a very quiet, retiring woman, and I was surprised that she was interested in guns. She had hardly spoken a word since we had left New York. But she proved to be a woman of action: she took the rifle and calmly shot down a dozen moving ducks and five clay pipes, and then she even shot out the flame of a lighted candle!

"You have a wonderful eye, Mrs. Dodge," Mr. Shepard said. "Where did you learn to shoot so well?"

"At home," she said.

After the shooting, Mrs. Shepard suggested that we look for more peaceful diversions. "All right, dear," Mr. Shepard said, "just wait until I tuck 'Dead-Eyed Dodge' back in her caboose and we'll be off."

The next stop was in front of a small confectionery store. Helen Anna and I went in with Mrs. Shepard to buy some Fralinger's Salt Water Taffy. A young man in an immaculate crisp white uniform stepped up to help us. He looked more like the resident physician than a candy salesman.

"Can I do anything for you, madam?" he inquired politely.

"Yes, thank you," Mrs. Shepard said.

"Some salt-water taffy, perhaps?"

"That would be nice."

"Would Madam like a small box or a large box?"

"I would like thirty pounds," she said.

He stared at Mrs. Shepard in amazement and said,

"Excuse me, lady, I'll have to get my father."

The father came running back with the look of a man who had just found oil in his backyard, and the transaction was completed with the help of two large scales which said, "Honest weight—no springs."

Then Mrs. Shepard explained that she was going to take thirty pounds of taffy back to New York, but she wished to mail a few small boxes from the store to her friends who lived out of town. She took out a list of names and called in Miss Stebbins and Miss Davis to help her write down the names and addresses on the small, individual mailing orders. There must have been over a hundred people on Mrs. Shepard's little list, arranged in alphabetical order.

"Miss Davis," she said, "you take from 'A' to 'J.' Miss Stebbins, you are responsible from 'K' to 'Q.' I'll write the names from 'R' to 'W.' "

I was left with "X," "Y," "Z." There wasn't much for me to do.

When Mr. Shepard came into the store to find out what was causing the delay, and saw all the activity he said: "Looks as if we'll have to hire another rolling chair." When the bill was paid, the proprietor and his son thanked Mrs. Shepard profusely and rather mechanically asked if there was anything else she wished.

"Yes," she answered, "twenty pounds of macaroons." "Son," said the proprietor, "get the macaroons. This is the biggest day we've had since the national clam and oyster-opening contest!"

That was the end of the buying spree, and we went outside. As the taffy and macaroons were arranged in Mr. Shepard's chair, he said, "I'm certainly loaded for bear." As we rolled back to the Marlborough-Blenheim, I wondered which friends of Mrs. Shepard would soon be eating taffy and macaroons. Certainly, her friends in Irvington and Roxbury,

Miss Quincy in Chatham, Mr. Ito in San Diego, and Mr. and Mrs. Tinsdale in Siam. It wouldn't be long now before a group of Siamese children in Bangkok would be chewing taffy by the big sitting Buddha near the Y.M.C.A.

The sun was going down, and it was beginning to get chilly. We started back and I thought we were through for the day. Not quite! We passed a store which had a large printed sign nailed above the door: **"auction tomorrow at three o'clock,"** and Mrs. Shepard reacted with fuss and flutter. She called to Mr. Shepard in the chair ahead and to Miss Stebbins and Miss Davis in the chair behind: "An auction, everybody! Look! An auction! Tomorrow we will all go. There must be many interesting things in there!"

From what I could glimpse of the interior of the store, I didn't think there could possibly be anything that Mrs. Shepard would want. It was little better than a cemetery for old furniture, books, gimcracks, and ship models. But Mrs. Shepard was determined to go. Who could tell what treasure she might discover! What priceless ornament might be hers for a few pennies!

Mrs. Shepard loved auctions and often attended them. She enjoyed the sing-song of the auctioneer, the competition, the suspense, and when she wanted it, the victory. But sometimes the price of victory was high. Once near Millinocket, Maine, she bid fifty dollars for a jade figurine, which she discovered later was made of soapstone.

All that evening at dinner and afterwards when we went out on the boardwalk to locate the three stars of Orion's Belt, Mrs. Shepard still had her mind on the auction.

"I know I'll find something interesting. I just know I will!"

Mr. Shepard did not share his wife's enthusiasm. "My dear, while you're at the auction, I think I'll go down and play skee ball."

Before we went to bed that night, Mr. Shepard discovered that his small leather toilet case was missing. A searching party was organized, and every suitcase was meticulously examined, but it was nowhere to be found. But the hotel drugstore was equal to the emergency except for a toothbrush. Mr. Shepard used soft bristles, and they only had hard bristles. "Send one up anyway," Mr. Shepard said, "I'll use just half my strength."

The day of the auction was overcast and depressing. Wisps of fog had blown in from the sea, and in the distance we heard the constant wail of fog horns. But Mrs. Shepard's spirits did not fall with the barometer. As the hour approached, she was more eager than ever. At two-thirty we gathered in front of the hotel, signaled for chairs, and were soon rolling on our way.

The weather did not interfere with the attendance at the auction. On the contrary, when we arrived, the room was crowded. We had difficulty finding seats and had to take single seats in various parts of the room, but we were not so far apart that we couldn't wave to one another.

The auctioneer stood on a raised platform in one corner of the room. He was florid of face and flamboyant of speech. He enthused over the most trivial items, praised the most worthless gewgaws, and rhapsodized on the beauty of the ugliest objects. When he tried to spark the bidding on a terra-cotta bust of Julius Caesar, he said: "Are we to witness the 'noblest Roman of them all' leave Atlantic City for a dollar and a quarter?"

"No, no," someone cried, "I bid two dollars."

"Thank you, madam," he said, "I see you have a sense

of history."

Following the departure of Caesar from the dais, an hour glass was exhibited, which the auctioneer looked at so admiringly, I thought he was going to bid for it himself.

"What am I offered for this graceful guardian of the hour? The sands of time! See how the seconds fall away to eternity!"

These words were not in vain, and I heard the familiar voice of Miss Davis: "Ten cents," she said.

"Ten cents!" the auctioneer repeated in disgust. He shook his head and embellished his sales talk with a quotation from Longfellow:

> *A handful of red sand from the hot clime Of Arab deserts brought,*
>
> *Within this glass becomes the spy of time.*
>
> *The minister of Thought.*

"Fifteen cents," said Miss Davis. She was bidding against herself.

"That's more like it. Now isn't there anyone here who will make it a quarter?" and he looked imploringly about the room.

"Twenty-five cents," someone said.

"Thirty cents," another voice added.

"Fifty cents," said someone else.

Miss Davis re-entered the bidding: "Forty cents."

"You mean sixty cents," said the auctioneer.

"I guess I do," she said rather sheepishly.

The bidding progressed by nickels and dimes. Miss Davis dropped out after two dollars and twenty cents. The sand had run more than half its course through the hourglass when the bidding closed at three dollars.

While the auctioneer was making the notation in his notebook, I heard him say to his assistant: "Imagine! The hour glass was sold for a dollar more than Caesar."

The afternoon was passing as a variety of things were exhibited, bid for, and sold. A "silver" tea service went for ten dollars, a set of Shakespeare minus "Timon of Athens" for five dollars, and a reproduction of the "Laughing Cavalier" for five-fifty. After the "Cavalier" was removed, a small native drum about three feet high was set up on the dais.

"This nineteenth-century drum," the auctioneer said, "comes from the Belgian Congo. Notice the beauty of the geometric carving, the simplicity of its design. It was made by the Bakuba tribe for important ceremonials: weddings, harvests, festivals, and funerals. It is a decorative reminder of ancient customs, and you can also sit on it. It is a valuable object. Now, who will open the bidding at a dollar?"

A hand went up; then a voice said, "Two dollars," another "three," and another "Five." Then a distinguished-looking elderly man in the back of the room jumped the bid to ten dollars. He evidently wanted the drum very badly, and his bid was probably made with the idea of stopping competition and to warn everyone that he wanted the drum and was willing to pay for it. Whatever his purpose, he succeeded. There was no further bidding.

"Sold to the gentleman in the gray raincoat," the auctioneer said. "Going, going," but before he could bring his gavel down and say "gone," a voice interrupted: "Fifteen dollars!" It was Mrs. Shepard. The bidding was resumed.

"Twenty dollars," said the gentleman.

"Twenty-five dollars," said Mrs. Shepard.

"Do I hear thirty dollars?" the auctioneer asked.

"Thirty dollars," said the old gentleman.

Mrs. Shepard was silent. The gentleman looked pleased, and he was smiling.

The auctioneer again went through the formalities: "Going, going," but before he could say "gone," Mrs. Shepard said, "Thirty-five dollars." She had waited again until the last possible second to place her bid.

The smile disappeared from the gentleman's face, and he frowned as though he were considering whether to go higher. After a moment, he made his decision: "Forty dollars."

"Forty-five dollars," said Mrs. Shepard.

This had developed into quite a contest, and some of the crowd turned around in their chairs to get a better view of the protagonists.

I knew that Mrs. Shepard wanted that drum. She was intensely, almost fanatically interested in African art and sculpture. She had countless friends who sent her gifts anywhere from the first cataract of the Nile, to the veldt in Kenya. A drum like this was irresistible. This was the unexpected treasure! This was an ornament beyond price —beyond expectations!

It looked as if the drum would soon be hers. The gentleman seemed to have given up, but the auctioneer still had hopes that he could fan new interest. He took his hand and beat out a little rhythm on the drum: "Rat, tat, tat—rat, tat, tat, rat, tat, tat." I had visions of white ivory, jungles of darkness, secret rites, mystic incantations, and almost put in a bid myself. The elderly gentleman, too, was moved by this sudden syncopation. He turned to the lady beside him and, after a brief consultation, he said rather timidly: "Forty-seven dollars."

"Fifty dollars," said Mrs. Shepard.

"Rat, tat, tat," sounded the drum again, "rat, tat tat," but it was no use. The spell was over, the illusion gone. The gentleman smiled sadly, threw up his hands, and shook his head. In a way it was rather pathetic. I felt like telling him that he was in an impossible situation. If he had bid five hundred dollars, it would not have done him any good. Hopefully the auctioneer hit the drum once more, but the bidding was over. "Going, going, gone," and Mrs. Shepard now owned a nineteenth-century Bakuba drum.

After a pair of brass candlesticks, a fine old compass from a whaling ship, and a cloisonne vase was sold, the auction was over. Mrs. Shepard put her drum under her arm, and we started toward the door. As we were about to go outside, the gentleman who had been bidding against Mrs. Shepard, came across the room.

"That is indeed a fine drum, madam," he said. "I can assure you it's worth a lot more than fifty dollars. I know. I'm an anthropologist. You have a bargain. Good day," and he tipped his hat politely.

"Just a moment, please," Mrs. Shepard said. "Would you do me a great favor?"

"Of course."

"I would like you to take this drum," and she put it in front of her.

"Thank you, madam, that's very kind of you, but I couldn't possibly accept it. You won it fair and square."

"I insist that you accept it," Mrs. Shepard said. "It would make me very happy if you took it, and very sad if you did not."

"But I couldn't madam, under the circumstances."

"If you don't take it, you will spoil my anniversary. Please, won't you take the drum?"

The gentleman looked at her determined face and

realized the sincerity of her offer. "Very well, madam, I accept your gift, but I insist upon paying you."

"No," Mrs. Shepard said. "I would consider it a privilege if you took it. You have more need for it than I." The gentleman took the drum, and I could see that he was struggling to hold back his tears.

"Thank you from the bottom of my heart. You don't know what this means to me."

"How sweet," Mrs. Shepard said. "How very sweet of you."

We went outside. It was dark and it was beginning to rain. There were no rolling chairs in sight. We would have to walk. Helen Anna and I linked arms with Mrs. Shepard and started slowly up the boardwalk toward the Marlborough-Blenheim.

Once when I looked back to see if Miss Stebbins and Miss Davis were following, I saw the anthropologist on the other side of the boardwalk, but he disappeared in the darkness. The rain began to come down in torrents, and gusts of wind blew in from the ocean. The waves were roaring and crashing violently against the beach, sending up fountains of spray across the boardwalk. The three of us huddled close together.

Suddenly, above the sound of the storm I thought I heard the muffled beat of a drum. I looked back, but no one was in sight except Miss Stebbins and Miss Davis. What was it I heard? Was it the echo of a distant drum, or was it the beat of a generous heart?

20

Batter Up

SIX MONTHS AFTER Gael was born, my husband and I left New York and moved to New Jersey. "It's better for children," Louis said, "and, besides, we can play golf there ten months out of every twelve."

For almost two years because of Gael we were unable to visit Mrs. Shepard at Lyndhurst in the spring or at Kirkside during the summer, though we did come into the city quite often. We went to 579 on Thanksgiving Day, New Year's Day, St. Patrick's Day, Ash Wednesday, and Easter Sunday. Occasionally also we came to town for a concert or to go to the theatre.

I remember the night that Mrs. Shepard took us to see Helen Hayes in *Victoria Regina*. It was a wonderful play, and I enjoyed it immensely, though not so much as Miss Stebbins did. In the second act, Prince Albert was writing at his desk. Suddenly the pen dropped from his hand. He tried to rise from his chair, but fell back. Victoria found him leaning on the table, his head on his arms. He reached out to her with a gesture of helplessness.

"Take me to bed! Take me to bed, *Weibchen*" he pleaded. "I am so tired. Ich habe kaum die Feder halten konnen!"

The queen threw her arms about him and held him tenderly as the curtain fell.

I looked at Miss Stebbins. She was weeping.

When we came out of the theatre, Miss Stebbins said, "I haven't had such a good cry since *Orphans of the Storm*."

And I remember other things about those years: unimportant things, and things that really mattered. I remember when Finley Jay lost his hat down the elevator shaft.

I remember the rejoicing when Olivia gave birth to another baby boy; and I remember so well when Mr. Shepard had to go to the hospital for an operation on his eyes. We were frightened and apprehensive, but everything turned out all right. After he got home, his eyesight was improved, and he soon regained his strength and gaiety. I went to see him often, and sometimes he asked me to read to him.

One evening, after I had finished reading a chapter from *Don Quixote*, he said, "Celeste, my dear, years ago a professor of mine told me that when he read *Don Quixote* as a boy in his twenties, he thought it was a comedy; when he read it again in his forties, it seemed more like a tragedy; but when he read it in his seventies, it was a comedy again. You know, Celeste, I think I'm just beginning to understand what my old professor meant."

Both Mr. and Mrs. Shepard always said that all invitations to 579 included Gael. We brought her in to town a few times, but Gael's first long visit with her grandfather and grandmother was at Kirkside during the summer of 1938. Louis had a month's vacation that year (two weeks without pay), and we stayed with his family the full time. Mrs. Shepard brought down a crib from the attic and filled it with picture books, rattles, and dolls. Mr. Shepard contributed a huge white teddy bear which, when wound up, played "London Bridge is falling down."

"Just think," Mrs. Shepard said, "Gael will be two years old this November, and you know, Celeste, as we grow older, we measure time by our children's birthdays rather than by our own."

It was good to be back at Kirkside again. Nothing was different. Our room was furnished exactly the same, the stairs creaked in the same place; not a picture had been moved from a wall, and not a chair was out of place: Neither a habit nor a custom had been changed.

One afternoon Mrs. Shepard asked me if I would care to accompany her on her afternoon motor trip with Miss Davis and Miss Stebbins.

"I would love to. Mother Shepard," I said. "What time shall I be ready?"

"The usual time, my dear," she said, "two-thirty"

At two-thirty sharp we assembled in the living room. Mrs. Shepard said: "We are going on quite a long trip today; are we all prepared?" Miss Stebbins and Miss Davis nodded together in the affirmative. I had an extra sweater and a coat over my arm so I felt I was adequately prepared for an afternoon drive but I didn't think it was necessary to reply. However, Mrs. Shepard wished a positive statement.

"Celeste, are you sure you are quite prepared?"

"Yes, Mother Shepard," I said, "as far as I know," and [held up my coat so she could see for herself.

Miss Stebbins smiled and said, "You see, Celeste, Mrs Shepard doesn't like to stop at any of the restrooms along the way."

Now I understood.

"Yes, Mother Shepard," I replied with a great blush, "I am prepared."

After Mrs. Shepard was assured that I was prepared,

we walked out to the car. We were immediately joined by the pack of dogs, but Mrs. Shepard would not allow them to come along.

"No, Spick, not today. I'm very sorry, Span, not today," and as we got in, she shooed them away. This was a drastic change in the dogs' regimen, and there was such a cacophony of barking that it looked as if they would go berserk. Speed was the essential thing, and Mrs. Shepard thought so too. She hurried us into the back seat, and we started off with a rush. The dogs gave chase, and by the time we passed the Roxbury Inn, they were still close behind. By the time we went by the Roxbury Hotel, they had all given up except the Boston bull, who continued bravely on until he saw a female Chihuahua.

I couldn't understand why the dogs were not allowed to come, but Mrs. Shepard's explanation was reasonable. "I hate to disappoint them," she said, "but we couldn't possibly bring them today. We're going to try to identify a few birds," and she took out a huge pair of binoculars from her bag. "Emily More told me this morning that she saw a 'fire-throat' at that lovely lake on the way to Haines Falls."

I didn't know what a fire-throat looked like, but Miss Davis explained it was a little bird smaller than a sparrow. "You can tell it by its flaming orange throat. It is often called a Blackburnian warbler."

"A 'wobbler'?" I asked.

"No, dear, not a 'wobbler,' a 'warbler.'"

Before we had the opportunity to do any bird watching, we classified a few larger objects. As we came around a curve in the road, Mrs. Shepard said, "Do you remember who lives there, Celeste?" and she pointed to a white frame colonial cottage.

"Mrs. Bronson."

"And whose house is that?" and she pointed to another large white house with green blinds.

"That is Louise More's house."

"How well you remember! You haven't been here in two years, and the blinds were painted red only last week."

I didn't know if I would recognize the "fire-throat" if we saw one, but I had done better than I expected on colonial houses. Before we did any bird watching there was still a bridge or two to cross. The first one was a small, shaky structure which traversed a stream that a man could easily leap across.

"Do you know the name of this river, Celeste?"

If this slight trickle of water was a river, it was a surprise to me. No name occurred to me, but having been right twice, I could afford to be wrong once.

"The Delaware River," I said.

"Almost right," Mrs. Shepard said. "It is a tributary of the Delaware — a distant cousin, you might say. We call it 'John Burrough's Creek.'"

A mile or so further on, we approached another bridge which crossed a rivulet. As we went over it, Mrs. Shepard asked me again: "And what is this river, Celeste?"

I thought for a moment, then I replied, "Another cousin of the Delaware."

"Yes, Celeste, indeed it is. You seem to have photographed this entire country in your mind."

The Delaware River was a ubiquitous body of water. No matter what brook we saw, what streamlet, what little puddle, each was a chink in the great river system of the Delaware. The East Branch of the Delaware, itself, flowed only three hundred yards behind Kirkside, and during one spring thaw, Louis said it flowed right through the kitchen.

It was only forty feet at its widest from bank to bank, but Mrs. Shepard seemed to think of it as the mother of waters. It was usually a mild-mannered river and in summer followed its course as gently as sheep follow the shepherd, but both Miss Stebbins and Miss Davis nodded in tacit agreement when Mrs. Shepard hinted darkly of whirlpools, quicksand, cascades, and dangerous rapids. From the way they talked, the East Branch of the Delaware must have been more dangerous than the Yukon.

When the children were younger, they had taken occasional canoe trips on the Delaware. Preparations for these voyages were so elaborate that Louis said you might have thought they were setting out to discover the Northwest Passage, except that they were never allowed to venture out of Mrs. Shepard's sight. In spite of constant vigilance and training, there was one memorable accident. Finley Jay and Louis' canoe capsized in two feet of water. No harm was done, but one of the paddles was lost. Sitwell and the lifeguard searched diligently for it in two-piece bathing suits, but after three hours, gave up. No one could figure out where the paddle went, but Mrs. Shepard had her theory: "The paddle has probably drifted downstream and gone over the rapids."

Mrs. Shepard was interested in the *land* bordering Kirkside as well as the water. She knew the name of every town in the county: Grand Gorge, Prattsville, Hunter, Tannersville, and Palenville were her favorites. She was acquainted with their history, the founding fathers, and the present fathers. "Ellery Jones owns that farm," she would say, pointing to a red bam. "He has eleven children."

Mrs. Shepard knew what towns had been subjected to Indian massacres and what the political sympathies of each had been during the Revolution: three towns had favored the Whigs, two favored the Tories, and one town never made up its mind. "I think the undecided one was Rannersville," Mrs. Shepard said.

At four o'clock we arrived at Lookout Point at Haines Falls and had tea in a restaurant on the side of a high mountain. After tea, Mrs. Shepard and I stood on a raised platform on the edge of the cliff.

"Celeste," she said, "from where we're standing, we can see five of our great states." She pointed her finger roughly toward the northeast. "There, is Massachusetts, the Bay State; and there," moving her finger over an inch, "is Connecticut; and there," moving her finger up an inch, "is Vermont." Then she looked through her binoculars.

"Yes, Celeste, 1 really do! I really think Vermont is Greener! See what you think," and she handed me the glasses.

I didn't think Vermont looked any greener than Massachusetts, but my sense of color is bad when I look at anything over a hundred miles away.

"What do you think, Celeste?" Mrs. Shepard asked again.

"Mother Shepard," I said, "I actually do think it looks greener."

Miss Davis came over to the platform and said that Vermont definitely looked greener, but Miss Stebbins had no opinion because she couldn't focus the binoculars.

"All I see is that sign up the road which says hot logs.'"

After a while Mrs. Shepard grew tired of Vermont. She looked at the Adirondacks for a few minutes, and then aimed her attention southward.

"What are you looking at now?" Miss Stebbins asked, "Slide Mountain?"

"No," she replied. "I am looking at Pennsylvania. Does

anybody want to look at Pennsylvania?"

Nobody wanted to look at Pennsylvania, so we went back to our table, had another cup of tea, and Mrs. Shepard wiped off the lenses of her binoculars with a napkin.

"Someday, Celeste," she said, "I hope we can take a longer trip, perhaps to Cooperstown, and stay overnight. I'd love to show you Natty Bumppo's Cave."

"I'd love to see it, too," I said. "I've read about Natty-Bumppo's Cave, but I've never been in it."

After tea, I assumed we would go home, but Mrs. Shepard had not forgotten the main purpose of the trip. "I think we should look for our birds now. Next to the very early morning, the late afternoon is the best time."

We started back the way we came, and after Mrs. Shepard pointed out Mount Ida in the distance, and we passed the largest oak tree in New York, we turned down a bumpy dirt road and stopped beside a small lake bordered by pine trees and berry bushes. We got out and followed a little path which hugged the shoreline.

"Now," Mrs. Shepard said, "let's be very quiet. There are secrets on every bush. Perhaps we'll see Emily More's fire-throat."

I thought Mrs. Shepard was very optimistic because I didn't see a bird of any sort. Half way around the lake we stopped under the shade of a tall spruce, and peered intently in all directions. Mrs. Shepard took out her binoculars and swung them slowly, counterclockwise around the lake but had no luck. She handed them to me but I did little better. I saw a cotton-tail rabbit and a dragon fly. Miss Stebbins and Miss Davis saw nothing although they heard a crow in the distance.

We all felt disappointed and looked at each other disconsolately while we listened to the monotonous drone of the cicadas—serenade to four ladies in search of a fire-throat.

Then Mrs. Shepard did the most unusual thing. She took the back of her hand and started to kiss it. Miss Stebbins and Miss Davis started to kiss the backs of their lands. I couldn't imagine what they were doing.

"This attracts the birds," Miss Stebbins explained. "If there are any around, they will often come out to find out what's going on."

"Smack, smack, smack," the kisses reverberated through the woods. I wasn't surprised that this attracted wild life. This was a sight I should think any bird would fly a long way to see.

But as usual Mrs. Shepard knew what she was doing. Suddenly I heard a plaintive, drawing whistle: "Pee-a-wee, pee-a-wee."

"It's a wood pewee," Mrs. Shepard cried. "Can you see it, everybody? Isn't it the cutest thing! See it, Celeste? In the branch of that small box elder tree!"

I didn't know a box elder when I saw one, let alone a pewee, but I could hear the bird without any trouble: 'Pee-a-wee, pee-a-wee."

"Are you sure it's not an olive-sided fly-catcher?" Miss Stebbins asked skeptically.

"Absolutely," Mrs. Shepard said, "the olive-sided flycatcher sounds like this: 'Whip whee wheer, whip whee wheer.'"

"And, sometimes," Miss Stebbins added, "'Hip-three- cheers!'"

Soon the pewee had company. Another bird appeared and sat on the branch of a pine tree. I knew this little fellow with the black cap. It was a chickadee and he joined the pewee in a duet: "Chick-a-dee-dee, pee-a-wee, chick-a-dee-dee, pee-a-wee." Then came other birds: a cedar waxwing, a robin, a myrtle warbler, and a bluebird that flew by with a worm in his mouth.

"And there is a towhee," Mrs. Shepard said, pointing to a large black and white bird rummaging among the leaves by a fallen tree. "You can always remember its call. It sounds as if it's telling you to: 'Drink-your teeeeeee, drink-your teeeeeee."

Mrs. Shepard knew the birds as well as she knew the flowers: she knew their names, their pipings and trills, their habits, and the exact time of year they flew south. And she certainly knew how to attract them!

Nevertheless, the afternoon was a disappointment. The birds we had seen were old and familiar friends. She wanted so much to spot a fire-throat, but no matter what she did, or where she went, she couldn't find it. We walked twice around the lake, through the briars and into the swamp, but in vain; the fire-throats evaded us.

"Do you think it might be in Prattsville?" Miss Stebbins asked.

Mrs. Shepard shook her head.

"Should we kiss the backs of our hands again?" I asked. "No, Celeste, that trick works once, but seldom twice.

No, I'm afraid it's no use."

"This is all very disappointing!" said Miss Stebbins.

"I have never seen a fire-throat," Miss Davis said plaintively. "Couldn't we search just a little longer?"

"We haven't time," Mrs. Shepard answered. "We must get home to see the ball game."

"The ball game! I almost forgot," Miss Davis said, looking at her watch. "We must hurry."

We had a long way to go. So Mrs. Shepard didn't protest when the speedometer in the car showed we were going at forty miles an hour. She wanted to see the ball game as much as she wanted to see a fire-throat. She missed the fire-throat, but she would not miss the game.

Almost every Saturday afternoon during the summer there was a baseball game between the Roxbury team and a team from a neighboring town. It was a popular event, and the local fans arrived early to find seats in the small grandstand behind the home plate.

The baseball field was part of the Kirkside estate, behind the Jay Gould Memorial Church. It was kept in perfect condition, and in all respects came up to major-league standards, except for the outfield. The East Branch of the Delaware River ran through left field. Mr. Shepard wanted to alter the course of the river by the judicious use of a stick of dynamite, but Mrs. Shepard thought it would kill the trout. The river stayed in left field, and any ball which a batter hit into the water, was declared a ground-rule double. This was acceptable to all teams in the league although the dour manager of the Margaretville nine had a counter suggestion: "Let's have a canoe tilt instead of a baseball game."

The Roxbury team was recruited from the population who worked or lived within the legal limits of the town as originally surveyed and recorded by Jay Gould as a young man in the year 1854. Though the players were subject to change without notice, the usual line-up was:

Pitcher	Assistant Superintendent of Kirkside
Catcher	Proprietor of the Roxbury hardware store
First Base	Assistant to the Proprietor of the Roxbury hardware store

Second Base	Theological student
Shortstop	Employee of Roxbury Creamery
Left Field	Lifeguard
Center Field	Dairy farmer
Right Field	Tree surgeon
Treasurer and Coach	Finley Shepard

When we arrived at Kirkside, the sixth inning was in progress, and Roxbury was ahead by the score of five to one. By the time we found our seats behind the wire netting, and greeted our friends, Roxbury was behind seven to five.

Mrs. Shepard often watched these games, although it was more out of concern for her husband than an instinctive love for the national pastime. In his younger days Mr. Shepard had been an excellent ball player. Now, as coach, he confined his activities to the third-base coaching line, but Mrs. Shepard was always fearful that he might be hurt. Once a hard-hit ball he did not see missed him by inches, but Mr. Shepard would confess to no weakness. He would no more favor his eyes than Mrs. Shepard would favor her heart. Neither Mr. or Mrs. Shepard would admit to human frailty.

During the first half of the seventh inning, the visiting team from Hobart scored three runs. The first man up struck out. The next batter knocked the ball into the Delaware River for a two-base hit. The next man up, knocked a grounder under the legs of the theological student covering second base, and the third man hit a home run over the head of the dairy farmer in center field. That made the score ten to five.

When the Roxbury team came to bat, they did a lot of damage but did not score a single run. One player hit a foul ball through the window of a chicken coop, and there was panic in the hen house. Mr. Shepard said there was no use appraising the damage until after laying time.

During the seventh-inning stretch, a baseball hat was passed through the stands, and everyone contributed something to the treasury of the teams. The hat was sagging with nickels, dimes, and quarters by the time it was passed to us. I put in twenty-five cents, Miss Stebbins and Miss Davis each put in a dollar, and Mrs. Shepard contributed ten dollars, saying:

"I do hope they can do something about that man's pants," and she pointed to the pitcher of the Roxbury team.

The rest of the game was exciting. Roxbury rallied in their half of the eighth inning, and the score became: Hobart, ten — Roxbury, nine. Mrs. Shepard knew enough about the game to follow it, but Miss Stebbins even understood some of the finer points. I heard the gentleman on her left say: "Don't you think that batter has a graceful swing?" and Miss Stebbins answered: "Yes, but I hope he doesn't hit into a double play."

Miss Davis, on the other hand, more or less followed the crowd. When the crowd clapped, she clapped too. When the crowd shouted, she shouted with the rest. But when the fans were in disagreement about "throwing the bum out," she maintained strict neutrality.

The score was still ten to nine in favor of Hobart when Roxbury came to bat in the last half of the ninth inning. The first man up was Sam Lutz, the assistant superintendent of Kirkside. He singled to first base, and the lifeguard sacrificed him to second. The next man up was the theological student. The first pitch was a strike over the inside corner. The next ball he swung at but missed. As he knocked the dirt out of his spikes and spat on his hands, he looked up at the sky, perhaps calling for divine assistance. But his call was unanswered. He struck out. "God," he said later, "was on the side of the team with the highest batting averages."

Two outs, now, and a man on second. There was still a chance for Roxbury to win. The dairy farmer was up, and I heard Mr. Shepard's voice ring out loud and clear: "Get a hit. You can do it. Just keep your eye on the ball."

"Yes, please do," I heard Miss Davis say behind me.

"Strike one," the umpire bellowed. The pitcher received the ball back from the catcher, rubbed it carefully in his hands, and stared at the dairy farmer as if he were his mortal enemy. Then the pitcher pulled back his arm, and the ball came toward the plate like a white comet. The farmer started his swing, and "smack" — the ball sailed in a graceful arc for a clean hit to center field. Sam Lutz, on second base, started for third, and I saw Mr. Shepard wave him on home with his arms and yell, "Dig for it, Sam; dig for home!" Sam did. He came running up to the plate as the center fielder threw the ball to the catcher. Ball and base-runner would reach home at the same time.

"Slide," yelled Mr. Shepard, "slide," and Sam slid in a cloud of dust as the catcher caught the ball and tagged him. "You're out!" the umpire shouted, and the game was over.

Hobart had won. There was no doubt that Sam had been out at the home-plate, but Miss Stebbins was outraged:

"Sam was safe. I know he was safe."

"Yes, I thought so, too," Miss Davis said. "What can we do?"

"We must abide by the decision of the umpire," Mrs. Shepard said.

The fans stood up, and the little grandstand was soon

deserted. Some of the people walked out on to the diamond and congratulated the players. Sam Lutz was standing with Mr. Shepard discussing the play that ended the game.

"I should have made it, Mr. Shepard. I should have scored the tying run. I hesitated, and that made the difference."

"No, Sam," Mr. Shepard said, "I should have held you on third base."

"I could have made it, sir. It was my fault."

"Let's forget it," Mr. Shepard said kindly. "It's just a game. We'll beat them next time," and he put his arm affectionately around Sam's shoulder.

Mrs. Shepard, Miss Davis, Miss Stebbins and I started back to Kirkside. We walked up Main Street past the church, and turned into our entrance way. Just as Mrs. Shepard opened the front door, a tiny bird flew down from a pine tree, darted into a hawthorn bush, and began to sing: "Zip sip sip sip titi tseeeeeee."

We looked at the bird in the fading twilight, and we all recognized it at once. "The fire-throat! The fire-throat!" It was unmistakable: Black and white and flaming orange about the head and throat. Zestfully alive! A beautiful, delicate creature! It hopped nervously from branch to branch, then stopped, cocked its head, and flew away. We waited, hoping to see it again, but it never returned.

"Perhaps it's on its way to South America," Miss Davis said.

"No," Mrs. Shepard said, "it doesn't leave until next month."

"Just think," I said, "we went all that distance and found a fire-throat almost on our own doorstep!"

"Sometimes, Celeste," Mrs. Shepard said, "the most beautiful things in the world are right beside us, and we never notice them!"

It had been an exhausting day. During dinner hardly a word was spoken, and immediately after coffee, Mrs. Shepard, saying she did not feel up to a game of backgammon, kissed us good night, and went upstairs with her nurse.

A half an hour later the living room was deserted. I read a magazine for a little while, but I must have dozed off. The next thing I knew the clock struck eleven. I had had a long nap, and someone had thoughtfully turned out the bright lights.

I got up and started for our room but stopped at the front door and opened it for a breath of fresh air. It was a still, clear night, and the milky way was a white highway across the sky. As I looked at the heavens, I thought I heard an organ playing. I closed the door behind me and wandered down the path to the church.

Yes, someone *was* playing. As I approached, I heard the music clearly, but whoever was playing at this hour was not playing sacred music. He was playing "Take Me Out to the Ball Game." But he was not playing boisterously; he was playing slowly and quietly. I walked up the steps of the church. The door was open, and I walked through the small vestry and down the main aisle. Halfway to the altar I stopped abruptly; I recognized the organist. It was Mr. Shepard. He didn't see me, and I didn't speak. I sat down in one of the side pews and watched him.

In the dim light, Mr. Shepard looked older, and I was aware that his hair was almost pure white, and his hands trembled as they moved across the keyboards. Yes, for all Mr. Shepard's jokes, and gaiety, and lightness of heart, he was an old man. Was he playing now in memory of some great victory in the years gone by—of a home run now long forgotten?

When Mr. Shepard finished playing, he walked up to the rail before the altar, kneeled, and began to pray aloud:

> *The Lord is my light and my salvation;*
> *Whom shall I fear?*
> *The Lord is the strength of my life,*
> *Of whom shall I be afraid?*

I felt like an intruder. I knew that I shouldn't be in the church. I was eavesdropping on his prayers and meditations. Quietly I stood up and walked out of the church, back to Kirkside, and hastened upstairs to our room. Mr. Shepard never knew I was in the church that night.

21

Gathering of the Clan

IN 1938, FOUR hundred people lived in the incorporated village of Roxbury, and most of them were related to each other. The responsibility for this state of affairs can be traced directly to John and Betty Taylor More, the first white settlers in Delaware County, circa seventeen hundred and thirty. They came from Forres, on the Firth of Moray in the north of Scotland, to seek freedom, find land, and to raise a family. Freedom in the New World awaited them; they bought land, and it was just a question of time before the footprints of their children mingled with the tracks of deer, bear, fox, muskrat, and mink.

John and Betty More had eight sons and one daughter, and in a few generations their descendants had almost a monopoly on the entire valley. After the Lewis and Clark Expedition of 1804, and the opening of the West, many of John More's descendants left the Catskills to find broader valleys and to scale higher mountains, but some remained and prospered on the shores of the East Branch of the Delaware.

It is understandable, if quaint, that today in Roxbury, forms of address such as "Mr.," and "Mrs.," and "Miss" are not used as consistently as expressions of kinship like "uncle," "aunt," and particularly "cousin." While it may be fiction that all men are brothers, it is a fact, according to Mrs. Shepard's genealogical charts, that most men in Roxbury are cousins. Every problem in the town is really a family problem; every argument among the members of the Town Council is really a family fight.

When I was in Roxbury, it was common to pass by the local garage and hear a gentleman say: "Hello, Cousin Robert! Give me ten gallons of gasoline, please," or if you entered a grocery store you might find a housewife bickering over her morning purchase with her relative: "I'd like five pounds of rump steak, Cousin, and mind, no fat this time."

"Anything else?"

"No, but the bread you gave me yesterday was stale. If I don't get better service, I'll take my business across the street to Cousin Stephen."

Mrs. Shepard knew every branch and twig of her fertile family tree; she could trace anyone's ancestors as far back as he had the patience to go. Her own father, Jay Gould, was descended from John More's third son, Alexander. This was the line that also led to Sabine Baring-Gould, the author of "Onward Christian Soldiers"; to Edward Harley More who invented the first friction guard for a mill saw; and to Daniel Dayton Tomkins More, a broom-maker. Daniel was so proud of his craftsmanship that he sent a consignment of brooms to London for exhibition at the World's Fair in 1852 and was awarded a medal and a diploma with Prince Albert's signature. The brooms were made in Albany, New York.

Not far from Kirkside, on the road to Grand Gorge, is a little cemetery where most of the More family are buried.

Mrs. Shepard often liked to walk between the rows of tombstones, recalling her ancient heritage and occasionally pulling out the weeds that threatened to hide the engraving of a name or epitaph.

The first place of honor in the cemetery belonged naturally to John and Betty More. Their names in large block letters were inscribed on a tall, handsome monument which stood beside the iron gate near the entrance. But John and Betty were not remembered in stone and script alone. They were remembered every five years by a reunion.

The reunions were held at Roxbury, and the descendants of John and Betty More came from every state in the union to pay homage to their ancestors. They came to Roxbury as faithfully as the Canterbury pilgrims went to the shrine of Thomas a Becket, as faithfully as the sons of Allah go to Mecca.

Mr. Shepard was also interested in the background of the More pilgrimages and gave me many old pamphlets, printed menus, and a 409-page book on the history of the More family. "You might find this book interesting," he said, "but there will be no test on it!"

I read this long volume from cover to cover. When I finished, I knew more about the history of the More family than about the history of the United States.

"You're an M.D. now," Mr. Shepard said, "Doctor of Mores."

The idea for a "More" reunion was born in the year 1889. A circular letter was mailed by David F. More of Newark, New Jersey, to all his relatives whom he could locate. The opening sentence of the letter asked the question:

Dear Cousin,

Why should there be a reunion of the descendants of John More and a monument erected to his memory?

The rest of the letter answered the question:

Our ancestors, John More and his wife, were noble, courageous, and heroic, enduring great hardships to make a home and rear their family in this land of promise. Their descendants are numerous and have prospered and can best show their appreciation of honorable and devout ancestry by the erection of a suitable monument. If not erected by this generation, now growing old, it in all probability will not be done by those who follow."

We are so numerous and able financially to do such a labor of love that we must do something adequate or we will subject ourselves to merited criticism. Not less than two thousand dollars should be freely contributed. Such a gathering on so large a scale and for so noble a purpose would be an event memorable for generations among those who shall follow us and will influence them for good.

Yours in the bond,
David F. More

The first reply to this circular letter came from Jay Gould with a check for five hundred dollars. Soon other acknowledgments followed, elaborate plans were made, and the first reunion was held in Roxbury one year later. The monument to John and Betty More was bought in

Scotland, except for the lower base which was bought in Barre, Vermont. Both base and monument arrived in time for the ceremonies and were unveiled by the oldest grandson in the presence of three hundred and fifty descendants, including James Franklin Frisbee from Carthage, South Dakota.

During the three-day festivities, there was an exhibition of family relics, games, concerts, a visit to John More's rustic cabin, a long historical lecture, and on the final day, nine short talks (limited to ten minutes each) on intimate family matters.

Arthur More, of Deposit, New York, gave a talk entitled: "The More Family in the Present." He said: "There are over seven hundred of our family still living, though I do not know of any of the family now in the State prison, or even in a common jail, although I must say it has been intimated that some of them ought to be there; but I feel like giving you all the benefit of the doubt as to that." (Laughter.)

Then in a more serious tone Mr. More said he was convinced that the present More family possessed the greatest of virtues — filial love and respect — due reverence for a worthy ancestor. Then after he quoted King Lear, "How sharper than a serpent's tooth it is to have a thankless child," he concluded:

"I am not a Jeremiah, weeping over the decadence of the human family. I do not believe that past generations possessed all the virtues, and the present generation all the vices. I believe that the present generation of the More family have 'kept the faith' of manhood and womanhood transmitted to them from honorable ancestors. Thank you." (Applause.)

I thought Mr. More made a very good speech, and I

silently applauded, thirty-five years after the event.

Mrs. Shepard enjoyed the More reunions immensely, and if she had had her way, they would have been held annually instead of every five years. On the way back from the cemetery that evening, she started to talk about them and continued all through dinner. She remembered all the reunions, but her favorite one was the reunion of 1915. Although it was held over twenty years ago, Mrs. Shepard remembered the most extraordinary details: who was present, who was the chairman of the reception committee, and who gave the address of welcome. She remembered that Henry More won the tennis tournament, that George M. More won the golf tournament, and that Mrs. Dilling won the potato race.

"I never liked the potato races," Miss Stebbins said. "They always seemed like such a waste of vegetables." Six hundred and twelve "Mores" attended the reunion that year—almost twice as many as had come to the first reunion in 1890. A mammoth tent was erected behind Kirkside for a luncheon, which was to officially begin the festivities. The luncheon was a fancy-dress affair. The men wore buckskin suits, and the ladies wore faded silk dresses over gently swaying hoops. A search of dusty attics and half-forgotten trunks had turned back the history of Roxbury one hundred and fifty years.

"We think in the present," one gentleman said, "but we live in the past."

The supporting pillars of the great tent were gay with evergreens, and bouquets of thistle and bon-bon boxes of green candy were set before each place. The seating was arranged according to ancestral line. The descendants of Alexander More sat at one table; the descendants of John More sat at two tables; but the descendants of Robert More sat at ten—ten tables jointed into one, which linked the punch bowl at one end of the tent to the huge coffee cauldron at the other.

During the fish course, a strange, shrill piping was heard faintly in the distance. One little boy perked up his head and said to his father:

"Daddy, what is that?"

"Well, son, perhaps I have a touch of the sun, but I think it's bagpipes."

It was bagpipes! They became louder and louder, and with a flourish eight sturdy bagpipers entered the tent in kilts of the Campbell Clan. Everyone rose and sang, "The Campbells Are Coming." It was a great day for Scotland in Delaware County. The Mores were there, and the Campbells were on their way!

This reunion was a subject close to Mrs. Shepard's heart and she talked about it as if it had happened yesterday. "We still have our costumes upstairs," she said. "Some rainy day we'll put them all on."

"I would love to see the old costumes again," Miss Stebbins said. "I hope it rains tomorrow!"

After we finished dinner, we went into the living room for coffee. Miss Stebbins and Miss Davis took their usual places on either side of Mrs. Shepard. Olivia, Helen Anna and Finley Jay occupied the window seat. Mr. Shepard pondered over his jigsaw puzzle on a card table in a far corner, and Louis helped him find some of the pieces.

After Sitwell passed the coffee, Mrs. Shepard asked him if he would mind fighting the fire. It was now the beginning of September, and the nights were becoming chilly. Summer was on the wing. Mr. Shepard said he had heard the honking of wild geese when he was taking a walk before breakfast.

After coffee was finished and Sitwell had removed the empty cups, Helen Anna had a romantic idea.

"Mother, let's turn out the lights and look at the fire."

"Your father is working on his puzzle," Mrs. Shepard said.

"It's all right, Helen Anna," Mr. Shepard said. "I can't do this confounded thing anyway."

We turned off the lights and silently stared into the fire. The flames bathed the room in a warm, amber light, and shadows danced across the walls. For a long time, the only sound was the crackling of the burning wood or the soft thud of a falling log.

As the fire began to die down, Mrs. Shepard began to talk again about the More reunion. She described the great allegorical pageant which dramatized the struggles and hardships that John and Betty More overcame when they first arrived in America. She talked intensely and quickly and for a long time. She could talk of nothing else. She seemed obsessed with the subject, but I thought I understood the reason why she kept harking back to her reunion of 1915. She associated it with her happiest and most fruitful years: her marriage, the adoption of her children, and her work. This period was in a way the climax of her life — the years when her energies and her spirit were at full tide.

But in the dim light, Mrs. Shepard did not want to return to the past alone. She wanted company even in her reveries. She looked toward the corner of the room where her husband was sitting with his head bowed against his chest.

"Finley dear," she said, "do you remember the pageant?"

There was no reply. Mr. Shepard was asleep. She spoke again a little louder, and this time Mr. Shepard awoke with a start as if he had been disturbed from some dream of his own.

"Yes, yes, my dear, what is it? What's happened?"

"I said, Finley, do you remember the pageant?"

"The pageant? The pageant? Yes, I think I do."

"You were the Spirit of Saint Christopher, and you guided John and Betty through the mountains and the storms of the great wilderness."

"So I did," Mr. Shepard answered, "so I did."

"You stood on the bridge, dressed in white and pleaded to the Spirit of Nature not to harm the travelers."

Mr. Shepard reached for Louis' arm and slowly got up and said in a deep bass voice:

"John and Betty More, remember that —

> *The Lord **is** thy keeper: the Lord **is** thy shade upon thy right hand.*
>
> *The sun shall not smite thee by day, nor the moon by night . . .'* "

"Yes, Finley," Mrs. Shepard said excitedly, "you do remember! Your voice rang out so loud and clear across the valley. Everyone was so proud!"

"Thank you, my dear," Mr. Shepard said and sat down.

Then Mrs. Shepard told us that she watched the pageant that afternoon with her neighbor, John Burroughs. Because John Burroughs loved the countryside where he was born, he enjoyed watching the enactment of its early history.

"Do you remember John Burroughs?" she asked Miss Davis.

"Of course, I remember him," Miss Davis replied. "What a handsome man he was with his long white beard!"

"He was like a prophet," Miss Stebbins said, "a great prophet!"

"Yes," Mrs. Shepard agreed, "he was Nature's prophet. I remember once when we were walking through the gardens behind Kirkside. It was springtime; the flowers were blooming everywhere, and a thrush was singing his wonderful flute-like melody. John Burroughs listened until the song was over, and then he said in that sweet, gentle voice of his: 'Behold, Mrs. Shepard, these are the wonders, these are the circuits of the gods; this we now tread is a morning star.' "

Miss Stebbins, who was preoccupied with her fancy-work, now stopped and suggested that perhaps Mrs. Shepard would like to go to bed. "In a little while, my dear, just a little while." Then Miss Stebbins whispered something to Miss Davis, who nodded, stood up, and quietly went out of the room, as Mrs. Shepard turned her attention to her children.

"Helen Anna, do you know that in the pageant, you were the spirit of spring? And Olivia, you were the spirit of summer. Finley Jay was the spirit of autumn, and Louis was the spirit of winter, but I don't suppose any of you remember. You were all so young."

Then Mrs. Shepard had a little lapse of memory and turned to Miss Stebbins.

"Do you remember. Miss Stebbins, who played the Indian chief?"

"No, I don't," Miss Stebbins replied, "but whoever it was, we couldn't get the paint off him."

Mrs. Shepard now asked her husband about the Indian chief, but he couldn't remember either. She tried to coax it out of the past, but no matter how hard she tried, she couldn't recollect the Indian chief. Over the years his name had faded from her memory.

Then Mrs. Shepard started to talk in disjointed

sentences: little fragments, unfinished thoughts, kindling hopes.

"It was a wonderful pageant," she said. "Two years from now there'll be another reunion. Perhaps we can have the same pageant again. Perhaps we can play the same parts. We are all a little older, but it won't matter. But you know, there's something sad about our reunions: so many of the faces you never see again."

The fire was now almost out. There were only a few faint glowing embers in the fireplace. I was about to suggest that Louis put on another log, when Miss Davis returned with the nurse. The nurse turned the lights on abruptly and told Mrs. Shepard that it was long past her bedtime. "You must come to bed now, Mrs. Shepard. You need your rest."

"Yes, I suppose so," Mrs. Shepard said, "I am a little tire,d. But tomorrow is another day, and we will all go to church together. The first time we have all gone to church together for a long time — a little reunion all our own!" Mrs. Shepard stood up, and we gathered around her and kissed her goodnight. "Goodnight, my children," she said, "sleep well, sleep well."

Mrs. Shepard started out of the living room, the nurse on one side of her, and Miss Stebbins and Miss Davis on the other. When she reached the door she stopped, turned around, and said to her husband:

"Finley dear, if John Burroughs were alive, I am sure that he could tell us the name of the Indian chief."

The day was done, and the last burning embers in the fireplace turned to ashes.

The next morning, we assembled in Mrs. Shepard's office a half-hour before services in the Jay Gould Memorial Church would actually begin. Although Mr. Shepard never arrived for worship until the Processional, Mrs. Shepard liked to arrive early to hear the organ prelude.

As the clock chimed ten-thirty, Mrs. Shepard said, "And now if everybody is ready, I think we should be on our way," and we started out the door. Mrs. Shepard took my arm, and we led the family procession: Miss Stebbins, Miss Davis, and the nurse followed directly behind; and then came Louis with Helen Anna, and Finley Jay with Olivia. Though we had plenty of time, Mrs. Shepard walked as though we were late for worship. "Slow down, Mrs. Shepard, please slow down," the nurse said, but this was a wasted warning. No voice, however kind or firm, could change the habits of a lifetime.

We approached the church and started up the few stone steps. And then suddenly, unexpectedly, Mrs. Shepard stumbled. With a little cry, she clutched my arm and fell. She was a heavy woman, and I didn't have the strength to hold her.

She was surrounded at once by her family. The nurse went quickly to her side, and we raised her slowly to her feet. Her face was pale and beads of perspiration stood out across her forehead. And she was shaking.

"Call Mr. Shepard," someone said.

"No," Mrs. Shepard said, "it is not necessary to call anyone."

"We will take you back to Kirkside," the nurse said.

"No, you will not, my dear. It is nothing. I am quite all right. I am going into the church."

"But, Mrs. Shepard!"

"Will someone please take me to church. I'm perfectly all right now."

"Mrs. Shepard, you simply cannot," Miss Stebbins said, almost frantically. "Please, Mrs. Shepard, let us go back to

Kirkside, I beg of you, for your own sake."

"No, I am going to church," Mrs. Shepard said quietly, "and there's no need making a fuss."

She straightened her hat, threw back her shoulders, and said: "We will now enter church calmly as if nothing had happened. Louis—Celeste, will you help me to go in?" There was nothing else we could do. No power in the world could stop her. She had made her decision. We all walked slowly toward the entrance and found our pew just as the organ began to play. Mrs. Shepard turned to me and said:

"I am glad we started early. We are on time."

Immediately after church Mrs. Shepard was put to bed, and this time she did not resist. Extra nurses were called, and both the doctor in Roxbury and her own doctors, who were summoned from New York, were constantly in attendance.

The main thing, they said, was rest and quiet.

"We will do what we can," Mr. Shepard said, "everything we can to keep her quiet. We must all do our best."

The first few days Mrs. Shepard was in bed she carried out the doctors' orders. She took her medicine, obeyed the nurses, and received no visitors. She was weak. She was very ill. On the steps of the church, she had had a stroke.

Once in a while Mrs. Shepard would rally, and there would be an interlude of feverish, almost hysterical activity. She would insist on seeing each member of her family and would send them off on all kinds of errands: to bring her a book, to fetch some memorandum from her file, to telephone a neighbor. She was particularly concerned about affairs at 579 and at Lyndhurst. She wanted to be sure that everything was being done exactly as she had done it. Mr. Shepard, Miss Stebbins and Miss Davis reassured her twenty times a day that everything was all right, that nothing was forgotten.

Mrs. Shepard was not only putting Kirkside in order—she was putting all her houses in order; everything must go on as though nothing had happened. After these exertions her strength would wane again. The doctors advised the children to leave so that Mrs. Shepard would accept enforced rest, for only in this way could her life be prolonged.

"If she could just stay with us a little longer," Mr. Shepard said. "If only she could have one more spring. It has all gone so quickly."

When Louis and I said goodbye to Mrs. Shepard, she was quiet and serene. She smiled as we kissed her and said cheerfully:

"Don't worry. I'm feeling much better this morning. I'm going to sit up in a little while. Please write me often and come back whenever you can."

"Of course, Mother Shepard," I said, "we'll come back, and I'll write to you every day."

"How sweet! How very sweet! I will stay here in Kirkside for a little while longer—perhaps until the snow falls." Louis and I went quietly downstairs, put our things into the car, and bundled up Gael in the back seat. The sun was out, but it was cold. There was a thin coating of ice on the Delaware. The valley had put on its autumn coat of many colors, and there were only patches of green left in the elm trees along Main Street. A few of the neighbors were raking dead leaves into little piles for burning. The song birds had left, and the woods were silent. It was the end of summer.

As Louis and I drove away, I looked up at Mrs. Shepard's room. She was sitting in a chair by the window, and Miss Stebbins and Miss Davis were standing on either side of her, like two guardian angels. I waved, and Mrs. Shepard waved back with her tiny handkerchief. Goodbye, Mother Shepard! Goodbye, Kirkside!

We drove quickly past the church, the inn, the drugstore, the bank, the hotel, and around the great bend of the valley. The white houses and the red barns gradually became dots of color and then disappeared. Soon even the highest mountain faded away in a haze of purple. Roxbury was far behind us. Our family reunion, like the Mores, was over.

22

Snowstorm

OUR VACATION HAD ended in sadness and apprehension.

After we returned home, I wrote Mrs. Shepard almost as often as I had promised. Hardly a day went by that I didn't write a few lines about our activities, the people we saw, the places we went. Louis wanted to return to Kirkside over weekends, but Mr. Shepard would not permit us to violate the doctor's orders. "But do keep on writing," he urged. "She enjoys your letters more than I can say. The arrival of the mail is the most important event of the day. She reads every letter over and over again."

So we wrote letters like this:

November 14, 1938

Dear Mother Shepard,

I do hope you are feeling better. Louis and I talk about you all the time and about the wonderful times we had with you last summer. Louis particularly remembers the baseball game, and I often think of that lovely afternoon we all went to Haines Falls to find the fire-throat. He's in South America now, as I remember you told me, but we will see him again next summer, perhaps in the same hawthorn bush.

We went down to Princeton last week and saw a lot of our old friends. Everyone asked about you and sends his love.

Mother Shepard, please don't bother answering my letters unless you feel up to it. We telephoned the other night and spoke to Miss Davis. She said that the weather was cold and that she wouldn't be surprised if there was snow. There are snow clouds here, too.

Now that you are not at 579, we seldom go into New York except to see my family. But you will be home soon, and we are looking forward to being with you again. We hope that we may visit you in Kirkside some weekend. Until then, we send you our love.

Greetings to Miss Davis, Miss Stebbins and Chinky.

Affectionately,
Celeste

To which she answered:

November 17, 1938

Dear Celeste,

It is sweet of you to write so often as I know how busy you must be.

Yes, I miss the fire-throat, too. And all the other birds. They will be back with us again in the spring. They always come. It is one of the laws of nature, and isn't it miraculous how they find their way! No one has ever been able to explain it. "The heavens declare the glory of God, and the firmament sheweth his handiwork."

All your letters are right here on the bed table beside me. I think of you often, and I am content because I know that you are happy. You and Louis have such a long, glorious life ahead of you.

Affectionately,
Mother Shepard

Mrs. Shepard answered all my letters. But these replies varied in length. Sometimes she wrote just a line, but there was always a heartfelt phrase, a quotation from the Bible, or a kind thought. On Gael's birthday, she sent her a lovely lace pinafore with blue ribbons, and for Thanksgiving we received an eighteen-pound turkey from the poultry farm at Kirkside. On Mrs. Shepard's little gift card there was a postscript from Mr. Shepard: "Eat this and remember your father. I picked it out myself."

I wrote a long letter thanking Mrs. Shepard, and I described in detail our Thanksgiving dinner: who was there, what we did, how much we missed her. I said that it was unnatural and strange not seeing her at the head of the table. "But next year, Mother Shepard, next year!"

Mrs. Shepard never answered the letter. In a few days we received a note from Miss Stebbins explaining that Mrs. Shepard was feeling so weak that she could not take pen to paper. "But I promised I would write for her," Miss Stebbins wrote in her graceful Spencerian hand. "I promised that I would write to all the children. Oh, Celeste, what can I tell you that you don't already know! And are there words to change it? I am afraid! I am terribly afraid! How can we comfort each other? We watch, and we pray, and then we fall asleep. Merciful sleep! It's the only way we can forget for a little while. Mr. Shepard has been magnificent—a knight in shining armor!"

The telephone call that we had been expecting since the day we left Kirkside came early on the morning of December ninth. "Long distance calling." It was Mr. Shepard. Louis listened intently to his father and then replied, "Yes, Father, we will come at once." Louis slowly put the receiver down and looked at me across the room.

"It's Mother. Better throw some things into a suitcase. I'll get the car ready." In an hour we were on our way.

As we were passing the Ashokan Reservoir, it began to snow. The snow came down lightly at first, but soon it was so thick it was hard to see, and drifts began to form along the shoulders of the road. It was cold and bleak, and there was hardly a car on the highway. The Catskills looked deserted except for a few children who were out with their sleds.

By the time we came around the last bend before Roxbury, we were fighting a blizzard. The snow was already a foot high in places, and most of the cars had chains on. When we arrived at Kirkside the blinds and curtains were drawn. The house was the same, but there was a shadow on its features, and we opened the door reluctantly and with heavy hearts. Olivia and her husband, John Burr, were already there, and Finley Jay and Helen Anna arrived shortly afterwards. Mr. Shepard told us simply and bravely that Mrs. Shepard was dying.

"She may live a little longer, a few hours, perhaps a few days. I have small comfort for you, but thank the Good Lord she is not suffering. For the most part while you are here, I will leave you to your own counsel."

The doctor was in attendance night and day, and nurses carried out their orders in a cold, efficient manner. Kirkside had a clinical aspect about it. I was glad when I learned that we were not going to stay there. Rooms had been reserved for us children at the hotel, but we were to have our meals at Kirkside. The meals, however, were little more than sandwiches and coffee.

No one at Kirkside except Mr. Shepard was able to function with the slightest semblance of self-control. No one had the will to do anything. I noticed that the wastepaper baskets had not been emptied, and the Seth Thomas clock on the mantle had run down. Mrs. Shepard's staff walked aimlessly, restlessly from one room to another. Selma, Mrs. Shepard's personal maid of thirty years, was taking care of Chinky. She walked back and forth in the corridor outside Mrs. Shepard's room holding Chinky close to her breast. She had transferred her love and affection to this bewildered little animal. She talked to it as Mrs. Shepard had talked to it. She tried to love it as Mrs. Shepard had loved it. Everyone clutched, as best he could, at something from the past.

Mrs. Shepard's children had lives, families, identities of their own. Life would go on for us. But as for those who had given so many years of their lives exclusively to Mrs. Shepard, their world was tumbling down.

Twice a day for five minutes we were allowed to see Mrs. Shepard. When we arrived outside her room, a nurse quietly opened the door, and we entered together: the children, Miss Stebbins, Miss Davis, and Mr. Shepard. Usually Mrs. Shepard did not know that we were there, but occasionally she would rally for a fleeting moment, and the faintest trace of a smile would form on her lips. When she spoke, it was at best a word or two: "My children, my dear children." Recognition and love. Memory and affection.

Sometimes after dinner we sat in the living room, talked, or played a game or tried to read. Mr. Shepard's jigsaw puzzle lay scattered on the card table unfinished, and Louis and Finley Jay would put a few pieces together and then listlessly pace up and down the room. No one had the spirit to sustain a conversation or game for very long. After an hour or so we would walk slowly back to the hotel.

Every night Mr. Shepard went over alone to the church and played the organ. It was Christmastime, and he played all the Christmas hymns and carols. One night on the way back to the hotel, we heard him playing "O Little Town of Bethlehem," and we stopped outside the church and listened. Then after the "amen," we walked on.

On December twenty-third about nine o'clock in the evening, we were summoned to Mrs. Shepard's room. The doctor was standing at the head of the bed holding Mrs. Shepard's wrist. The lights were on, but they were carefully shaded. On the white table beside the bed I saw the letters that she had received from friends all over the world, and there was a Bible lying open, opened perhaps to some favorite passage that comforted her during her illness. On a chiffonier by the window there was a small vase filled with blush roses. The things that Mrs. Shepard had treasured: flowers, letters, the Bible, and now her family.

But we were here for the last time. This was the final visit. This was the last escaping moment before eternity. Miss Davis asked Mr. Shepard if she might say a prayer. He nodded, and she knelt down by the side of the bed and buried her face in her hands. Almost inaudibly, she began to recite the Twenty-Third Psalm:

> *The Lord is my shepherd; I shall not want,*
>
> *He maketh me to lie down in green pastures,*
>
> *He leadeth me beside the still waters.*

> *He restoreth my soul.*
>
> *He leadeth me in the paths of righteousness for his name's sake.*

As Miss Davis was speaking, I saw the doctor gently let go of Mrs. Shepard's wrist, and then he, too, bowed his head.

> *Yea, though I walk through the valley of the shadow of death,*
>
> *I will fear no evil: for thou art with me;*
>
> *Thy rod and thy staff they comfort me."*

Then Miss Davis stopped. She tried to get control of herself, but Miss Stebbins saw in an instant that she could not, and with hardly a pause, she finished for her:

> *Thou preparest a table before me in the presence of mine enemies:*
>
> *Thou annointest my head with oil; my cup runneth over.*
>
> *Surely goodness and mercy shall follow me all the days of my life:*
>
> *And I will dwell in the house of the Lord forever.*

Miss Davis and Miss Stebbins had lived with Mrs. Shepard through most of her life. Now, together, they had said the words that they knew she would have wanted them to say.

We were crying unashamedly. We walked quietly out of the room, down the stairs, and into the library. Immediately, Mr. Shepard called Louis and Finley Jay to one side and said in a whisper, "Will you phone the newspapers? I am sure they will want to know. We are going to take your mother to Woodlawn. She wished to be buried with her father and her mother."

Then Mr. Shepard went up to Olivia and tenderly kissed her, and then to Helen Anna, and then to me.

"Remember in your sorrow," he said, "that your mother lived a glorious and splendid life. God granted her the promised three score years and ten." Mr. Shepard turned and walked toward the door. As he passed the table where the guest book lay, he stopped, looked at it, and slowly turned back a few pages as if he were looking somehow on the history of a happier day; then slowly, but with finality, he closed the big leather volume. The last entry had been written; the last name signed. Olivia and John Burr, Helen Anna, Finley Jay, Louis and I walked silently and thoughtfully out of the front door of Kirkside and down the porch steps. The stars were out, but I saw only the dark spaces between them. I was thinking of Mrs. Shepard. She had been an important part of my life. I would miss her terribly. I would remember her as long as flowers grew, as long as the birds sang, and the wind blew.

Somewhere a clock tolled the hour. It was late. Roxbury was asleep. We passed the church, but tonight there was no music. The only sound in the little village was footsteps on the snow—the slowly fading footsteps of Mrs. Shepard's children going back to the hotel.

www.ingramcontent.com/pod-product-compliance
Lightning Source LLC
Chambersburg PA
CBHW051350290426
44108CB00015B/1958